New Hope for Urban High Schools

New Hope for Urban High Schools

Cultural Reform, Moral Leadership, and Community Partnership

LISA GONSALVES AND JOHN LEONARD

Foreword by Lee Teitel

Westport, Connecticut
London

Library of Congress Cataloging-in-Publication Data

Gonsalves, Lisa.
  New hope for urban high schools: cultural reform, moral leadership, and community partnership / Lisa Gonsalves and John Leonard; foreword by Lee Teitel.
p. cm.
  Includes bibliographical references and index.
  ISBN 0–275–99165–2 (alk. paper)
1. Urban high schools—Massachusetts—Boston—Case studies. 2. Education, Urban—Massachusetts—Boston—Case studies. 3. School improvement programs—Massachusetts—Boston—Case studies. I. Leonard, John (John Ellyson), 1948– II. Title.
LC5133.B6G66 2007
373.9744'61—dc22   2006038811

British Library Cataloguing in Publication Data is available.

Library of Congress Catalog Card Number: 2006038811
ISBN-10: 0–275–99165–2
ISBN-13: 978–0–275–99165–4

First published in 2007

Praeger Publishers, 88 Post Road West, Westport, CT 06881
An imprint of Greenwood Publishing Group, Inc.
www.praeger.com

Printed in the United States of America

The paper used in this book complies with the Permanent Paper Standard issued by the National Information Standards Organization (Z39.48-1984).

10 9 8 7 6 5 4 3 2 1

Dedication

We dedicate this book to the students, past and present, of Dorchester High School and the Dorchester Education Complex.

"A knowledge of history, as detailed as possible, is essential if we are to comprehend the past and be prepared for the future."

—Pearl Buck

Contents

Foreword

This is a book about connections—the kind of connections that those of us who care about urban education need to understand.

It is a book that connects a high school to the city that owns it (and appears to have disowned it at various points). It is the story of Dorchester High School—an ordinary school, a district high school like a dozen others, coexisting in a system with prestigious examination schools like Boston Latin. It is a school with its share of ups and downs over the decades: middling for some years, sinking to the lowest in reputation and test scores for others, rising again in a renaissance, and ultimately being dismantled and reborn as a trio of small schools in 2002.

Lisa Gonsalves and John Leonard connect the history of this once-proud high school to the larger societal movements of a city, to stormy forces swirling around desegregation, blockbusting, and redlining. Against this backdrop, the book plays out the educational drama as waves of school reform and renewal wash over the school: administrative redesign, school-based decision making, school site councils, magnets, small learning communities, and ultimately the breakup of large high schools into small schools. Lisa and John use the school and the people who live in it as a way to personalize this history, to put a human face on it, and to connect what could be dry and abstract history into a compelling tale of a school buffeted by forces it can only begin to control.

The book focuses on other types of connections critical for an urban school: partnerships with businesses, universities, and non-profits. It tells of the benefits of forty-year long relationships with the University of Massachusetts Boston and Verizon, the local telephone company—consistent partners, bringing programs, resources and ideas. We learn how critical these and Dorchester's many other external partners are and how delicate a task it is to manage dozens of partnerships so they really contribute to the lifeblood of the school.

The book is also about people and the personal connections they make. Institutional partnerships only work when they bring together people who care about each other, and each other's mission. I have been honored to play a bit part in the history described here, when as part of the creation of a professional development school partnership between the school and UMass Boston, I volunteered to spend half my time at the school for two years, working closely with teachers and administrators, and getting the partnership running. It was a profound learning experience, helping me, as a professor of educational leadership, truly understand the challenges and the possibilities of an "ordinary" urban high school. While there, I had the opportunity to be on the hiring committee for one of the authors, John, and when I was phasing out my involvement at Dorchester, I was thrilled when my faculty colleague Lisa stepped in to breathe new life into our teacher training partnership, each year bringing ten skilled and committed teacher interns to the school. The connections that grow out of the partnership, and the back and forth of university faculty have unquestionably benefited UMass as much as it has Dorchester High School.

At its core, this book is about the challenges of connecting children and youth to learning and to the adults that teach them. The book sings to us about the pockets of hope, the experiences of community when bands of teachers have connected to one another, to the students, and to outside partners to bring about the cultural changes needed to make a difference in the lives of children. The book anchors us as we see adults connecting to students and to each other in ways that bring meaning and learning into what could be an otherwise impersonal institution.

And finally, the book should connect powerfully to readers. Its carefully and elegantly framed analysis connects the authors' concluding lessons to the history of Dorchester High, and more importantly, to us as readers in our own settings. So read on, immerse yourself in the story, connecting people, time, and place, and most important, make the connection between this story and your own school in ways that connect your students to their schools, their communities and their worlds.

Lee Teitel
Professor and Associate Chair
Department of Leadership in Education
University of Masschusetts Boston

Preface and Acknowledgments

Pick up almost any comprehensive history of secondary education in America and at some point the author will mention a great shift in the challenges faced by high schools that came about in the mid 1960s. This shift has been described as "the 'unraveling' or 'fragmenting' of America;" as "a time of great turmoil," and as a "turning-point" in the history of public education.[1] Up through the early 1960s "it was still possible to describe the United States as a country with a strong central core of shared values."[2] Many parents relied on the schools to reinforce, if not instill, these core values in their children. Of course, the schools were far from perfect on many fronts. In fact, two of the events leading up to this "unraveling," the 1954 Supreme Court ruling against segregated public education and the 1957 Soviet launch of Sputnik, were a direct reflection of the profound failure of the schools to provide children from all backgrounds and abilities with a rigorous education.

Education became so much more complex after 1960. Diversity within the student populations continued to grow between 1965 and 1975. Schools were mandated to include minorities, students with special educational needs, and bilingual students, plus immigration brought many new faces and cultures into the country. At the same time, the postwar values of America were challenged by civil rights, women's rights, and the growing ethnic diversity of the country. Last, the overall purpose of education changed dramatically throughout these years.

The Supreme Court desegregation ruling and Sputnik ended up defining the themes that would dominate educational debates up through the present time—access and achievement. Teachers and administrators were expected to comply with two mandates at the same time—raise student achievement levels while providing equal educational access to a massive influx of students from various racial, class, and ability back-grounds—mandates for which they were not prepared. The turmoil of the 1960s also added new dimensions to the role that secondary education was expected to play in America. Up through the 1940s the main role of a high school education was to prepare students for the jobs they would hold as adults. Developments during the Depression and World War II caused the high school population to swell, leading some to believe that schools should serve a "custodial" role and focus more on the "problems of youth."[3] The civil rights and women's movements led others to believe that the role of a high school education should be to raise student awareness of racial prejudice, gender discrimination, and the political process.

The mandates of the federal government and the conflicting versions of the role of secondary education put tremendous pressure for reform on the nation's high schools. These pressures were felt most keenly in urban school districts. Because of these mandates however, we have seen tremendous strides in high school education. More young people, of all races and backgrounds, are graduating from high school, with more credits in tougher courses, than ever before. Nevertheless, particularly in urban high schools, our dropout rate is still too high, far too many graduates are not prepared for college, and we still fall short on international competitions. Too many teenagers cannot read properly. We agonize that, despite our best efforts, many of our students are disengaged and alienated from their own schools. High school reform for city schools has been particularly challenging where poverty and racism undermine the high school experience.

Education writers have documented the frustrating inefficiency of high school reform efforts in the past half century and urban education is even more challenging.[4] We will not add to this commentary. Instead, we offer a new approach.

We believe our book is unusual in several respects. First, we focus on just one high school in Boston—Dorchester High School—never the best but not always the worst school in Boston. When we began this book, our hope was that a richly detailed case study would provide lessons in education reform work that would be useful for urban school districts across the country.

Second, we study the school in the context of the surrounding history, both nationally and locally. So, in following the course of the high school history, the reader will learn about the Boston School Committee and how busing impacted the high school. The school history cannot be understood without the city history. Similarly, the reader will notice the local impact of national policy changes, such as the change in curriculum during the civil rights era or, more recently, the impact of the 1990s education finance reform. The impact of large-scale economic recessions and national immigration policy are noted as well.

Third, we study the school in the geographical and sociological context of the local neighborhoods and community partnerships—all the people and institutions who were engaged with the high school. For Dorchester High School, the history is less about parental engagement and more about the commitment and engagement of community partners. There are valuable lessons to be learned about helpful collaboration. The study of relationships, within the school and among the community partners, leads us to a new model of school change emphasizing cultural reform.

THE LAYOUT OF THE BOOK

This book has two main sections. The introduction lays out the broad themes of the book and explains our focus, which is on the most challenging urban schools in cities throughout this nation. Chapters two through nine present the history of the school from 1945 to 2006. We begin, in chapters two and three, tracing school roots back to 1945 and then presenting in great detail how this urban high school community unraveled between 1962 and 1982. This history demonstrates how, by 1980, Dorchester High School, similar to many urban schools, was a place where overcrowding and violence meant that very little learning was taking place.

Chapters four through nine describe the impact government mandates had on Dorchester High School and how local businesses, universities and the state legislature influenced the reform efforts. These chapters are rich with historical detail and reach far beyond the school as community partners became increasingly involved. Specifically, these chapters demonstrate how, by the late 1980s and early 1990s, communities began to form among the city's business and legislative leaders. These business and legislative communities began to work together to reform schools based upon the values they drew upon to run businesses and state government. While the process was often "three steps forward and two back," there was a gradual alignment of forces which all focused on school reform. Once this happened, there was significant reform at Dorchester High School.

The reader will encounter many characters in this section of the book. These characters peopled Dorchester High School at various points throughout the 60 years covered in this history. Some of them agreed to publicly share stories of the role they played at and for Dorchester High School. These include Pam Trefler, a local philanthropist who made a tremendous difference at the school, not only with her material resources, but also with her personal time, support, and commitment to the children and teachers at Dorchester High. Charles Desmond, a vice chancellor at the University of Massachusetts at Boston from the 1960s through 2000, who took it upon himself to bring the resources, faculty, and special programs of the university to the school. Samuel Tyler, head of the Boston Municipal Research Bureau, worked with the business community in their fight to change school governance. Last, Neil Sullivan, who was deeply involved with school issues during the tenure of Mayor Raymond Flynn, and is now head of the Private Industry Council, which provides jobs for Boston's high school students, shares the story of how local government also fought to reform school governance, ultimately winning Boston an appointed School Committee.

Teachers and administrators also shared their stories with us. Most prominent among these is Paul Casilli who taught at DHS from about 1983 until 2003. He worked with Compact Ventures and was one of the founding teachers of the Academy of Public Service. Robert Belle, headmaster from 1996 and now overseer of the three small schools that make up the Dorchester Education Complex, also shared his invaluable insights about what it takes to run a troubled urban high school. There were others, both inside and outside of DHS, who shared their stories. For various reasons, these individuals have decided not to be publicly acknowledged, but their stories are also included in this history. Theirs are the quotes attributed with a description of the role they played at and for Dorchester High. Our deepest appreciation goes out to these valiant teachers, administrators, school partners, and community members who struggled to make Dorchester High School work for urban children.

THE LESSONS LEARNED: THE SECOND SECTION

The second section stands back from the historical account and offers lessons learned and recommendations for urban high school reform work. The section begins with chapter 10 and presents our conceptual framework, based upon the theories of the late developmental psychologist Urie Bronfenbrenner (1979). Bronfenbrenner takes an ecological systems approach to human development. We examine the history of DHS through this cultural/developmental approach and suggest an ecological systems model for reforming urban high schools.

The following chapters (11, 12, and 13) look specifically at the impact of community partners, at the unique challenges that face urban teenagers, and at the role of school leaders as cultural change agents. Finally, in chapter 14, we take an even broader view and examine the values that have come to dominate our efforts at urban high school reform.

ACKNOWLEDGMENTS

There are many people who deserve mention for the part they played in bringing this book to fruition. We want to thank Bobby Belle, headmaster of Dorchester High School, who brought author John Leonard on board as an administrator, thus beginning ten years of work with the school for him, and who has always worked tirelessly as a true partner with the University of Massachusetts Boston.

We want to thank the many administrators, teachers, and former students who brought color and detail to the project through their informal conversations and more formal interviews. We are especially grateful to Chris Caperneros, for her insights into the long history of Dorchester High School. We want to thank Kim Leonard for her detailed transcriptions and Jessica Wilmot for her detailed descriptions and thoughtful analysis while collecting and coding the field data.

We are also grateful to the many community partners who shared their stories, such as June Kuzmeskus and Charlie Desmond of the University of Massachusetts Boston, Pam Trefler and Linda Kutsch of the Trefler Foundation, and Karen James Sykes of Verizon Corporation.

We appreciate Charlie Glen and Karen Boatman of Boston University, and Lee Teitel, of UMB, who supported the initial writing and asked the tough questions. We are also indebted to the Senior Project Editor Aimee Sands, who really pushed us and helped make the book accessible to a wider audience. Rachel Cummings pointed us to an ecological approach with her kind gift of a favorite book. Last, our most heartfelt thanks is reserved for Susan Slesinger, our original editor at Praeger, whose belief in this project made this book a reality.

This work builds upon and extends the analysis and insights of the many theorists and educational researchers who have come before us such as Urie Bronfenbenner, Karen Louis, and Matthew Miles, Elijah Anderson, Anthony Bryk and Barbara Schneider, just to name a few. Louis and Miles actually did their own case study of Dorchester High School in the mid 1980s. Their analysis has informed our work.

Finally, but foremost, we thank our families. John thanks his wife Lee who believed in him throughout this project and his three boys, Joe, Dan, and Phil, who brought some excitement to an academic life. Lisa thanks her partner Diane Pullen whose support and confidence in this book sustained her throughout the process, and the children in her life, Aisha, Leila, Marina, Kyle, Jasmine, Jessica, and Janyce, who constantly remind her why this work is so important.

List of Abbreviations

APS   The Academy of Public Service
BBURG   Boston Banks Urban Renewal Group
BPS   Boston Public Schools
DHS   Dorchester High School
DYS   Department of Youth Services
EBA   Economics and Business Academy
ILT   Instructional Leadership Team
ISA   Institute for Student Achievement
LAB   The Northeast Region and Islands Education Laboratory at
         Brown University
MCAS   Massachusetts Comprehensive Assessment System
MERA   Massachusetts Education Reform Act
METCO   Metropolitan Council for Educational Opportunity
NAACP   National Association for the Advancement of Colored People
NBA   Noonan Business Academy (Former EBA)
NEASC   New England Association of Schools and Colleges
NET   New England Telephone
PIC   Private Industry Council
SLC   Small Learning Community
SPED   Special Education
TBA   Tech Boston Academy
TNY   Teach Next Year
UMB   University of Massachusetts Boston

CHAPTER 1

Introduction: Reforming Our Most Troubled Urban High Schools

Dorchester High gets the leftovers for the students, like people that just got out of jail, people that's coming from different countries and stuff, like they, they just throw them here....Dorchester High has a reputation of not learning, a bunch of bad people, people that's crazy, ghetto people and people that just have no home training, that type of thing. (African American female student)

Dumbchester, it's called Dumbchester, and it's supposed to be one of the worst schools in Boston. (African American male student)

Welcome to Dorchester High School (DHS). When it's not called "Dumbchester," it is called "Dumpchester," for it is well known to be the "dumping ground" for the Boston Public Schools' most intractable students. Located in a poor, black Boston neighborhood, it is a place where students have been mugged at gunpoint on their way home from school, where dead bodies have been discovered on the school grounds. Its students have the lowest reading and test scores in Boston, and the highest rates of emotional and behavioral problems. It is also a place that has attracted millions of dollars in foundation funds, and a cohort of talented young teachers determined to make a difference in the lives of their struggling students.

I'm not here for the money I'm getting, I could take my two masters degrees and go make a fortune. I'm doing this for summers off? Are you kidding? I'm doing it because I think— because this kid over here is adorable, he's adorable, pure—he's gold, and this young man over here doesn't speak, but he is adorable too. (white male math teacher)

The students are bright—contrary to popular opinion most of the students are bright and know the system, know how to work the system probably better than anybody else, they are street smart. (white male history teacher)

But despite years of effort and literally millions of dollars, Dorchester High School is on the verge of closing. How did this once proud school community descend into chaos and violence in the 1970s? Why is the recent campaign to turn it around failing? What can be learned from the history of one inner city high school—from its mistakes and from its hidden successes? The answers, we believe, can point the way toward truly effective reform of the nation's most troubled high schools.

THE WORST URBAN HIGH SCHOOLS

I have been here for ten years. I have seen a whole lot of reform efforts, and reform projects. A lot of money has been spent on this school. From the time I came in 1999, I spent through hundreds and hundreds of thousands of dollars...and we don't see a whole lot of impact for what we are doing. (Former Assistant Headmaster)[1]

There remains a class of inner city high schools that has proven impervious to reform. Almost every U.S. city has at least one; our largest urban centers have several.[2] Their problems are familiar to those who work with and study urban high schools: standoffs between administrators and teachers, bitter struggles with school district headquarters, the frustration of knowing that the needs of one's best students are not being met.

We are talking about the worst high schools in a city. You can find them in Boston and Cleveland, in Detroit and Louisville, in New Orleans, Los Angeles, and Milwaukee. These schools come in last on every indicator of success. The students are invariably poor, and usually black, Latino, or from immigrant families. Education does happen in these schools, and we will demonstrate that. But too often the best efforts of teachers and their students yield at best mediocre results.

Why are certain urban high schools so troubled? Why do our attempts to reform these schools fail again and again? This book is about these schools; it examines what undermines them, and what we, as a community, might do to restore them.

IT TAKES A COMMUNITY TO SUSTAIN A SCHOOL

The average headmaster will say, "This is my school and this is the way it's got to be." But you know what, I cannot run this school by myself, and I'm not even stupid enough to think that I can. I need help. (Bobby Belle, Former Headmaster DHS, 1996 to 2003)

Ample research exists on urban high schools and their problems. We believe that these studies contain one fundamental error: they usually analyze the problems that exist exclusively within the four walls of the school, and recommend primarily school-based reforms. We take a different view. Rather than compare snapshots of more than one school, or present a generalized history of urban education, we look at reform efforts in the context of one urban high school over a sixty-year period.

Looking at one troubled urban high school over time allows us to tease out what is often missed in comparative or generalized studies. To this end we have gone back over sixty years to the point just before *Brown v. Topeka Board of Education* and the horrific desegregation battles that rocked many cities. We then travel with the school through the major reforms since then—the inauguration of special education and bilingual education, standards-based reform, systemic reform, education finance reform in the 1990s, and, finally, the high school restructuring movement of today. We are convinced that the average urban high school cannot pull itself up by its own bootstraps. A school like Dorchester High needs sustained outside support to succeed. Equally important, clumsy co-ordination of outside agencies can actually spell disaster for a school.

Therefore, our study extends beyond the schoolhouse walls to all of the people and institutions that are engaged with Dorchester High School. For example, we trace the neighborhood demographic changes around the school as immigration forces and economic pressures forced people to move. We examine the school's partnerships with local businesses and universities, and its relationships with philanthropists. Finally, we analyze the role of the central administration of the Boston School Department in the school's struggle to right itself.

As you will see, many of the problems uncovered in this history grow out of Boston's infamous racist legacy. Despite this fact, it is not accurate to blame the problems of Dorchester High on racism alone. Institutional racism still undermines the school's best efforts at success, but other external forces buffet the school as well. Today, poverty appears to be the number one culprit in terms of damaging student outcomes. The "code of the street"[3]—a product of the persistent economic and racial disenfranchisement of the surrounding African American ghetto—also has a profound impact on the school. Mental illness and/or substance abuse in some families create a subgroup of troubled students who regularly disrupt their classes.

Urban institutions like Dorchester High are besieged by overpowering forces that knock them off balance. In addition to the pernicious long-term effects of racial, economic, and social factors, these schools are locked into myriad district, state, and federal mandates, as well as multiple contracts and stakeholder expectations that constrict every attempt to make change.

The general public still tends to hold the local high school accountable for successfully educating all its students to high academic standards. But the power to effect true change has long since shifted to levels well beyond the school. Therefore, this is not simply an isolated history of one urban high school, but the story of a community that includes a high school. For us, context is everything.

THE ARCHAEOLOGY OF SCHOOLS

Our study presents a longitudinal examination of reform efforts at a single troubled urban school. We wanted to see how one urban high school fared through the monumental social changes since the 1950s. "One of the first things a physician or psychotherapist does is to review a patient's history. That's the only way to make an accurate diagnosis of a current condition. Likewise, leaders need to initiate, one way or another, an in-depth and comprehensive history of their school."[4]

There is another reason why we choose a historical approach. We believe, along with many education reformers, that understanding the history of a school is one of the most important elements in understanding the culture of that institution. For in the end, it is a school's culture that makes or breaks educational reform efforts.

> Parents, teachers, principals, and students have always sensed something special but undefined about their schools—something extremely powerful but difficult to describe....We believe the term culture provides...a way... to understand a school's unwritten rules and traditions, norms, and expectations that seem to permeate everything: the way people act, how they dress, what they talk about or avoid talking about, whether they seek out colleagues for help or don't, and how teachers feel about their work and their students....One scholar suggests that culture is "the way we do things around here."[5]

Like archeologists, we believe that the only way to understand the broken cultures of urban schools is to unearth the past. Culture and history are intertwined. One cannot understand institutional crisis without understanding how its culture was formed over time. Unfortunately, the history, and therefore the culture, of our most troubled schools, is often ignored by the schools themselves, by school districts, and by the overall education reform community—with usually disastrous results.

"THE WAY WE DO THINGS AROUND HERE": THE ARGUMENT FOR CULTURAL REFORM

Oddly, school culture has been largely ignored in the educational reform movements of the last forty years. Instead, researchers have recommended changes in the curriculum and structure of schools. Even the recommendations of the landmark report, *A Nation at Risk*, published in

1983, focused on curricular and structural remedies. Among other measures, the report called for a core academic curriculum and standardized testing.

The trend continues today with No Child Left Behind, which prescribes national curricular standards, annual exams to measure student progress, and consequences for school systems that fail to meet those standards. At local levels, reformers—including those at Dorchester High—have attempted to restructure large urban high schools into smaller "schools within the school" in hopes of duplicating the healthy cultures often found in small schools.

But history shows that curricular and structural changes alone do not raise student achievement, especially when expectations for students are low. High standards, combined with low expectations, have little effect. Neither restructuring schemes nor new instructional practices raise student achievement unless they are accompanied by raised expectations for student performance.

A third type of school reform—cultural reform—is needed. Cultural reform aims to change the climate and culture of high schools and to raise the expectations that schools have for students. Cultural reform also focuses on community building and the relationships between all school constituencies: trust between administrators, teachers, parents, and students is indispensable to the success of a reform effort. When trust is absent, there is tremendous resistance to mandated reforms, even those with a proven track record in urban schools. When trust is established, miracles can occur, even at schools like Dorchester High.

> There was a huge amount of excitement around the restructuring plan. Dorchester High School got its accreditation back early, like three to four weeks after the plan was put in writing and presented. The entire school dressed in matching T-shirts the day they got their accreditation. There was a huge amount of positive energy around the idea of taking this high school that was known as "Dumpchester" and turning it into an institution that people could be proud of. I think that extended to 99.9% of the people who were involved, and I'm including the students and faculty as a huge portion of this....We felt that in the past, students and faculty were usually ignored. They were dictated to; told what to do; no one paid attention. The fact that we were well known faces [meant that] we had very friendly relationships with a number of the faculty and we also knew a large number of the students. (Pam Trefler, Philanthropist)

Relationships are vital to this work. We know that learning is a social exercise. Students do not learn in isolation and for urban students, in particular, social relationships are vital to cognitive success. Far too little attention has been paid to the network of relationships in which the urban student learns. We explore, in detail, that social network.

Throughout this historical case study, we notice two startling facts. First, we are surprised at how easily and how often we lose sight of the student as the center of those networks and, indeed, as the focus of all our reform efforts! Second, we are impressed that the social network of responsibility that surrounds the student is far more broad and complex than we imagined.

With this in mind, we return to the claim made above: "the average urban high school cannot fix itself." Far too often, curricular and structural reform efforts begin with the false and unexamined assumption that "if those people in the school did what they are supposed to, then everything would work fine." Our findings indicate that the circle of responsibility extends far beyond the walls of the school and that a cultural reform strategy in this expanded community is a requirement for real school improvement.

The History of Dorchester High School 1945 to 2006

CHAPTER 2

Demographics, Discrimination, and Decline: The Destruction of Dorchester High 1945 to 1970

It is the fall of 2002. Gloria is on her way over to Dorchester High School yet again. Her daughter Aisha was late to school, and because of the school's lock-out policy, Aisha cannot enter the building unless Gloria comes and signs her in. This is the third time this week. Last week, Gloria had asked her supervisor if she could change her shift at the nursing home where she works. Her supervisor hadn't been pleased. Now Gloria will be late for work again.

Gloria knows Aisha is acting out because she is afraid of the school. When they talked the night before, Aisha told her that she was worried someone was going to try to start a fight with her out of nowhere. She said she'd seen it done to other kids, and felt that it was going to happen to her. Aisha told her mother that her grades were slipping because she didn't want to stay after school alone. Gloria had already tried to transfer Aisha to Madison Park High School, but without success. There was nothing they could do. They were just going to have to wait it out and hope that her grades didn't slip any further.

Gloria is deep in worry when she is suddenly startled by a phalanx of blue flashing lights. A wall of police cars blocks the Dorchester High parking lot. As she drives around to the front of the building, she sees it: a body is lying in front of the school, covered by a sheet. She looks up. Students are in the windows of every classroom looking out.

"How long has that body been out there?" she asks, when she finally finds parking and enters the building. "All morning" she is told. She finds Aisha standing in the front foyer with about twenty other latecomers.

"And you want me to sign my daughter in here?" she says to the teacher stationed at the front desk. *"Where is the headmaster? What's going on here?"* The
teacher just looks at her. Gloria signs Aisha in with clenched teeth. She has to get
back to work, but she vows to come back and speak with the headmaster, and the
police chief, the mayor. . . .

———————

This is what Dorchester High had become by the year 2000: a source of
worry for parents too overworked and overstressed to properly monitor
their children's schooling, and a source of fear for students, who con-
tended with frequent outbreaks of violence. In short, it had become a lost
school that stood as a symbol of the crisis in America's urban high
schools.

It hadn't always been this way. Dorchester High School began as a
solid, if segregated, educational institution, whose reputation steadily
improved over the first forty years of its existence. Few people, even in
Boston, know the full story of the school's decline.

> All the teachers were wearing a suit coat and a tie, okay, and the women
> were dressed up, you know, with a necklace. Everybody was bedecked.
> The boys had to wear a tie. If they didn't have a tie, you would rent them
> one and it would be one of the most God-awful ties, from a Good Will bag
> somewhere, you know? And it would teach them a lesson. (white male
> teacher, 1950s).

The Dorchester High School of the fifties and sixties was a place where
"the teachers were like a deity in the classroom." Tardiness was not tolerated. Students were openly tracked: one group in the college prep track,
one in a business track, and one in an industrial track that focused on
woodworking, carpentry, and upholstery.

> Those kids could type, and they got jobs. They were really good at it. My din-
> ing room chairs were done there, too. They would do them and you would
> pay for them. (white female teacher, 1960s)

The school building itself was constructed in 1923 to accommodate a
huge influx of immigrants into the surrounding neighborhood, including
17,000 Jews displaced by a fire in the nearby city of Chelsea. A total of
150,000 people lived in Dorchester by 1920, rendering the old Dorchester
High building as obsolete as the nineteenth century wood frame structure
that had preceded it.

The 1923 structure is an impressive, symmetrical brick building with
expansive windows and wide corridors. But it is oddly concealed. It is
completely engulfed by its neighborhood and cannot be seen until one
comes right up on it. (See Figure 2.1) The school is literally ringed by
triple-decker housing. The front of the building faces an expansive athletic field, but this also is surrounded by triple-deckers. The school is so
well hidden that if one were to walk around the block of homes that

border the schoolyard, one would never know that a large, urban high school stood right behind them.

Until the 1960s, the school was overwhelmingly white. Those who attended the school in the 1940s have no memory of seeing even one black student at DHS. Ethnic conflict trumped racial conflict in those years, but the scene was the same—police cars lining Peacevale Road after school to prevent the Irish and Jewish kids from hurting each other. It is not until the 1951 yearbook that we see a lone black student.

Figure 2.1   Aerial view of Dorchester High School with surrounding residences. (Aerial and satellite imagery provided by GlobeXplorer.com)

A 1948 graduate described the school as a "general" high school, not well known for its academic or athletic programs. If there were second language learners or special education students at the school, teachers were not obligated to acknowledge or even identify their educational needs in any way. Everyone in the school spoke English, even though the yearbook names reveal immigrant roots. There were no free lunch programs for low-income students; the only way a child could get a free lunch was by working for it during lunchtime.

Despite the prevalence of Jewish children, Christian values and religious language comfortably permeated every aspect of the school. Religious ideas were unabashedly proclaimed in the curriculum. The introduction to the 1957 general science curriculum stated, "As the pupil learns of the great order of the Universe and of the beauties of nature, he must invariably come to a greater appreciation of the Divine plan in creation." "Faithfulness" was assessed, along with other student character traits. The annual Christmas pageant always included the Nativity scene, a fact that very likely disturbed the Jewish students. They would have had little recourse to do anything about it, however, since the notions of inclusion and diversity, and the laws that would eventually enforce those notions, were still about twenty years away.

John Gibbons, bespectacled and portly, led DHS from 1954 to 1964. Dr. Gibbons graduated from Harvard University and was described as a real scholar and a gentleman by those who taught at the school during his tenure. He freely quoted Scripture and the classics, as this quote from his 1957 yearbook greeting illustrates:

> Shakespeare in Troilus and Cressida reminds us, "time hath, my Lord, a wallet at his bark, wherein he puts alms for oblivion."

Gibbons nurtured his relationship with Harvard, initiating social exchanges between the university and the high school. By the end of his tenure he was given a Harvard chair in recognition of his efforts to bring the two worlds together. Gibbons also brought many "firsts" to DHS. He instituted the first cooperative office-training program in the Boston Public Schools (BPS), where female students attended classes for two weeks and then spent two weeks working in offices around the city. A student newspaper was created in 1956 called the Dunbar Chronicle. The paper had a staff of thirty-five juniors and seniors who took pride in reporting on local and national events.

Gibbons was described as never coming out of his office; one former employee said the aloof and learned leader was "like God." The students never saw him except for an occasional address, most likely at graduation. As leader of DHS, Gibbons' main concerns were making sure the students made it through their 180 days of school and then went on to good careers or post-secondary education. A teacher from the 1950s described the headmaster's job. "You only worked two days more than the teachers. You worked 182 days...the day before and the day after and that was it. That was what made it attractive." Gibbons led DHS for ten years and was the last leader of his type at the school.

Gibbons did not supervise his teachers. That notion was not introduced until the 1960s when many new teachers began to join the ranks. In the 1950s, teachers were evaluated and promoted more for their loyalty than their teaching ability.

> If you wanted to get promoted in those days, you had to do all these jobs. I did everything under the sun. I ran the yearbook; I ran dances; I did programming, and I did graduations, proms, just to get one thing—to have him [the headmaster] give you a good mark. The headmaster gave the rating, but he never came to visit [my classroom]. (white male teacher, 1950s).

The students of the 1950s could choose from thirty-three different after-school clubs and social activities. There were literary, science, Spanish, French, and Latin clubs, junior Red Cross, drama, glee, and band clubs, photography, rotary, chess, and radio clubs. There were committees for the prom, yearbook, senior class play, class day, talent show, and the Christmas Dance. In 1954, so many students wanted to be involved in planning these activities that a lottery had to be created in order to choose who would be able to serve. The school also had an active student council made up of two elected representatives from each homeroom. One senior from 1964 described his years at the school as "a joyous whirlwind of never ending activities."[1]

Academically, however, the students at DHS were not stellar. A quote from the 1963 yearbook describes "many students pleading with teachers to pass them" so they could graduate with their class. The curriculum was easygoing, as it was assumed that "most students would not go on to college." There were no advanced placement courses taught at the school throughout the 1950s and only basic math courses were offered.

Nevertheless, there were always enough college-bound students to take advantage of the few courses offered in art, foreign languages (Spanish, Italian, French, and Latin), and English. Overall, the school enabled some students to excel, while allowing many others to patch together very spotty transcripts and still graduate. Many, of course, dropped out. The school had a 50 percent graduation rate throughout the 1950s,[2] with girls graduating at a slightly higher rate than the boys.

Dorchester High was very much a neighborhood high school in the 1940s and 1950s. It sat right between a Jewish and an Irish neighborhood. Jews began moving into the Irish section in the early 1950s, sparking an upsurge in ethnic tensions. The animosity between the two communities was often vented on the grounds of Dorchester High School. Those who attended the school in the 1940s and 1950s recall that police cruisers were stationed outside the school and along Peacevale Road at the end of the day to break up fights between Irish and Jewish teenagers. At times the playing fields in front of the school served as a battleground for gang fights between the two.

The fights rarely found their way into the hallways of the school, however. It seems that in the late 1940s and early 1950s, adolescents knew not to take their physical conflicts through the schoolhouse door. Discipline problems found inside the school were minor, consisting mainly of students who skipped classes or were caught smoking cigarettes. This was most likely a reflection of the times, when drugs and deadly weapons were rarely, if ever, found inside the classroom.

Despite its mediocre academic program and the neighborhood-based prejudices of its students, Dorchester High School began the 1960s with great potential. Academically, the course offerings were expanding, due in part to the National Defense Act of 1957, which prompted a new emphasis on academic achievement. Reflecting the technology of the day, there was an entire course on aviation, including information on engines, flight theory, navigation and the history of aviation. In the early 1960s students could take four years of English as well as courses in Spanish, Italian, French, and Latin. The Art program, large enough to constitute a graduation track, drew students from across Massachusetts.

The school was also beginning to develop relationships with academic institutions in the area. In 1965, Dorchester partnered with the University of Massachusetts Boston (UMB) on the first Upward Bound program in the country. As part of Upward Bound, students received academic support, and experienced college life at the university on weekends and during the summer. Also in the 1960s, students could take summer classes at the Massachusetts Institute of Technology in calculus, computer programming, probability, and chemistry. Harvard University also offered a cultural exchange with DHS students, bringing 150 teachers and students to the school in 1964.

Meanwhile, ambitious student forums at the school tackled such topics as the problems of democracy and U.S. foreign policy, demonstrating the students' growing political sophistication. The most telling statistic during this time was the school's graduation and attendance rates. Between 1960 and 1965, 57 percent of DHS students graduated from high school, and 90 percent of students attended school daily. This remains the school's highest graduation rate for any period from 1950 to today.

Black students began attending the school in these years. Before 1960, black students made up 1 percent of the graduating class, but by 1964 that number had risen to 15 percent. It can't have been easy for these students to enter this traditionally white school. As one white, male teacher said candidly, "It was the first time I had met any really black people."

Many of the school's black students participated in citywide school boycotts in 1963 and 1964, to protest segregation in the Boston Public Schools. However, according to most reports from this time period, this was not accompanied by an outbreak of racial strife at Dorchester High. As one black teacher who was hired in 1964 explained, "There was more trouble between the Irish and Jewish students, than between the blacks and the whites at DHS in the early 1960s."[3] A white, female teacher who taught at DHS in 1963 emphasized, "We never had racial problems. We had about 20 percent minority, and we never had racial problems. Never."

Seven out of sixteen senior class superlatives went to black students in the 1964 yearbook, including most likely to succeed, best dressed, and most talented. In many ways, Dorchester High was on its way to becoming a model for successful racial integration.

Perhaps one factor that contributed to the lack of racial strife at DHS during this time was the fact that the traditional, semi-religious values from the 1950s still prevailed at the school. These values provided strict moral and behavioral standards that were expected to guide student and teacher behavior. Another factor may have been that character traits were graded at DHS throughout the 1960s, including "Initiative, Seriousness of Purpose, Industry, Influence, Concern for Others, Responsibility, Emotional Stability and Social Adjustment."

Sometime around 1965, things started to change rapidly at DHS. A number of social shifts were taking place that would impact the school in monumental ways. The first of these began in 1963 in Roxbury, the neighborhood from which most of DHS's black students came.

Boston has always been a city of neighborhoods, and in order to understand the social forces that impacted DHS, one must understand something about the changes that were taking place in the city's neighborhoods during the 1960s. Two neighborhoods in particular are important to our story: Roxbury, home to most of DHS's black students, and Dorchester, including North Dorchester and South Dorchester, where DHS is located.

In 1960 Roxbury was 80 percent black and South Dorchester was 1 percent black. Starting in 1964, black families began moving south, and by 1966, half of the school's black seniors came from South Dorchester. White families, meanwhile, began to disperse, the Jews moving further south, and the Irish further north (See Figure 2.2, a map of Boston).

What precipitated these population shifts, and why is this significant to the story of DHS? The answer to the first question is urban renewal. In 1963, Roxbury's Washington Park became the first urban renewal project in Boston. Even though the goal was residential revitalization, city planners determined that at least 10 percent, or 2500, of the buildings in Washington Park would need to be demolished. These were replaced with 800 new residential units with rents that were too high for many of the former tenants. Those blacks who could no longer afford to live in the revitalized Washington Park neighborhood moved—into South Dorchester, prompting the "white flight" of the resident Irish and Jews.

Now to our second question: why is this significant to the story of DHS? First of all, these developments led to a poorer student body. The blacks who moved from Washington Park were low-income families,

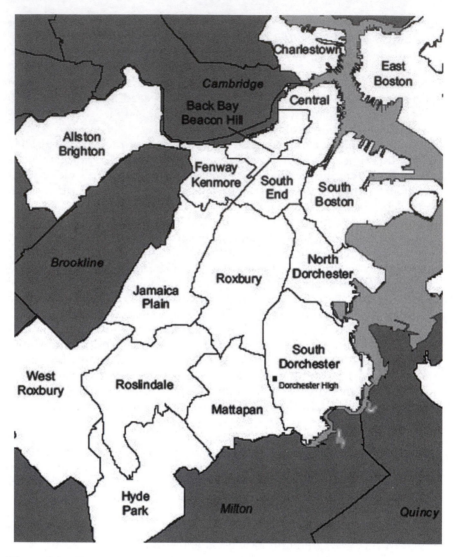

Figure 2.2 Boston is a city of boroughs and ethnic neighborhoods; Dorchester High School is located in South Dorchester.

poorer than families in other parts of Roxbury. At the same time, the white families remaining in South Dorchester were also poorer than their white counterparts in other sections of the city.

While the school was experiencing this shift in population from middle and working class to poorer students, another equally significant social change was brewing. In 1954, the U.S. Supreme Court had ruled in *Brown v. Board of Education* that it was no longer legal to educate children in segregated schools. In 1961, the National Association for the Advancement of Colored People (NAACP) of Boston took action, filing a complaint with the Boston School Committee, which led to the busing crisis of the early 1970s. The story of busing in Boston has been recounted amply since then. For the purposes of our story, we will summarize these events to show their enormous impact on DHS.

The NAACP based their complaint on a study they conducted of the Boston Public Schools. That study documented de facto segregation in a number of Boston's schools. The School Committee and the superintendent dismissed their complaint. It was not until 1963, under pressure from state leaders, that the School Committee agreed to hold a hearing on the original NAACP complaint. Local media reports fueled the flames by publishing statistics on the differential spending patterns and the condition of school buildings in black and white neighborhoods of Boston.[4] When the hearing finally took place, it became apparent that the School Committee had no intention of taking the NAACP complaint seriously.

The black community responded by staging the school boycotts mentioned above. The first boycott took place in June 1963; 9,000 black students stayed out of school. A second boycott was held in 1964. This time 20,000 black students stayed out.[5] The most significant aspect of these boycotts for our story was the fact that they helped politicize the students.

Instead of going to school, students attended freedom schools during both boycotts. At these schools, they learned about black history, civil rights, and the struggles their community has engaged in for equality in America. For many of the students this was the first time they were learning about such things from members of their own community. The experience was very empowering for students. The seeds of empowerment planted during these boycotts would, in a few years, grow into the black students' struggle for student unions at the city's high schools. As we shall see, these struggles were particularly difficult at DHS.

The NAACP complaint and the student boycotts prompted the state to get involved. First, the state Board of Education conducted a study on "racial imbalance." This study came to be known as the Kiernan Report. It documented racial imbalance in forty-five schools in Boston and recommended the busing of some elementary school students. It held the School Committee directly responsible for the elimination of these imbalances.

Once again, the School Committee did not take these recommendations seriously. In 1965 the state legislature stepped in and, with the backing of the governor, passed the Racial Imbalance Act outlawing school segregation in Massachusetts. This law gave the state, not the city, power to oversee the desegregation of all schools. Now the state could require that schools submit desegregation plans or risk losing their state funding.

The Board of Education began their attempts to enforce the Racial Imbalance Act in 1965 by asking the School Committee to submit its first desegregation plan. When the plan was ruled inadequate in 1966, the Board suspended state funding for Boston's schools.[6] Amazingly, this too had little impact on the School Committee. Instead, the Committee embarked on a nine-year struggle in both the courts and the legislature to get the Racial Imbalance Act overturned. Finally, in 1972, Boston's civil rights leadership took matters into their own hands, filing its famous desegregation lawsuit. As is well known, the court ruled in favor of the NAACP in 1974, two long years later.

Even though the Racial Imbalance Act did not have an immediate impact on the segregated schools in Boston, the law did validate the black community's struggle for desegregated and quality schools. In the face of continued School Committee inaction, and growing frustration with Boston's emerging black leadership, black parents in the community took matters into their own hands and formed the Roxbury-North Dorchester Parents' Committee for Better Schools.

> The parents slowly reached the conclusion that whereas the civil rights leadership had wasted its energy trying to change the School Committee, the parents would ignore the School Committee and act on their own. We really didn't know where our plan would take us; we just decided that by sending our children to other schools, people in the city would know we were there and might start to understand the problems that existed in the schools.[7]

The parents began by taking advantage of the BPS open enrollment policy that allowed any Boston student to transfer into any Boston public school that had available seats. Using this policy, the parents organized what came to be known as Operation Exodus, a program that bused black children to better schools in other parts of the city. When the School Committee refused to reveal where the vacancies were, the *Boston Globe* published articles detailing which schools in the city had vacant seats.

In 1966, Operation Exodus led to a voluntary urban-suburban partnership called METCO (the Metropolitan Council for Educational Opportunity), which bused Boston's black students to suburban schools. At first funded by grants, the state legislature began funding METCO in 1969. Three years later, METCO was busing 2,500 black students out of Boston. Many of these students were from black middle class families, once again leaving behind poorer students, with less active parents, to attend the Boston Public Schools.

Meanwhile, DHS was still on its way up. The graduating class of 1966 was the third largest since 1954 with over 300 students, 20 percent of them black. Ninety percent of the students attended school daily. Black students were being successfully integrated into the social life of the school. Then came the pivotal year of 1967.

During the summer of 1967, Boston's first racial riot took place in North Dorchester, which experienced three days of looting and arson along Blue

Hill Avenue. It was clear that by this point both the country and the city of Boston were beginning to explode over civil rights for blacks in general and school equality for black children in particular. In Boston, frustration continued to build on all sides as each constituency met with failure in their struggle to gain control of the schools. Black parents were frustrated with the civil rights leadership over what they saw as a futile fight with the School Committee, while their children continued to languish in failing schools. Civil rights leaders, state legislators, and the state Board of Education officials were frustrated with the School Committee, which continued to defy every legal order that came down against it. And white parents were frustrated by what they perceived as their growing lack of control over their children's education.

Also, in 1967, the population shifts set in motion by the 1963 urban renewal project in Washington Park began to manifest themselves more clearly at DHS. By 1967 DHS was 25 percent black. For the first time, the majority of black seniors—over 50 percent—came from Dorchester. Also, black students were coming from poorer and poorer neighborhoods, as were many of the white students.

Two things happened in 1968, one that would drastically alter the population of the high school and another that would have the same impact on the surrounding community. First, in a move that would turn Dorchester High almost overnight into a black school, the Boston School Committee voted to add the ninth grade to the student body. To understand the significance of this, one needs to understand the Byzantine, racially motivated school assignment system of those years.

In order to avoid desegregating Boston's schools, the School Committee relied upon a complex system of feeder patterns designed to move students along a specific path from elementary through high school. In the early and mid 1960s Boston had both middle schools, which served grades six to eight, and junior high schools, which served grades seven to nine.

According to the feeder-pattern system, junior high school graduates were sent to high schools that were from grades ten to twelve, and middle school graduates went to high schools that were from grades nine to twelve. It just so happened that the junior high schools tended to be in white neighborhoods and the middle schools tended to be in black neighborhoods. Adding the ninth grade to DHS, therefore, made the school "black by intention," a term used by the courts to indicate deliberate segregation.

A look at the statistics tells the story. In 1967, when DHS was still a ten to twelve grade institution, 25 percent of the students were black. Most of the starting tenth graders were assigned from the junior high schools that were in white neighborhoods. This helped keep the school racially balanced, even though the neighborhood itself was becoming more and more black. In 1968, when the School Committee changed DHS from a ten to twelve grade school to a nine to twelve grade school, 50 percent of the students were black. For comparison purposes, blacks made up 16 percent of Boston's overall population and 33 percent of the students in the Boston Public Schools at that time.

At the same time, the student population jumped from 960 to 1,300. By 1969 it had climbed to an unimaginable 1,578 children, an almost 40 percent leap in two years. Overcrowding, previously unknown at the school, was now severe. First, the School Committee deliberately turned Dorchester High into a black school, and then they abandoned it.

While the School Committee was creating chaos in the high school, Boston banks were putting policies in place that would disrupt the surrounding neighborhood. In 1968, the Boston banking community created the Boston Banks Urban Renewal Group (BBURG). The program was announced in May of 1968 as being a national model for urban home ownership. Twenty-two Boston banks would commit up to $50 million in loans "to accelerate housing rehabilitation and provide mortgage money for greatly expanded home ownership in the inner city."[8] The Federal Housing Authority agreed to guarantee all loans made through the program, making them more attractive to lenders. What made this program unique, however, was that the mortgages were only available to those who bought property in a specific geographic area. This area was designated the "Model Cities area." The Vice-President of the then Suffolk Franklin Bank explained the rationale behind this decision as quoted by Levine and Harmon, in their book, *The Death of an American Jewish Community.*

> A contiguous neighborhood, with an attractive housing stock, was clearly needed to make the program a national model. The South End of Boston, which lay directly to the north of the Model Cities area, was already showing signs of gentrification. To the west of the Model Cities lay Jamaica Plain, long the most stable of Boston's neighborhoods. The neighborhood was a favorite for Boston politicians, police and city workers. From the perspective of the bankers, Jamaica Plain had a large "do not disturb" sign hanging from its doorknob. To the east of Model Cities lay the largely working class Irish sections of Dorchester [a population that had proven to be violently opposed to what they perceived as "black encroachment"]. What remained was an area that almost to the house, corresponded to the precise inner-city locus of one ethnic group—Boston's Jewish community of roughly 40,000 people. It was there, and only there, that low-interest small down payment loans would be made to the city's minority home-seekers.[9]

The story of how the real estate agents "persuaded" Jewish homeowners to sell their property has been well told by Levine, Harmon, and others. Unfortunately, their blockbusting tactics were very successful. Within three months of its inception, the BBURG had financed 171 mortgages for inner city families. Within five months that number grew to 314 mortgages. By 1970, just two years later, the black population in the BBURG Model Cities area would grow from 2000 to 21,000. It just so

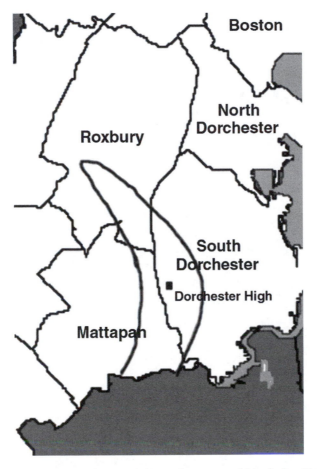

Figure 2.3   The crescent shape outlines the route of black families who left Roxbury in the face of urban renewal and moved south toward the school.

happened that this area formed a crescent bubble around Dorchester High School (see Figure 2.3).

Banks, of course, do not usually consider the impact of their actions on schools. But urban renewal and blockbusting—as well as the School Committee's decisions—took a profound toll on DHS. The incremental improvements the school had been making in the 1960s were cut short, and a decline was precipitated that would continue for the next twenty years.

CHAPTER 3

The Fragmentation of Culture and Community: The Long, Slow Decline of Dorchester High School 1969 to 1982

Nineteen sixty-nine held a lot of promise for the teachers at Dorchester High School (DHS). The school had just embarked on the first school-business partnership in the state, and the oldest in the country, with New England Telephone (NET). Also the teachers were becoming more empowered through the formation of the Boston Teachers Union. In the early 1960s, Boston teachers were represented by two organizations. The Boston Teachers Alliance, which had over 2000 members, served elementary and middle school teachers. High school teachers had their own union, which was much smaller. At the time, there was a bitter rivalry between the two unions because high school teachers were paid a higher salary. The catalyst for empowering Boston teachers began in 1965 when the two unions merged creating the Boston Teachers Union. Teachers from DHS were very involved in these events. One teacher was the vice president of the high school teachers union and participated in the early merger negotiations.

The relationship with New England Telephone was a well-functioning school-business partnership. A company representative regularly visited the school and consulted with school officials in the 1970s. NET provided funds for special projects at the school (such as a student art exhibit) and internships for students. These efforts reflected the desire of the company to help while also signaling reluctance to interfere. NET made one very powerful investment in the school in 1970 when they provided leadership training to a group of teachers. This training at the Sloan School of Management at the Massachusetts Institute of Technology provided the school with "a core set of people who knew how to react, to form communities, and take hold of change."[1] These teachers, dubbed the "class of 1969," and the skills they acquired during the training, would end up impacting the school for the next twenty years in ways that no one would have imagined. The teachers formed a team that helped reinforce the school's common professional interests and build mutual trust and support, significantly shaping the culture of the school.

These two events prepared the teachers to fight not only for internal school reforms, but also for their own interests with the wider district administration. Their first opportunity was district-wide, when in 1970 the newly formed Boston Teachers Union voted to hold the first teacher's strike in Boston's history. Seventy percent of the teachers picketed for three weeks.[2] The major concerns on teacher's minds during the strike were job security, wages, and benefits. Still, most observers saw the teachers as militant and less intimidated by authority and the law. Some contributed this "militant unionism"[3] to young college graduates who had been shaped by the civil rights movement and now, as teachers, were transforming the teaching profession. At DHS the strike strained relationships among teachers who had worked side by side for many years.

> A lot of ill feeling occurred because of the teacher strikes too. During that first strike, the people in the vocational education department didn't go on strike....None of the guys in there went out on strike. They were older guys who were members of their own unions, which were upholstering, carpentry, or whatever. And they crossed the picket lines. Do you know that no one spoke to those people for years after that? (white female teacher).

In terms of cultural cohesion, the strike hurt more than helped DHS. On the one hand, DHS teachers began the school year in 1970 more empowered, better paid, and more informed about how to bring about educational change within the building. On the other hand, there was more division and tension, not only between the administration and the teachers, but also among the younger and older colleagues within the building.

At the same time that the adults in the building, still 94 percent white, were having trouble communicating with each other, the student culture was changing drastically. Not only were there many more students enrolled in the school, but the students themselves were also different in three significant ways. First, the racial composition of the student body changed drastically in four short years. The student population went from 20 percent black in 1965, when there were about 950 enrolled, to 50 percent black by 1969, when enrollment jumped to 1575 students. (By 1974, 2000 students were enrolled in DHS, 55 percent of whom were black.) Second, due to the social manipulations described in chapter

one, both the black and white students were poorer and more disenfran-
chised than those who had attended the school five years earlier. Last,
because of the School Committee's decision to change DHS to a nine
through twelfth grade school, the students were up to a full year younger,
bringing the attendant problems of early adolescence to the school for the
first time. At the same time, the 1970s ushered in an unprecedented focus
on rights and access in American society and American schools. This
focus on rights and access opened the school doors even wider, providing
access to students who spoke English as a second language and to those
with special educational needs. Unfortunately, adjusting to these events
prevented the new teacher leaders from focusing their energies on internal school reforms for many years.

It is important to remember that the 30 percent rise in the black student
population that occurred between 1965 and 1969 was not the first drastic
change in the racial composition of students at the school. There was also
a 20 percent rise in the black student population between 1960 and 1965,
from one percent to 20 percent. As described in chapter one, DHS had
been able to absorb the first jump quite painlessly with the potential of
becoming a model of racial integration for the city. What made the second
increase so difficult? In order to answer this question we need to look in
two directions—outward toward the wider social context surrounding
the school and inward toward the internal culture that sustained the
school.

Internally, the semi-religious cultural values and the strict moral and
behavioral standards that sustained DHS through the first wave of integration had started to unravel at the beginning of the 1970s. For example,
by 1970, the list of character traits upon which students were graded was
shortened to three, "reliability, initiative and concern for others." Gone
from the revised list were those qualities that fostered leadership, such
as "influence and seriousness of purpose." Still the new list encouraged
traits necessary for both student and community success. By 1975, DHS
no longer attempted to grade character, ending the focused attention, by
both teacher and student, on the level of personal behavior and responsibility exhibited at school.

Dress codes at the school were also beginning to relax by the early
1970s. A quick look through the 1969 yearbook reveals that all the male
faculty, and a substantial number of male students still wore suit jackets
and ties to school. There were also no photos of girls in pants in that year.
By 1971, however, the male students were no longer wearing ties. This
trend was also evident among the younger male faculty. Also in 1971,
about half the girls were wearing pants to school.

Another cultural change moving through the school between 1968 and
1972 was the relaxation of the strict moral and behavioral standards to
which students were expected to conform. Prior to 1968 tardiness and
even hallway chatter were not tolerated.

> The discipline was very rigid in those days. You couldn't talk in the hall.
> Kids were not allowed to go to their lockers between classes. The period
> started at 8:20 and if your foot wasn't over the threshold when the bell rang,
> you were tardy. One day, I was talking to this girl in the hallway, and the as-
> sistant Headmaster came running down the hallway yelling, "What are you
> talking in the halls for?" That's how rigid and strict it was. It was pretty tight.
> (white, male teacher).

The focus on student character and the strong adherence to personal
and behavioral norms as expressed through the dress code and public
orderliness had all but unraveled by 1972. The erosion of these cultural
norms made it much more difficult for DHS to withstand the changes
being brought about by national, state, and local policies. Ironically, many
of those policies sought to improve schools in general and the quality of
education for disadvantaged and minority students in particular. However, between 1970 and 1974, the impact of those policies swept through
DHS with such speed that they challenged the schools cultural moorings
by overwhelming the staff and the students, leaving chaos and confusion
in their wake.

Externally, the disintegration of DHS must be understood within the
context of the struggle to integrate the Boston Public Schools. More than
anything, DHS was a victim of this struggle. During the struggle for the
integration of Boston's schools, a series of decisions was made by constituents from all sides that resulted in rapid, in some cases overnight,
changes at DHS. The first of these was the Boston School Committee's
decision to add the ninth grade to DHS in 1968, which, as was explained
in the previous chapter, increased the school's population from 960 to
1300. When teachers left DHS in the summer of 1968, the student population was familiar and manageable. When they returned in September,
they had 340 more students with whom they had to deal.

At the same time that DHS was being flooded with students, the teachers and the black students inside the building came to see themselves
more and more as constituent groups, rather than as members of one unified school community. For the teachers, this lead them to accept the
"new militant unionism," described above that was sweeping across the
country, especially among those of the baby-boom generation.

The black students were also growing more politicized. Building on the
student strikes from 1963 and 1964, black student unions were unoffi-
cially organized in all Boston high schools during the summer of 1969.
The black students at DHS were very involved in these unions and held
frequent strikes to protest conditions in the school. One teacher described
the black student unions:

> They were a very highly active, highly politicized black voice. They were
> excellent students. The administration at that time didn't agree because they
> were seen as troublemakers. They had teachers who advised them, but these
> kids really met on their own; they were very politicized. This was a period of

growing black consciousness. I remember the students very well. They would come into class and tell me in advance; let's say the class started at 9:00, they would tell me that at 9:30 there would be a walkout. So I'd say, in that case, let's get our work done. When 9:30 rolled around, they would all get up and walk out. Because we knew the students, we were looked at by the administration as instigating them, which was totally wrong.

The black student unions were very active in 1970. In January, Dorchester High was closed for two days due to student demonstrations over a teacher's racist comment. An African American female who was a junior at DHS in 1970 lamented:

Our junior year at Dorchester High was one of turmoil and trouble. Students throughout the city were striking. So many students leaving school early hurt club activities. There were accusations of abuse and disagreements between students and teachers which triggered our problems. There were false fire alarms almost every day and we finally had to have students guard the alarm boxes all day. The sad thing was the disagreement between blacks and whites which rarely happened during my first two years here. It seemed that all the Boston high schools were about to explode for about two months but we survived.[4]

In 1969, the School Committee, ostensibly to relieve the overcrowding at DHS, but really to avoid sending black students to white schools, approved the construction of the "satellites" behind Dorchester High School. The "satellites" were two long cinder block buildings that stood face to face in the yard behind the school. Each building provided six classrooms, but they could only be reached by going outside. The rooms were small and poorly equipped, with low ceilings, and no labs. The heat was uneven and the location of the bathrooms necessitated walking through other classrooms. Both staff and students had to go to the main building for lunch, gym, and student assemblies.

The satellites were reserved for the new ninth graders. One student remembered her first year at DHS:

We felt we were missing a lot by being pretty isolated from the main building activities and in addition we had to wait quite a while for a lot of our equipment. When all the lockers, chairs, and tables arrived we settled down, but the weather was something else. It rained almost every day during the fall and we were ankle-deep in water changing classes many times.

Since seasoned teachers refused to work in them, the new ninth grade teachers were also assigned out there as well. One veteran from the 1960s remembered, "Nobody wanted to work out in the satellites. That meant that you were low man on the totem pole. . . . That was considered to be the worst job out there."

At best, the satellites could hold 360 (twelve times thirty) students. Combined with the main building, this raised the official capacity to 1380 students, but enrollments were already hitting 1500 and climbing.

By 1970, with 1578 in the school, the decision was made to rent the Pierce building, three blocks away. The Pierce was a miserable building with little equipment, few supplies, and poor communication with the main building. New students came to school and spent their first year in the satellites or the Pierce. Yearbook pictures from 1972 showed fourteen teachers on the Pierce staff; over 300 students went to this school until 1974 when it burned down in the middle of the school year in a suspicious fire.

For the next two years, the school rented the Whittier, another building that was a few blocks away from the main school. Total school enrollments peaked at over 2000 in the 1974–75 school year. DHS had to hold double sessions in order to accommodate all the students. The huge ninth grade class started school at noon. The school that just five years prior had prided itself on harmony was being severely challenged.

The arrangements left people disgruntled. One teacher complained that after five years in the Boston Public Schools, he was transferred to DHS and placed in the Whittier in 1974. To him, it was a slap in the face and he contemplated leaving teaching altogether. Many students, especially those new to the school, felt isolated and cut off. And some local folk were not excited. When DHS proposed renting a seventh building in 1974, the Gilbert Stuart, in the Lower Mills neighborhood for the burgeoning ninth grade class, the mostly white neighbors took matters into their own hands. One teacher explains:

> When they heard that the Gilbert was going to be turned into an annex for Dorchester High School, just before the April vacation, the principal of the school got a call from somebody—probably had a handkerchief over the phone—saying, "tell your teachers to take anything that they have of value home." You know, before the April vacation. And then they burnt it down. It burnt down during the April vacation.

The overcrowding at Dorchester High School left the staff splintered, exhausted, and disgusted. Relationships inside the building and with the district administration deteriorated even further. By 1976 the situation had gotten so unbearable that teachers wrote the following letter to Judge Garrity in an attempt to remedy the situation:

> The teachers at DHS protest the unbearable condition under which the bulk of the 9th grade classes (320 students), four twelfth grade English classes and all music classes must be taught. Nine classes of ninth grade students are permanently located in the schools auditorium for the entire school day. All classes are conducted within earshot of each other. The students have no desk surfaces on which to write. It is impossible to use audio-visual equipment and the seating is extremely poor. Four senior English classes must meet in the cafeteria since five other ninth grade classes are using classroom space. Most deplorable, there are music classes meeting continuously in the auditorium balcony. We demand that a solution to this problem be found immediately.[5]

The decision to include ninth graders, who were less mature and self-controlled, only aggravated the situation. The strikes and turmoil continued for the next four years, turning more violent as time progressed.

> We had 1300, 1400, 1500 kids. It was a mad house in there. It was just constant fighting between the blacks and the whites and of course it always happened around lunchtime. Just like any place where you have too many students. Every single seat was filled in every single class. And when you have that many students in there and somebody starts fighting, it just spills. I remember many times they would have a code on the intercom and you'd have to lock your doors and not let anybody in and not let anybody out. (white, female teacher).

This white former student recalled the terror of his last days at DHS:

> I got chased out of there in the Spring of '73. I was late for school, and a friend of mine gave me a ride. I couldn't get in the front door, so I started walking around the building and about seven black guys started chasing me and they had sticks, you know, like broom handles...I ran around the whole building and I scaled this tall, 15-foot fence and my friend was still driving out, and I waved to him and jumped in and drove out and that was the last that I saw of Dorchester High.

Finally, in 1974 teachers experienced a near race riot at the school.

> We had an absolute full-fledged race riot....When all hell broke loose. We're seeing 400 white kids running [away from the school] toward Ashmont and the dust is flying—it's like a Cecil B. DeMille epic—and they were being chased by 400 black kids and the noise of the feet, the dust, the yelling and screaming. I mean it was horrifying. Right there on Rogers Field. We're watching it from the windows. Then all of a sudden the leaders turned this whole crowd around and they made a charge at the school. And they went in the door at Armandine Street. So we thought, "Oh Jesus, they're coming out here." My heart, it was in my throat. Fortunately they made a rampage through the school and then ran out the other side..... But it was frightening.
>
> After all the dust settled, and the police had rounded up all of the clubs and sticks, they asked all of the teachers to go into the auditorium and the area superintendent got up in front of the faculty and he says, "you know, this is all your fault." I just stood there. I couldn't believe the man had just said that. I had hardly recovered. But some of the more outspoken teachers...they let this guy have it. They walked out of there, and it was just frightening.

Violence was not the only thing disrupting education at this time; drugs hit the school hard in the early 1970s. Teachers and students from that era recalled rampant chemical use: "drinking, smoking pot, taking pills." Teachers and students smoked openly in the classrooms, sometimes smoking pot. One teacher related the incredible story of a student who would come into class, light up a cigarette, and then just go comatose. The cigarette would "burn right down to his fingers and you could smell the flesh burning." The other students would lift up the back of

his shirt and squirt lighter fluid on his back and then set it on fire. The
teacher had to keep a bucket of water in the room to put out the fires.

For many students, it was the pervasive drug use, more than the violence and racism that made education impossible at Dorchester High.
Sadly, it appears that both students and faculty were hooked. One veteran teacher recalled the cliques of teachers that hung together after
school. There was one crowd that always drank and another that turned
to drugs—hallucinogens, marijuana, mushrooms, and harder stuff.
"Some of them never made it. They died."

Meanwhile the METCO program, which bused black students to
schools in white suburbs around Boston, was growing so rapidly that by
1972 METCO was busing 2,300 black students out of Boston, leaving
poorer students, with less active parents, behind..

Unfortunately, there was way too much headmaster turnover at DHS
during these turbulent times. From 1969 to 1982, DHS had six headmasters. During this period, the Boston School Committee made all personnel
decisions including selecting and replacing headmasters, as well as delin-
eating much of their day-to-day work. Patronage was rampant throughout the system. The Mayor's Committee on Violence, appointed in 1976,
concluded that

> the patronage method of making appointments still pervades the Boston
> school system. Friends, neighbors and relatives of School Committee mem-
> bers ask for and get special consideration for jobs. Who you know often
> counts more than what you know.... Job and employment questions per-
> vade and poison the entire operation....The result is low morale and
> cynicism by teachers and parents and substandard performances by many
> mid-managers in the system.[6]

Teachers at DHS shared in this cynicism and, of course, the growth of
the teachers union and the rapidity of administrative dictates coming
down from Court Street in the years of Garrity's leadership certainly did
nothing to warm teacher-administrator relationships. (The school district,
or central administration, in Boston is called Court Street, due to the
address of its headquarters at 26 Court Street.) With few exceptions, those
at DHS during this period struggled to recall the great leaders. One former teacher said, "certainly there were no scholars." Another added,
"you have to remember, they were mostly Phys Ed People." A third
added, "These guys were gym teachers; how much do they know about
teaching?" In fact, of the six headmasters who served during the 1970s,
three were former coaches or physical education teachers.

The 1970s marked a transition in headmaster styles. Prior to the 1970s
the headmaster's role was to maintain stability; during the 1970s the focus
was on school reform and change. The earlier period was characterized
by long headmaster tenures and few dramatic initiatives. The latter
period was characterized by crisis management, many initiatives, and
more turnover. With the daily threat of violence, in addition to struggling

with aging buildings, isolation, and overenrollments, whatever leadership there was at the school during this time was reduced to crisis management rather than purposeful innovation on most days. Even though the school had some programs that worked well, it was difficult to maintain their successes under violent conditions. Also, since the "average student who arrived at DHS during the mid-to-late 1970s had already been in six different schools in the system"[7] what the students needed most was stability, "not innovation."

On top of all of these changes within the school and the city, the Massachusetts State Legislature, building upon the Racial Imbalance Act, made two key decisions during this period that further impacted DHS. The first was their passage of the Transitional Bilingual Education Law in 1971. The first of its kind in the nation, this law mandated that bilingual students be educated in their own language so their learning could proceed while they tackled English. Bilingual education came to DHS in 1974 with three teachers "handling 85 Haitian students on a full or part-time basis."[8] By 1979, DHS was specializing in both Haitian creole and Spanish bilingual education.

In 1972, the Massachusetts State Legislature passed the Special Education Act known as Chapter 766. Again at the forefront of providing equal access to all students, the law mandated that students with special needs be educated in public schools in the least restrictive environment. The law gave parents more rights to question their child's placements and required schools to maintain individual education plans for each student.

The fruits of Chapter 766 began to manifest themselves at DHS in 1974, with the hiring of the school's first special education (SPED) teachers. While special education had existed in Boston for years, the students were educated primarily at the elementary and middle school levels and tended to drop out before high school. The turmoil of the late 1960s, and the white flight that followed, led to the shrinking of the elementary school population in Boston even as the high school population was growing; consequently, elementary SPED teachers were allowed to apply for the new high school positions. Therefore, the SPED teachers hired at DHS in 1974 came with elementary school certification, as previously there had been little reason to prepare for high school special education.

The SPED classes at DHS began with one classroom that was partitioned to make space for three or four classes. In those days, providing access was considered paramount to academic achievement. Therefore, the curricular emphasis was on accommodations and adaptations. Lesson plans were "success-oriented," making it easier for teachers lacking secondary certification to concentrate on making students feel good about themselves. This also allowed the district and school leaders to bypass providing the teachers with content focused professional development. Without a focus on content knowledge, the guidelines for mainstreaming were quite lax and measured more by the student's level of success in the

SPED classroom. This allowed teachers to move students in and out of the program, mainstreaming them as needed.

Increasingly, students with disabilities were given greater access to the regular education classroom. This caused friction between the SPED and regular education teachers who were dismayed and overwhelmed by the unrelenting emphasis on access over achievement. Since professional development was almost nonexistent at the time the teachers were left to figure out the proper balance between providing a rigorous academic experience on the one hand and making appropriate accommodations for students on the other. One teacher from 1969 recalls the impact this had on the school.

> One thing that really upset the whole structure of DHS was the whole thing with special education and mainstreaming of students. Before desegregation there was a very clear-cut breakdown of courses—we had the college courses and we had resource rooms for your SPED students. As time went on, more and more of those special education students were mainstreamed into our classes and so the whole chemistry of the class began to change. For example, I was teaching U.S. History in 1971. I was using original sources, by 1975 up until this very day it has become impossible to use those sources in class. After 74, 75, 76, 77, that's when it started to blur. We no longer had the college [track], the business, vocational. This school became heavily ... you know, it was suppose to be a comprehensive high school ... in reality it was a special needs school. They did away with all the special educational programs and started offering just regular education and special education. (white, male teacher).

These conclusions were common to regular education teachers at DHS from this period. Unfortunately, the district had no system-wide plan for how to implement Chapter 766 in the classroom. From the teacher's perspective, this dilemma seemed unique to Dorchester High School, and they began to lament the loss of tracking, the gradual disappearance of the college, business, and vocational programs, and what they called the "dumbing down" of courses. Once again, the teachers at DHS had to figure out how to deal with the influx of students with varying ability levels on their own.

> I taught psychology and sociology. Kids were put in my classes with no ability grouping. They were just thrown in there. You had seven or eight kids who just didn't belong in there because you spent a lot of energy on discipline, behavior, lack of interest. Those kids set a tone. We asked for them to at least allow ability groups. The more we said that, there was a reaction from the special needs people, not only from within school but from downtown, because there was this idea like "that is tracking. You're ruining the poor kid." (white male teacher).

Rather than do what was right for the students, this became one more point of contention between the teachers. Soon, the situation also pitted departments against each other. As the administrators prepared to mainstream students, they tended to look for elective courses with minimal prerequisites. A social studies teacher from that time maintains that it was the death of his classes:

> At that time, in the mid '70s, the chemistry and physics teachers, they were assigned thirty students, they could remove ten or twelve students who could never do chemistry or physics. They would cut that class down to the kids who were capable of doing that. Those kids then went into our electives, right? ... It seemed like social studies was a catchall.

What became clearer over time was that the system-wide effort to mainstream students with disabilities was a desegregation issue as well, backed by the power of the district court. As one teacher explained,

> These issues ran into each other [desegregation and mainstreaming]. The majority of these special education classes were made up of minority students. The college level classes had a majority of white students. The assumption was that there had to be some sort of discrimination in place... So mainstreaming of special education students and desegregation really began to blend into one another.

As student enrollments eased after 1975, more and more students with disabilities were sent to Dorchester High School. In time, the school had one of the largest populations of students with disabilities in the city. Roughly 20 percent of the student body was classified as special education. By the end of the decade, the SPED department counted twelve teachers out of an entire staff of ninety-seven teachers and aides, or about 12 percent.[9] Resources were limited. Both students and teachers began to feel that they had been dumped.

The events outlined above finally began to take their toll on teachers. Between 1974 and 1976, DHS had an unprecedented rate of teacher turnover. Seventy-nine teachers left the school during those years. At the same time, with up to 2000 students in 1974, DHS hired 89 fresh, young teachers to match the growing enrollments and to fill the ranks as older teachers retired in the face of the increasingly violent and challenging atmosphere. Special education teachers and bilingual education teachers were also joining the staff for the first time. Hiring 89 new teachers in two years had a significant impact on academics at the high school. Previously, the teacher's examination and competitive application process had ensured that most teachers were competent in their subject matter, so ongoing evaluation was not considered necessary. One teacher, hired in the late 1960s, recalls the arduous process of getting hired to teach in Boston and the level of supervision that followed.

> In those days, in order to get a permanent appointment in Boston, you had to take a six-hour examination, three hours in your major in the morning, and then two one-and-one-half hour examinations in the afternoon. Seventy-five percent of the people who took those exams failed them. That's why they ran the system in substitutes because very few people could get a permanent

appointment. Also, in order to get appointed, you had to put on a classroom demonstration to the board of examiners, or they had to come to the school that you were working at and observe you for a period. Back then, Boston teachers always had to take exams. We were tested. Absolutely. So many people wanted to teach in Boston because Boston paid the best. (white, male teacher).

This teacher claimed that he was "the first permanent teacher appointed to Dorchester High School in four years." A teaching position at Dorchester High School may have been difficult to obtain but it was also almost impossible to lose. As for poor teachers who might need to be removed, he replied, "Well, all those teachers never would have been appointed years ago. They never would have passed the exam and they never would have been appointed."

When you were appointed permanently in the Boston public schools you went on immediate tenure. There was no supervision, nothing. Immediate tenure. If you passed the exam and you passed the observation and you were recommended for that job they put you on immediate tenure. And you were never supervised. I was supervised when I was subbing. . . .But after that I was never supervised again.

In the early 1970s, as minority students crowded the Boston schools, it was important to identify competent black teachers. But the Boston Teacher's Examination was designed to give preferential treatment to Boston graduates, so black teachers often scored poorly. "Many of the black teachers were weeded out by a local examination, the 'Boston Teacher's Examination,' which was never formally validated. Once this examination became controversial, the Committee substituted it with the Educational Testing Service's National Teacher Examination."[10] Soon after they made this change however, all teacher testing was dropped. There were just too many young teachers coming and going in the 1970s to confidently test every teacher. When the test was dropped, the BPS was not accustomed to nor were they equipped to properly evaluate new teachers.[11]

What impact did all of this social turmoil have on the academic program at the school? In 1965 three tracks defined the curriculum, vocational, business, and college. Tracking by both program and degree of difficulty was still an acceptable practice. The vocational programs included woodworking, upholstering, and cabinetry. Graphic arts and electronics were introduced in the early 1970s. The business program, serving up to 60 percent of the students, offered many options that included a work-study component. There was also a topflight art program at DHS in the early 1970s. "Dorchester is listed as a principal site for art education in the city of Boston. It lists itself as the place to go if you wish to major in art."[12] Students could take two different courses in art each day. There were three art teachers and three classrooms during most of the 1970s, but limited supplies. Students came to DHS to major in this subject from inside and outside the district. This small department was the one magnet program at DHS that pulled in students from the suburbs. Last, the college program offered many and varied electives, not only for the 30 percent of students enrolled in that track, but for the general school population as well.

From 1968 on however, these academic tracks began to fade. The focus on access and equity brought by the civil rights movement opened the doors to minorities, students with disabilities, and bilingual students, but the faculty and staff was not prepared to teach the new students to their highest potential. As the school got more and more crowded, there was a growing population of students who could not access the topflight courses because they were bilingual, had special educational needs, or were academically unprepared. This meant that more and more students fell short of college. As a result, DHS began to focus on the basics, targeting mathematics, and reading and writing in the curriculum. The social studies department shrank in comparison to the English and mathematics departments. The art program was cut back and finally eliminated altogether by 1980. Electronics also died in 1977 and graphic arts was gone by 1978. The business department also lost 10 percent of its students by 1977. Most telling of all, by 1980, special education was the largest department in the school. This shift in curricular emphasis was slow, however, and teachers give up their favorite courses reluctantly. By the end of the decade there was a discernible lack of focus in the curriculum.

The final blow for the DHS community came in 1981 when declining school enrollments throughout the city led to the closing of twenty-seven schools and the layoff of 1206 teachers system-wide. The schools were still under court order to maintain racial balance, and Judge Garrity insisted on fair minority representation among Boston teachers as well, pitting the notion of union seniority against that of affirmative action, leading to massive layoffs of relatively senior white faculty. At DHS, almost all of the white teachers with less than ten years seniority were let go. This left the younger black teachers who remained to deal with bitter hostility among their colleagues. One white teacher who survived explained, "It was a difficult time ... it didn't help morale; it didn't help race relations." The business program fell from 22 to eight teachers. Faculty morale hit an all time low, resulting in an 89 percent staff attendance rate for the year. Students at DHS were so upset at having lost some of their favorite teachers that they staged a walkout in April of 1981 to protest the layoffs.

Sadly, the social and political climate and the resulting loss of a clear academic focus at the school severely impacted student achievement. The watershed arrived in 1975 when things really fell apart for the students. The attendance rate dropped from 90 percent in the late 1960s to 73 percent. The graduation rate fell similarly, from 56 to 20 percent. By the end of the 1970s, fatigue had settled in at Dorchester High. There were still protests and walkouts, but the battles were over for the most part. The Federal Court was pushing the development of magnet schools and they transferred many students out of DHS to boost magnet enrollments. This, combined with poor attendance, meant that there were only about 700 students in the building on any given day, even though the official student population was listed at about 900. The relief of student congestion helped restore some normalcy to the building, but the reduced enrollments meant the loss of more faculty. By the end of the decade, the classes were smaller, the behavioral problems were minimized and the collegiality revived among the survivors. A new community was created, a new cultural ethic formed, but unfortunately, it was one that was more distrustful, fragmented, and guarded.

CHAPTER 4

Help Is on the Way: The Community Comes to Dorchester High School 1982 to 1989

From The *Boston Globe*, February 9 & 10, 1982:

A 17-year-old Dorchester High School student was shot in the head by another student yesterday with a gun the second student may have thought was not loaded. The student was shot in the right side of the bridge of her nose by a male student just after school ended. The shooting occurred in Room 103, an 11th grade history class.

The shooting again raised questions about violence inside Boston's schools. The latest figures for this school year, through Jan. 8, show there have been 18 assaults with dangerous weapons before yesterday's shooting, 165 armed and unarmed robberies, four stabbings and cuttings and 47 assaults on staff members. Students at the scene yesterday appeared to be more angry than frightened.

"I can't even come to school. Situations like this one make me not want to go to school. I just want to get out and get a fulltime job," said a male student who asked not to be identified. An 18-year-old senior added, "A lot of students will say that this is a bad school. That bothers me a lot. They talk about guns and stuff, but they don't really know. It's a good school. That was a freak accident."[1]

The student survived her shooting, but it was clear that Dorchester High School was at the bottom. Violence inside and outside of the school had shattered what little morale was left among students and faculty. The surrounding neighborhood was decimated in the wake of years of urban renewal, blockbusting, and redlining. Students had to walk to school through an area that was "dilapidated, dotted with boarded-up buildings, abandoned cars, and rubbish-filled vacant lots," according to a local newspaper. A new school choice plan was in place citywide as part of the desegregation order, but Dorchester High was now the least chosen school in Boston. "This was a dead school," recalled one teacher. "There was no identity—not among students, not among the staff."[2]

The school needed help. It needed coordinated, sustained intervention from the outside. For the next six years, Boston's major institutions actually came together to provide that help, and for some students, Dorchester High came close to being transformed.

THE COURT CONVENES THE COMMUNITY

The groundwork for change had been laid seven years earlier by the desegregation orders of Federal Judge Arthur Garrity. A former campaign manager for John Kennedy, Garrity was "essentially obsessive in his details."[3] In early 1975, having already ordered that Boston Schools be desegregated, he issued a second, voluminous "Report of the Masters." The Report laid out the most ambitious and comprehensive plan for the Boston Public Schools ever devised. Its legacy remains with the system to this day.[4]

Several key recommendations specifically impacted Dorchester High School. One dragged the system into compliance with federal and state law, forcing the city to obey the new 1970s legislative acts on bilingual and special education. Another called for the fazing out of the outdated vocational programs like those at DHS. A third called for the creation of "school/community partnerships" with every school in the city.

Garrity had ambitious ideas for the partnerships. He specifically challenged Boston's businesses, trade unions, community organizations, colleges, and universities to involve themselves directly in the daily life of the city's schools, and to "establish the role to be played by each in educational planning, curriculum, development, instruction and research."

The Court's order was a catalyst, a kind of convenor of "the community." The leaders of the major business and educational institutions in Boston quickly stepped forward to endorse the judge's mandate. Six months later, when school started in September 1975, 24 colleges and universities and 21 businesses were partnered in some way with all 17 of Boston's high schools. Dorchester High School was officially partnered with Boston State College and New England Telephone.

> We have a huge entry-level workforce, which does not necessarily require a college degree....operators [and] technicians. The high schools are a big customer for us in terms of future employees, so it makes sense for us to work with the students that are going to be graduating and entering the workforce.[5]

But the partnerships did not go far enough initially. Relatively superficial opportunities were offered to students: guest speakers, field trips, and career development activities, along with some jobs and internships. In 1976, a new report called on the business community to push for real, sustainable reform: to "address the problems of central school administration,"[6] and to "think in terms of developing, initiating and supporting a job placement program."[7] In 1979, business leaders responded with the creation of the Private Industry Council, or PIC, which to this day sets up summer and after-school jobs for Boston students.

> You can't succeed in urban education just in the classroom....You can't go after poverty with delayed gratification. You have got to put some money in kids' pockets as positive reinforcement for academic achievement and good behavior. (Neil Sullivan, Executive Director of the Private Industry Council)[8]

As business leaders became increasingly involved with the Boston Public Schools, they grew increasingly frustrated. Too often, students were so poorly educated that they were virtually unemployable. As one business representative said, "We want to hire the kids...[but] we're not able to get the students to pass [our] tests." The CEOs wanted to institute standards of accountability for the schools, a business-oriented system to measure the schools' success and failure rates. They found a ready ear in Robert Spillane, who became superintendent of the Boston Public Schools in 1981.

THE BOSTON COMPACT: THE COMMUNITY GETS ORGANIZED

Robert Spillane had a three-year contract, an unheard-of vote of confidence from the Boston School Committee, which was notorious for hobbling its superintendents.[9] Spillane lost no time in using his new mandate. In one of his first major initiatives, he called together business CEOs and college and university presidents to discuss a more formal agreement between the school partners and the district as a whole. These talks led to the Boston Compact.

> The Compact was a result of that agreement. The business community would give priority access to jobs....Higher ed would give priority admission and scholarships. [Boston University President] John Silber delivered fifty-one full boat scholarships as part of the original compact deal. In exchange, the school system would fix itself...as measured by lower dropout rates, higher test scores, and better attendance. (Neil Sullivan)

The Boston Compact was unprecedented. It was a signed agreement between the business community, local colleges and universities, and the school system. The CEOs and higher education presidents pledged to increase by 5 percent each year the number of BPS students either hired by local businesses or accepted into the state's colleges and universities. The educational partners also pledged to work with schools to reduce the dropout rate.

In return, the BPS agreed that the graduation rate would increase by 5 percent each year. In addition, the BPS agreed to implement a district-wide assessment system to document student competency in reading and math. With this new system in place, the BPS pledged that all BPS seniors would achieve the minimum competency needed for employment and college acceptance by 1986. They would also track student attendance, test scores, and the dropout rates with the goal of yearly improvements. Last, the agreement contained a provision for the evaluation of high school headmasters according to these benchmarks.

> The Compact was a way to pull together the business community and the higher ed community....It was a construct. It remains a great construct; a great set of measures of accountability for the school system, and a list of commitments that the business community and higher ed would make to the schools and the school kids. (Neil Sullivan)

"The Compact was acclaimed nationally as the first and most ambitious effort by the business community to support public education in response to *A Nation at Risk*."[10] It immediately brought millions of dollars into the school system. The New England Merchants bank committed $300,000 to fund awards of $6,500 each for excellence among BPS teachers. Next, the Bank of Boston used $1.5 million in funds to create the Boston Plan for Excellence in 1984. The Plan was designed as a "self-sustaining" endowment that would fund educational reforms over time.

Once the Plan was in place, other corporations made major donations, too. John Hancock Financial Services created the HEART fund with a $1 million donation to support middle school education. The New England and the Boston Foundation created a $5 million endowment for financial aid counseling and college scholarships. Finally, the law firm of Goodwin, Procter and Hoar created the SEED program to fund innovation in early childhood education. These and other funds were managed and administered through the Boston Plan for Excellence. As we shall see, the Plan itself later became a force to be reckoned with in the continuing struggle over the Boston Public Schools.

POCKETS OF CREATIVITY AT DORCHESTER HIGH

Coincidentally, just as the Boston Compact was signed, and only a year after Robert Spillane was hired, Dorchester High School got a new headmaster. It was a fortunate confluence of events. Carl Cohen was a canny administrator who, though he often took credit for others' ideas, was skilled at the art of institutional reform. With Spillane's strong leadership to back him, and with the help of DHS's new business and university partners, Cohen was able to implement a broad range of initiatives—including, ultimately, a Compact-funded program called Compact Ventures.

But first he had to face an exhausted and demoralized faculty. Those teachers who were left at DHS by the early 1980s—those who had survived the overcrowding, the racial animosity and violence, and finally, the layoffs—had taken one of two paths. Some had closed their doors against the larger school, managing their own classrooms as best they could.

> I had union protection and good benefits...I kept myself going for years by teaching night school to adults – that was a lot more enjoyable.[11]

Fortunately for the school, and for Headmaster Cohen, there was another group of teachers who had taken a different path. These teachers, members of the progressive "class of 69," had created pockets of creativity in the school, small educational "clusters" which became both inspiration and foundation for Cohen's reforms.

> The faculty who remained were people who enjoyed teaching. And we enjoyed teaching city kids. We felt comfortable there.[12]
> During our darkest hours we gravitated toward collegial networking. We had a hard basis of caring and respect to see us through. We could share our goals, support each other.[13]

The first of these smaller "educational clusters" was called LEAP, for Law, Education, Allied Health and Public Service. It offered a series of introductory courses in those subjects. One teacher, who would become a key resource for reform at DHS, explains the impetus for LEAP:

> So I can remember walking into Jimmy's class, this is like the early '80s, and I said, "Look, this school needs some kind of theme to set it apart, to give it some kind of direction" because it seemed like we were just floundering at that time. (LEAP founder)

Meanwhile, the science faculty was developing a program of its own. These teachers were housed together on the third floor of the building, a circumstance that allowed them to create a small community of colleagues who shared the same ideas and values about education. They put together Allied Health, a multi-year program of courses and internships focused on health careers in 1982.

Both LEAP and Allied Health attracted support from outside the school. Once again, the Federal Court was pivotal. Judge Garrity, in an attempt to halt re-segregation in the schools, had declared DHS too black. In order to remedy the situation, the Judge demanded that efforts be made to attract more white students to the school. This in turn made school district headquarters more open to these small, theme-based academic programs, because they believed the programs would attract more white students to the district high schools.

They wanted to find something that would be more exciting for white students to come back because so many white students were fleeing from the public schools, so I think the superintendent's theory was that if you had some very interesting themes in high schools, the kids would want to stay in the Boston public schools. (white, female staff member).

After one year, the School district administrators felt that Allied Health had the potential to attract more white students into the system, so they provided the funds for a fulltime coordinator. Allied Health slowly became a strong program with partnerships and internships in health careers. LEAP and Allied Health were very small, however. LEAP served only about 100 students and Allied Health served fewer than that. From their inception, both programs were accused of serving only the most able students at DHS, a charge that would resurface repeatedly as school reforms unfolded.

Four other small communities developed at DHS, including one that involved bilingual students, and two that served special education students. Each functioned independently of the rest of the school, as teachers tried to wall themselves off from the intractable problems in DHS as a whole.

The bilingual department served Spanish-speaking students. These students, and their teachers, tended to embrace their language and culture, and the bilingual program became a tight-knit community. An unintended consequence of this was that large numbers of Spanish speaking students failed to move on to English-only classes. Although the students were well served and supported in other ways, their overall academic achievement ultimately suffered.

The special education program for "substantially separate" students—whose disabilities ranged from severe cognitive delays to emotional and behavioral challenges—was housed in the satellites. By this time, the satellites not only had inadequate lights and heat, but also had leaking roofs. "All we needed was ducks," said one administrator later. A 1982 accreditation report fiercely criticized the school for this, and for the lack of communication between the SPED teachers and the regular education staff. Similar complaints were aimed at the bilingual program. Said the report, "They appear to function independently while occupying the same facility."[14] The accreditors did not realize that the same could have been said for the staffs of all of the small communities in the beleaguered school.

THE COMMUNITY COMES TO DORCHESTER HIGH

When Carl Cohen arrived at Dorchester High in 1982, the faculty had very little love for administration of any kind. Previously, Cohen had been an athletics coach, and some teachers regarded him with disdain, believing that he didn't know much about the kinds of curricular reforms the faculty were trying to initiate through their small learning communities.

In some ways, this was a plus for Cohen. In reality, he didn't have many ideas of his own about reforming the curriculum, allowing him to readily support the faculty's ideas for curricular innovation. Cohen was also aware that if he was ever going to win the faculty's trust, he would have to first address their concerns about violence and the deteriorating building. As one teacher said:

> When he first started, I'd talk with him about curriculum issues and he'd say, "No, I've got to get discipline under control first," or "I've got to get the building renovated first." Naturally I didn't believe him."[15]

To this end, Cohen spent his first year focused on improving discipline and cleaning up the facilities. He began by instituting new attendance procedures, including a provision to call the parents of absent students. He also reorganized his three assistant headmasters to focus all of their time on discipline.[16] In 1984, DHS hired school police for the first time.

> Mr. Cohen didn't waste any time. And he was very direct. If you were a troublemaker or causing problems, you were suspended right there. He didn't play games. Everybody knew it and I think that's why things ran so well. Because everybody knew it. But on the other hand, he would find time ...like I was on the softball team and he came out and he watched us play our games. He didn't have to do that. So he was involved on both ends, like discipline, but he was also there to encourage and to motivate and you know that was nice. You don't find that all the time. (former student and teacher)

Cohen also succeeded in renovating the physical plant, convincing Court Street to let him use $1 million from the desegregation fund for the renovations. The rattling windows were finally replaced, new student lockers were installed, the one chemistry lab was refurbished, the auditorium renovated, glass backboards were added in the gymnasium, and lots of new paint applied everywhere. One other first was a computer lab on the second floor. Mayor Ray Flynn came by to cut the ribbon on the "new" school.[17] (Unfortunately, those 1980s windows were made of a new unbreakable material that clouded over in the sun giving students a bathroom-like view of the outside world for the next twenty-five years.)

Next, Cohen brought a number of new social support programs into the school. In 1983, DHS got its first Junior ROTC program and a parenting program for teenage girls. Resources were found to hire a coordinator of the "Student Support Team," a team of school personnel who meet weekly to match students with needed social services.

Then, Cohen called in the community, starting with the University of Massachusetts Boston. UMB had been providing academic remediation to selected students since 1965 through its Upward Bound program. This program, the first Upward Bound grant in the country, brought promising students to the university on weekends and in the summer to have a college experience. The UMB representative brought more than college help to DHS; he brought a valuable new perspective on the students.

> Essentially what we did was to specifically go into classrooms, which is what I would do. This is where I met my good friend Carl Cohen, who...was extremely skeptical at first about whether I would in fact find any talented youngsters, or any kids at that school who would be worthy of participating in this program...The direct quote was—he went inside to talk with the students first of all—and when he came out, he looked me right in the eye and said, "They're animals!"...And they were out of control, I will admit. I'm not going to deny it. They were definitely out of control. They were bouncing off the walls, but they were teenagers. They were just young teenagers. And my issue was that I thought I had something to say to them, and I did have something to say to them, and I think it was substantive and meaningful and I think once they started getting the message that I was serious about their future, that it was meant for them, they gave me their full attention and I was successful in recruiting from that class a couple of students who I still remember to this day. (Charlie Desmond)[18]

In 1983, UMB created a second program called Urban Scholars, which they designed specifically for gifted urban students from DHS and the university's two other partner schools.

> Clearly what I could see was in the three schools that UMB was concentrated in, there were students that were just exceptionally gifted young people that simply had skills that were far beyond anything that one would have reasonably expected "in the neighborhood school." Certainly they were skilled beyond what was being provided to them academically in those schools. What we thought was why not develop a series of strategies and programming support that would enable these students to achieve at the limits of their potential? Which is different that simply giving them the skills and motivation necessary to pursue higher education (which is what we were trying to do through Upward Bound). (Charlie Desmond)

Urban Scholars allowed DHS, for the first time, to effectively serve those students with college potential.

Cohen's decisions to focus first on safety and the school environment were critical to fostering readiness in the staff for more substantive changes. The faculty and staff were impressed with his efforts and their "skepticism diminished, but they were still not convinced"[19] that Cohen's reform efforts were the ones they wanted to support. Perhaps one reason for this was that about half of the faculty had their own little "schools" within the school to keep them busy.

Cohen turned once again to the community for help, this time in the form of DHS's business partner, New England Telephone (NET). Cohen wanted teachers to be more involved in systematic reform planning school-wide, rather than just in the smaller clusters. Louis and Miles, who studied DHS in 1984, describe how NET helped Cohen by sponsoring a day-long retreat on planning strategies and skills which was attended by administrators and department heads. The day was a success, but Cohen and NET realized that teachers needed to be more involved. The NET partnership coordinator, "located a program used for NET management training called 'Investment in Excellence.' The workshops emphasized enhanced self-esteem, motivation, and personal goal setting; administrators who attended were so enthusiastic that another workshop was done for more staff."[20]

Reports of dramatic personal change such as weight loss and smoking cessation circulated throughout the school after the workshop series was completed. Even though these changes were more personal than educational, it was Cohen's the first step in trying to entice and prepare faculty and staff to participate more fully in reform planning.

The next push came from UMB. According to Louis and Miles, UMB's liaison worked with the department heads "to improve their curriculum planning and their supervision skills, so individual faculty could in turn improve their own planning and self-evaluation strategies." UMB also worked directly with DHS teachers by establishing "think tanks and running summer institutes that focused on curricular issues of interest to them." DHS teachers had to write proposals for think tank projects that focused on classroom instructional issues. The teachers were then paired with university faculty to work together on their projects. By this time, both the NET and the UMB liaisons were spending over half their time in the school.

NET's deepening interest in DHS proved to be a boon for the school. NET was a power in Boston business circles, and a leader of the Private Industry Council. The company played a key role in bringing the needs of DHS to the attention of the PIC. In 1984, the PIC brought the full weight of the Boston Compact to Dorchester High for the first time.

COMPACT VENTURES: DORCHESTER HIGH ON THE WAY UP

The PIC had been working with DHS since 1983 to place students in summer jobs. In the summer of 1984, representatives of the PIC approached Headmaster Cohen and a group of teachers at DHS about working more closely with the school. Together, the PIC, the teachers, and Cohen wrote a $135,000 proposal to the state for a program called Compact Ventures that would focus on a cluster of at-risk ninth graders.

Ninth graders were having a particularly difficult time at DHS. They had an 80 percent attendance rate, a 22 percent dropout rate (the overall dropout rate was at 50 percent), and their Metropolitan Achievement Test scores were the worst in the city. In reading, the ninth graders scored 22 percentile points below the city average of 42. In math they were 13 percentile points below the city average. Even if the school had a plan for turning these statistics around, it would have been very difficult to impact students since only 39 percent spent a full four years at the school, leaving DHS with the highest mobility rate in the city.

The PIC/DHS proposal was aimed squarely at this problem. The proposal was funded, and Headmaster Cohen promptly went out to recruit the most talented urban teachers he could find.

> The way I remember it…Carl Cohen was actively recruiting people that he heard of and knew about and he actively recruited me and I believe Ann Todd.…He made a real effort to recruit people that he wanted and he told us about this program, if you want it, I would like to have you be the English teacher and I would like for you to be the math teacher. (Paul Casilli)[21]

Casilli, Todd, and the other Compact Ventures teachers began teaching in the program in September 1984. They were responsible for 110 of the incoming ninth graders.

> We had some tough, tough kids in that Compact. All freshmen. I got cut with a razor blade from a student in Compact Ventures who almost killed a kid in my room, you know. She almost cut her jugular with a razor blade, right down the side of her face. And when we found out, I remember going down and testifying, that she had done it the year before and no one told us. In the eighth grade, in the middle school. It was real, real tough. (Paul Casilli)

The Compact Ventures program was painstakingly structured. Each teacher was a member of a cluster of four teachers who met daily to discuss student progress. These teachers were able to develop close relationships with the students because the students moved through their classes as a cohort, taking English, reading, math and science with the same teachers. This allowed the teachers to catch problems early, whether personal, social, or academic. The cluster also employed a youth worker and three teaching assistants to work in the classrooms. Tutors were available to work with the students in all subject areas.

Headmaster Cohen gave the Compact teachers ample leeway to run the program as they saw fit.

> One thing I remember from Carl Cohen…is that, he trusted us enough to say run with this. Do what you want. Just run anything by me. I just want to know so I am not caught in the media headlights. You know you're outside doing some community service; I want to know about it. Pretty much carte blanche…[He] trusted us enough to make the judgments and calls with what we were doing with the students. So he did do that. He empowered the teachers in that Compact Ventures to do the planning; to do the extra kinds of things we wanted to do with the students. (Paul Casilli)

Common planning time was a key feature of Compact Ventures. The teachers' daily meetings were a subject of great interest to the students.

> It was funny, I remember the kids would always say, "You are in there talking about me today aren't you?" And sometimes we would say, "You know what, we are, we are real concerned. We are in there talking." "Well, what are you talking about?" "Well, if you want to come to the meeting, you can

join us," and a lot of times they would be there...We used to put a seat right there and maybe it wasn't in the textbooks or anything, we said, "This is the hot seat and you sit there and you are going to listen to us. Why we are so concerned about you. Let's talk, how is he or she doing in your classes and so forth."

They were just overwhelmed. You know it was kind of like they gave up, they weren't even going to have a pretense anymore that I am making it, that I am making an attempt. No you are not making an attempt. We would call them on the carpet. They felt that someone was concerned about them. They might not have liked hearing what we had to say at that point, and sometimes we were more tactful than others, but even if we were not as tactful, that was concern. (Paul Casilli)

The first Compact Ventures class received much media attention, perhaps due to the growing interest in education sparked by the publication of *A Nation at Risk* in 1982. The *Boston Globe* published a year-long series on the program, visiting Ann Todd's classroom five times in the 1984–85 school year. It was the first time that the city's media had given the school any positive coverage. As we shall see, this and other *Globe* reports during this period were indispensable to the success of the education reform efforts in Boston. The *Globe*, in fact, was an important member of the community.

According to the *Globe* reports, 46 of Todd's students failed the first term, 33 of them because of absenteeism, the rest because they didn't do any homework. She also lost and regained 22 percent of the students during the first five months of the year. Ten percent of the girls in her classroom were teenage mothers.

One of her students, 17-year old Michael Clougherty, had dropped out of seventh grade the year before (which he was repeating), and had now returned to the ninth grade. "I was happy to go back to the ninth grade," Michael told the *Globe* reporter. "It would have looked funny, a seventeen-year-old in seventh grade." Michael failed Ms. Todd's class in the fall of 1984. "That was because of my homework," he said. "I did none of my homework. I didn't really catch it." For the second term, Compact Ventures provided Michael with a tutor four days a week, bringing his average up to a C. Although Michael was improving, he had already missed six days of school. One more, and Ms. Todd would be forced to fail him.[22]

Ms. Todd then sent Michael out of class each day to work with an aide for individual attention. Having the aide was a great help, Ms. Todd told the *Globe*. "You could spend ten to fifiteen minutes every class just going over things for the kids who were out."[23]

Progress was slow. The *Globe* reported that by the end of their first term in the program, 50 percent of the students failed, most because of absenteeism. By midyear, half of the students received notices that they were at risk of being held back. However, there were some real improvements by June. Of the half who received warning notices, twenty were still failing, eighteen because of poor attendance, but fifteen were passing, and thirteen had the potential to pass, and only four students had dropped out altogether.

There were also signs of academic success. In September, half of the students in the cluster were reading at a fifth grade level. By June, their reading level had jumped to midyear seventh grade. The most telling sign of success was revealed in the 11 percent dropout rate for Compact Venture students as compared to DHS' 22 percent dropout rate for ninth graders the previous year.

Compact Ventures was so successful that it expanded to the entire ninth grade the following year. By this time, LEAP, Allied Health, and the other small learning clusters were becoming more established and more identified with DHS. Even though these communities served small numbers of students and tended to isolate themselves within the building, the students did come to identify more and more with DHS. This identification lifted the entire school culture.

Signs of this could be seen in the 1985 yearbook, one of the most positive school yearbooks in the last ten years. The yearbook had one of the highest percentages of senior photos and many candid shots of students. There was even an poem dedicated to the changes evident at the school:

> May God bless your heart,
> When you come to Dot.
> Our name is number 1 on the chart ;
> We rock the spot!
> We fixed up our school, now we
> Go by certain rules.
> So don't come to school and act like a fool
> By putting your name on the wall or the floor.
> Because the way they fixed up Dorchester
> We couldn't ask for more.[24]

Another indication of the increasingly positive school spirit was the winning sports teams. In 1985, DHS had four championship teams citywide and two statewide. That year, the Boston Globe recognized DHS for overall excellence in athletics.

Louis and Miles describe a healthier and happy climate at DHS in 1986:

> As of late 1986...weekly staff meetings to discuss at risk students were well carried out; external agencies were beginning to deliver services within the school. The Junior ROTC was popular. The ninth grade cluster program staff had high esprit as a team in creating a personalized environment for students. Furthermore, all students were involved in one or more of the various program components, both in and out of the classroom....Administrators were involved and getting a great deal of support and training in goal setting, planning and supervisory skill. At least three departments, English, math and bilingual education were undertaking serious efforts at curriculum development. [At the teacher level] implementation was more uneven [and]

ranged from the highly committed teachers who were excited with their new autonomy...to the apathetic and angry.[25]

Meanwhile, Headmaster Cohen had developed increasingly congenial relationships with Superintendent Spillane and the city's business community. He used these contacts to bring badly needed resources into the school. Between 1985 and 1987, DHS acquired at least four fulltime positions to assist and manage student support: one in job development, one for Compact Ventures, and one in social services. The school also had a fulltime development officer. These resources were in addition to those provided by DHS's business and university partners—New England Telephone, UMB, and the Private Industry Council.

These improvements led to measurable gains in student achievement, even outside of Compact Ventures. Student attendance rose 10 percent between 1982 and 1986—from 73 percent to 83 percent. Math scores on the Metropolitan Achievement Test went from the eighteenth to the thirty-first percentile. The ninth grade Metropolitan Achievement Test reading scores rose 15 points from the twentieth to the thirty-fifth percentile. Last, only five seniors failed the district-wide reading test in the Spring of 1986, "when more than sixty had failed the previous" year.[26]

With the steady, active support of the community, things were most definitely on the way up for Dorchester High School.

CHAPTER 5

Reports from the Circus: The Community Goes After the School Committee 1982 to 1991

While Dorchester High was making strides towards educational reform in the mid 1980s, things were not going so well downtown. The problem was the Boston School Committee. Already notorious for its behavior during the busing crisis, the School Committee had done little to redeem itself in the intervening years. Meetings were frequently chaotic, sometimes deteriorating into catcalls and shouting matches. Committee members spent more time on hiring and firing matters than on educational policy—even custodial positions made the agenda. Patronage was rife.

The Committee had its supporters. It was an elected body, and those with political ambitions in Boston had found it an effective first rung on the political ladder. Nine of the thirteen Committee members were elected directly from the neighborhoods, and this had enabled a few black and Latino candidates to enter the traditionally white power structure.

But many others were disgusted with the Committee precisely because it was elected. Constituent services—the bread and butter of a candidate's career—too often trumped concern for the school children of Boston.

> The School Committee was thought of as a stepping-stone to higher office—not about concern with the school system. They had their own staff. It would drive the superintendent crazy because the staff would be asking questions related to constituent issues—but it never really resulted in policy recommendations....We used to say that they had constituents, but they were the adults [of the city], not the children. (Samuel Tyler)[1]

The business community, in particular, had long ago lost patience with the School Committee. It was not only a matter of the Committee's problematic behavior; business leaders felt that they were not getting their money's worth out of the Boston school system.

> They got tired of having to do the remedial training for Boston graduates in order for the students now in the workforce to be productive and able to do the job.... That was a constant source of complaint.... Why are they paying these taxes and a big chunk of those taxes are going to education and they have to pay it again in terms of training those students? (Samuel Tyler)

The Boston Compact had only heightened business leaders' concerns about the Committee. Essentially, the CEOs had made a bargain with the Committee: they would provide the resources, and the Committee would fix the schools. Despite the progress at Dorchester High and other schools, business felt the progress was too slow. In their view, the School Committee was not honoring the bargain.

> Accountability is a big thing in the business world, we're always measuring, we're always talking about how did we do, where did we meet the mark, and you know, that kind of stuff. I could see people saying, "We have this agreement and we're holding up our end. We've been investing this amount of money in educational initiatives and what are we getting back from it?" (DHS Business Partner Verizon)[2]

Business had previously made two attempts to weaken the School Committee, including a 1982 legislative proposal, but both efforts had failed. In 1987, they decided to go back to the state legislature, this time with a proposal to "dramatically strengthened the superintendent's role."[3] Most notably, the measure sought to transfer the ability to hire, fire, promote, and transfer from the School Committee to the superintendent. The bill passed, and the CEOs thought their fight was over.

> We did at the time think that this was going to be the last step—this created a superintendency that was and probably still is legislatively the most powerful superintendent in the country. (Samuel Tyler)

But the Committee proved to be a wily adversary. It had already defied a Federal judge in the 1970s, and it found ways to ignore the new state law as well.

The CEOs went back into a huddle—almost literally. Their favored meeting place was a vault in the Boston Safe Deposit Bank, and they were becoming known as "The Vault"—the 25 top business leaders in the city from banking, finance, insurance, utilities, and manufacturing.

> This goes back to a time where good corporate citizens of Boston wanted a good viable city, knowing that a good educational system is an important part of that.... The only Fortune 500 company in Boston now is Liberty Mutual. If we were in the late 1980s now under the current conditions, I don't know that the business community would be so much involved. It used to be

where the heads of the companies had more time for these issues, particularly the involvement with the schools. (Samuel Tyler)

The Vault decided to try to talk directly with the School Committee. This time, they brought the Mayor into the process. After many months of negotiation, an agreement was reached between the "parties," as they came to be known.[4] The consensus emphasized school-based management and admonished the Boston School Committee to follow the letter and spirit of the new state law: that is, the Committee would stick to educational policy matters and allow the superintendent to oversee day-to-day operations.

One year later, not much had changed. "[The] elected school committee still saw itself as politicians whose role was to provide constituent services which inevitably meant [it] would get involved in daily operations and would tie the superintendent's staff down with work that [had nothing to do with establishing] policy guidelines." (Samuel Tyler)

THE MAYOR STEPS IN

By now, Mayor Ray Flynn was getting frustrated too. Flynn prided himself on being a "neighborhood" mayor. When he'd been elected in 1983, he'd hired "a bunch of community organizers" to carry out his agenda, which included affordable housing, rent control, restoration of public housing, and an end to racial violence. But he'd been able to do little for the schools, primarily because the School Committee had control of the school budget. Now, as he entered his second term, Flynn wanted the Committee out of the way.

> Remember, we are a bunch of community organizers, we come in and we suddenly controlled the city budget and most of the spending was in the schools. It was our biggest account and we have no control over how the money is spent. That wears on you real quick. (Neil Sullivan, former Education Advisor for Mayor Flynn)

The Mayor did have the power to allocate the annual school budget; but only the School Committee could decide how to spend it.

> There would be the annual contest of how much money would be allocated from the city budget to the School Department and the pathology started at this level and then ramped up to triple the noise. It was clearly destructive. There would be a big City Hall versus the School Committee fight over the allocation and the School Committee would say, "The schools are failing because the Mayor doesn't give us enough money." And then the Mayor would say, "I gave them the money, but they waste it." The one thing everyone agreed upon was the schools are failing. (Neil Sullivan)

> I can remember State of the City addresses where the Mayor wouldn't even mention education. . . . It was a matter of making sure that the School Department had just enough money so you couldn't be criticized for underfunding it. . . . The political advice was stay away from schools, you can't win because

you don't have the control over the schools so don't even bother. (Samuel Tyler)

But Mayor Flynn was determined, and besides, he knew the Vault was behind him. In October of 1988, shortly after he started his second term, Flynn made his first move against the School Committee, appointing an advisory committee on school reform. Three months later, the racially diverse panel concluded that the present School Committee had outlived its usefulness. They recommended that Committee members be appointed by the Mayor, not elected.

Next, the City Council got involved with its own study commission. This commission split its conclusions: some members favored an appointed School Committee, but others wanted a half-elected, half-appointed board. The one thing they all agreed on was that the present School Committee had to go. Said one commission member, "If the School Committee doesn't realize it's over, it will pretty soon."[5] The Vault weighed in immediately. The half-elected/half-appointed option was unworkable, they insisted. Only an appointed Committee could be expected to run the schools well.

Just as this debate was beginning to heat up, The School Committee added its own fuel. It was July of 1989, and the Committee was facing a key decision. There were 4,000 excess seats in the city's high schools, and one school was going to have to be closed. The Committee had appointed a special commission to make the controversial decision, and had agreed to be bound by the Committee's recommendation.

But when the special commission voted to close a high school in a politically powerful white neighborhood, the School Committee reneged on its promise. Instead, they closed a predominantly black school by merging it with a predominantly Latino school.

> The profound nature of the mistake is, in retrospect, that they made it in the middle of rising gang activity....To take an African American High School, to pick it up with a prestige name like English, drop it into Jamaica Plain High School, a predominantly Latino school and here is the kicker: to take a predominantly Spanish speaking school and to call it 'English'! At that point, the media turned on the School Committee. You know, Brian Leary started doing "Reports From the Circus." It was on the 11:00 news. (Neil Sullivan)

Despite the uproar, School Committee members dug in their heels and refused to budge. It was the beginning of the end for the embattled panel.

But it would take another year and a half to finally abolish it. Community members didn't yet agree on what kind of Committee they wanted next: all-appointed, or half-elected/half-appointed. The ensuing debate eventually drew in the entire community: the media, business, city and state power brokers, black politicians, black parents, and black religious leaders.

THE FINAL BATTLE

In December of 1990, after two failed referenda, innumerable meetings, and a flood of media coverage, the City Council and the Mayor finally agreed to abolish outright the Boston School Committee. They proposed an all-appointed Committee in its place. The measure would go before the state Legislature in 1991.

Soon after, representatives from the black and Latino communities reignited the push for a half-elected, half-appointed school board. They reiterated that the School Committee represented a valuable entry-level opportunity for aspiring politicians of color. They argued that the loss of all the elected Committee positions would leave their communities once again in a political backwater.

But the Mayor, the *Boston Globe,* and the Vault wanted an all-appointed board, and when the proposal reached the Legislature in April, it was a proposal for an appointed School Committee of seven members. Accordingly, the Black Legislative Caucus led the fight to defeat the proposal in the Massachusetts Senate. Initially, they were successful in persuading Senate Republicans to side with them. But pressure from the Vault quickly convinced the senators to reconsider the alliance.

Then, a disagreement surfaced in the black community. On May twenty-third, the Bay State Banner, the city's only African American weekly newspaper, published an editorial and political cartoon in support of the abolition of the School Committee. "Some political activists in the black community have campaigned against the appointed School Committee on the grounds that it would reduce the number of black elected officials," said the editorial. "And indeed it would, but if the black elected officials have not been able to do the job for their constituents, why should the constituents be concerned about keeping them in office?"

The next day, the Interfaith Ministerial Alliance of Greater Boston—a black organization—held a press conference on the steps of the Statehouse, and announced that they too supported an appointed School Committee. They sent a letter to all 40 of the state's senators urging them to vote for an appointed School Committee.

The fight was almost over. Later that day, the Senate voted 26-11 to abolish the elected School Committee. Many in the Senate attributed their vote to the actions of the Bay State Banner and the ministers. As one Senator remarked, "there has been a suggestion that the black community was monolithically opposed to the petition. I think the intervention of leaders—the Bay State Banner and the ministers—belied that."[6] However, the black legislative delegation credited the defeat to aggressive lobbying of Senate Republicans by the Vault and business leaders. "The significant factor was that the Vault got into it and had various campaign contributors contact senators. I don't think the ministers had any influence. I think they saw a win coming and rode the wave of a win."[7] The House followed suit in early July.

Now it was up to the state's Republican Governor William Weld. The governor owed political debts to people on both sides of the School Committee debate. In a tough election fight the year before, Mayor Ray Flynn had supported him.

> Flynn had appeared at JJ Foleys, lifting a beer with Bill Weld on the front cover of the Boston Herald, which was about as an effective cultural endorsement as Bill Weld could get....Basically Flynn then called on Weld, politically, this is democracy, and he asked for two things. We asked for the summer jobs campaign...and the other thing we wanted was the appointed board. (Neil Sullivan)

On the other hand, the black community had also supported Weld's election. The Governor hesitated.

> He thought that this would be a pretty good deal to try and gain some foothold in the minority sections in Boston, and he had an idea of maybe vetoing the bill. And that is where the business leadership really got involved because they basically went to Weld and said, "Look this is not politics. You've got to keep your hands off of this. This is too important to play around with," and he backed off. I don't know if he would have if the business leadership—the main contributors to the Republican Party—hadn't weighed in on that. (Samuel Tyler)

On July 5, Governor Weld signed the bill into law. A nominating panel presented Mayor Flynn with a list of 32 nominees in December 1991. He appointed a new School Committee of seven members three weeks later.

> I hated giving up the elected Committee. I hated it....We were electing dog-catchers back then because we believed that enfranchisement came from electoral work....So to be positioned at the end of the decade to get rid of the elected Committee, I mean, it just didn't go down easy....It has been a loss for the town because the community of color, and I will argue the white community as well, has lost entry-level political positions. Therefore, less people get experience in running for office. I don't think achieving that, however, is sufficient trade off. I don't think a dysfunctional school system is an acceptable trade off for that....We did realize our grandest aspiration, which was the next mayor would completely embrace the school system. Be willing to be held accountable and through the Board appoint a superintendent to have the power and stability necessary to turn things around....I mean, when is the last time you heard anybody blame anybody else for the condition of the schools. It doesn't happen any more. (Neil Sullivan)

The new alignment of power downtown would indeed turn things around in the Boston Public Schools, even at Dorchester High. The concentrated attention of the entire community had produced a new School Committee that would eventually back groundbreaking reforms at DHS. But first, more change was needed in the educational superstructure. The next big push for reform came—as in the 1970s—from the courts.

SCHOOL REFORM TAKES HOLD IN MASSACHUSETTS

Just as the new School Committee was taking office in Boston a pivotal 15-year court battle over school reform was finally being resolved at the state level. The stakes were high in the suit: the plaintiffs argued that Massachusetts was perpetuating a system of unequal schools through its school funding formula. The Supreme Judicial Court agreed, and ruled that the state had failed to meet its constitutional mandate to adequately educate all children. Schools in poor communities—like Dorchester High—were entitled to more money.

The state legislature moved swiftly to remedy the problem. In 1993, the Statehouse approved a new funding formula that would double state aid for education over the next seven years. As we shall see, some of that money found its way to Dorchester High.

But the legislation went much further. Business leaders had been quietly lobbying legislators for the same educational reforms that they'd pushed for in Boston: more accountability, more standards. The legislature responded with the sweeping Massachusetts Educational Reform Act (MERA), which standardized curriculum statewide, and instituted a controversial state exam for students in grades four, eight, and ten. The grade ten test in particular drew fire: no student could receive a high school diploma without passing it.

The law also established new standards for teachers, including two rigorous tests, and professional development requirements. Even schools themselves were given progress and performance criteria, and the state Department of Education was directed to take underperforming schools and districts into receivership.

Finally, the law opened the doors for the first Massachusetts charter schools. Charter schools are publicly funded schools that operate free of district requirements but are directly accountable to the state. The new charter schools, which threatened to draw off students and money from the BPS, compelled Court Street and the Boston Teachers Union to support the creation of ten innovative "pilot" schools in Boston, including one which was located at Dorchester High. The pilot schools were small and operated with unprecedented freedom from union and School Committee oversight, while still remaining part of the Boston Public Schools.

THE COMMUNITY IN ALIGNMENT FOR REFORM

A solid platform for the launch of school reforms was taking shape all around Dorchester High. In addition to the new School Committee and the new state law, a new Mayor was taking office in Boston. Tom Menino's tough, nuts-and-bolts style worked in the city, where voters appreciated his attention to basic services: snow removal, potholes, clean streets, crime prevention—and education.

Menino declared himself the city's first "education mayor." "I want to be judged as your mayor by what happens in the Boston Public Schools," he said in a State of the City address. "If I fail to bring about these specific reforms by the year 2001, then judge me harshly."[8] He outlined an agenda that included higher standards for student achievement, a district-wide extended day program, and a commitment to reaching a one-to-four ratio of computers to students in all the schools. The *Boston Globe* praised him, and pointed out that Menino was one of the first mayors in the country to wield real power over the school system. Business leaders quietly congratulated themselves.

> I can remember State of the City addresses where the Mayor wouldn't even mention education....Really, the political advice was stay away from schools, you can't win because you don't have the control over the schools so don't even bother....Now, you have some addresses that it is all about education because the Mayor is fully responsible for education which he wasn't before. Prior to the appointed board it was a matter of making sure that the School Department had just enough money so you couldn't be criticized for under funding it. (Samuel Tyler)

But despite the promising developments downtown, all was not well at Dorchester High. The school was on a downward slide again, and it would be three more turbulent years before the community finally stepped in to help for a second time.

CHAPTER 6

Back to Square One at Dorchester High School 1989 to 1995

It is a very tight story, what happened in Boston [in the late '80s and early '90s]. The mob was convinced not to go into crack distribution...so crack didn't show up here for about 3 years after it had taken control over the Bronx and Brooklyn and there was this big vacuum, and a guy by the name of Darryl Whiting came up; he bought a video shop on Bowdoin Street; he set up in Orchard Park; and he started recruiting teenagers right into a gap with the most addictive poison anyone has ever put out. He literally brought the crack in from New York, but armed the teenagers. He started giving them turf and guns...It was chaos, we had a twenty percent local aid cut at the very time that gang violence [took off]. We had 152 murders in 1990, seventy-five of which involved kids eighteen years or younger. It was out of control. (Neil Sullivan)

Even as the School Committee battle was heating up downtown in the late 1980s, everything was collapsing at Dorchester High. First, Compact Ventures was cut, just when it was taking off. By 1987, the program had expanded from the ninth grade into the tenth and eleventh grades. It had even spread to eight other schools in the district. The program now included many features designed to keep students connected: drama productions, team teaching, clustering students, plus extra counselors and social workers. The program was so well staffed that "every day one staff person does nothing else but telephone or visit the homes of absent students to find out what is wrong." The school had also done away with the use of out-of-school suspensions to deal with disruptive students and instituted a "time-out" room instead—a very innovative approach to dealing with troubled students. The program was doing so well that the state had become its principle funder, donating $400,000 in 1988.

> But then the funding was cut....We were dumbfounded. How can you come up with a positive report from the Education office and the State saying this is working, and then cut it. People kept saying teachers there are jaded; teachers are very cynical and they were, a lot of us, including myself at times. It wasn't the kids so much; it was that kind of thing that made you jaded and cynical. You saw something working for the kids and you saw people from the outside prove that it was working. It wasn't just us saying it was working for the kids. And then it gets cut. (Paul Casilli)

Part of the problem was the economy. A severe economic recession in 1988 forced deep cuts in the school budget. The recession also sent Vault members scurrying to protect their companies; the business focus on DHS waned, and there was little interest in renewing the Compact. As if the cuts weren't bad enough, Dorchester High also started hemorrhaging leadership. Carl Cohen, the diligent headmaster, left in 1989 to work for the central administration.[1] The vigorous representatives from the Private Industry Council and New England Telephone were replaced. The carefully built relationships between the school and the business community tottered, as the new headmaster and the new company representatives encountered each other for the first time.

Then there were problems with the overall curriculum. Compact Ventures did a fine job of educating the students who moved within its protective parameters. But many more students at Dorchester High needed the same concentrated attention. These students, frustrated in a school that offered them no clear route to success, tended to act out in class, skip school, fail, and drop out. Nobody thought to redesign the entire curriculum with a coherent scope and sequence.

The outcome of this over a 10-year period was that test scores improved for the ninth and tenth graders, while declining for the eleventh and twelfth graders. Had things not changed so drastically, DHS most likely would have been in a good position to deal with this. But the opportunity was lost.

DUMPCHESTER

The overriding factor that knocked DHS back into chaos was the growing neighborhood violence. By the early 1990s the climate at DHS had once again sunk to toxic levels. The School Committee was partly to blame. The Committee's fateful school closing decision in 1989 forced many of the burgeoning Dorchester gangs to attend school together. These gangs, and those from Dorchester's other high school, often clashed on school grounds, leading to the shooting of one student in front of the school in 1988.[2]

Then there was the problem with "dumping." By now, the term referred to young criminals recently released from the Department of Youth Services' juvenile lockup.

> We always had a joke, anybody that came into that building after October or November was most likely coming out of jail or lockup somewhere, and they were. A lot of times the judge would say, "Look, you either go back to school or I am going to incarcerate you for another six months. Where would you like to go?" "Oh, let me go back to school," and at that point, the only place that had openings in October, November, December, guess where? Dumpchester again. So we had a cast of characters walking around that building that were really tough. I mean really tough kids. I am not talking about just little stealing a car, but assault and battery, attempted murder, sexual assault, some tough hombres. It was like "oh my God." Walking down this corridor or that corridor, and that is why a lot of the kids wouldn't go to the cafeteria. They would come down and sit in our rooms and eat. (Paul Casilli)

The *Boston Globe* published a story during this time about a street-gang member "convicted of six charges of car theft, assault and robbery," who was given the choice of going to prison or going to school.[3] This student was a member of the Humboldt gang, a gang which was a sworn enemy of the DHS-based Castlegate Gang. At his sentencing the judge proposed that the student, who dropped out of the tenth grade, "finish high school, work after school, go on to a junior college and stay out of trouble for five years." The student enrolled in DHS the following day.

Some teachers at DHS believed this "dumping" was intentional. But in fact, Dorchester High was one of the only high schools in the city that had room for extra students after the start of the school year. The school was drastically under-enrolled as a direct result of changes in the school desegregation case. Federal Judge Garrity had released the Boston school system from his control in 1987; high school students in the city could now choose which school they wanted to go to, instead of being assigned by the court. Hardly any students chose Dorchester High. The only students who came were those whose families had never gotten around to making a choice; and those who, however unwillingly, needed the school's bilingual or special education programs. The resulting student population was a strange, disaffected mix of kids with disabilities, new immigrants, and kids from chaotic families. There were always empty seats at the school, and there was always room for a violent young juvenile just released from lockup.

Between the dumping and the surge in gangs, it didn't take long for crime and violence to spill over into the school. In early 1990 a female DHS student was killed in an attack in Roxbury, the same weekend that nine other people were wounded—an unusually violent period in the city. The DHS student had been a senior, had applied to college, and was hoping to study nursing in the years ahead. She was only seventeen.[4]

Police charged three girls with the stabbing, growing testimony to a new phenomenon of girls' violence. Another DHS girl was seized inside the school with a .38-caliber handgun.

Barely 20 days later another DHS student was murdered, this time a sixteen-year old male sophomore from the Dominican Republic. He was apparently the victim of mistaken identity, catching the bullets intended for his older brother, who was slated to testify in regards to a neighborhood shooting. Similar to the female student, he "went to school every day, not like some other kids. He really liked school...He was a very good kid. He used to go to church every Sunday with his mother. His friends are going crazy; they can't believe this."[5] Students at DHS made posters in his memory to hang on the walls. The family returned to the Dominican Republic.

The violence lasted for several years, into the mid 1990s. School programs died in this climate. The sports programs of 1985, which had won so many championships, dwindled. There was no money for police security, and violence prohibited student attendance. School officials stopped announcing games for fear that rival gangs would appear. As school funds shrank and spirits dipped, even the yearbooks grew thin. The 1994 yearbook was a tiny piece of work with only a few pages on sports and activities. Much of the yearbook was devoted to the Six Flags class trip, the Prom, and Graduation (which suggests that this yearbook was produced very late in the year). The yearbook did more boasting about "how good we look" and less about "how much we have accomplished." Even the Senior Superlatives smacked of superficiality: best legs, most greedy, baddest attitude, most facial expressions, and most unusual. In terms of sports teams, the school had lost volleyball, hockey, badminton, and swimming. There were only three cheerleaders.

THE CLASS OF '69 REGROUPS

Once again, DHS teachers were on their own in the midst of chaos, and once again, some of them formed small, self-protective learning communities. As before, the now middle-aged "class of '69" was at the center of these efforts, but with a new member. Paul Casilli, recruited to DHS to work with Compact Ventures, was "feeling jaded" as a result of the loss of the program. But he hadn't by any means given up on DHS students.

> I felt strongly, and a few of my colleagues felt strongly, that we had a large group of kids in that building who want to do the right thing; who aren't hard core, yet they're not being motivated at all because that ten percent or twenty percent walking around this building are dragging them down. This kid who has got a record this long is sitting next to them on the left, and on the right is another kid who has a record this long. And you have this student there who wants to learn something, and those needs aren't being addressed.

It is always the students who are hardcore; they're in interventions left and right or kids who have severe special needs and whatever and yes, their needs need to be addressed, but what about this whole group in the middle? We used to say, their education is really getting stolen here from the disruptions that are going on, on a daily basis in the classroom. (Paul Casilli)

Then came a threat that spurred Casilli to action. The high school zone superintendent, concerned that DHS was becoming the least-selected school in Boston, called a school-wide meeting. Those who were present described him as being "pretty blunt." He told the teachers that they just weren't producing anything that anybody wanted, and if they couldn't come up with something that would draw more kids to the school, then it was going to get shut down. Deep down, the teachers knew he was right.

We were in the newspapers all the time for being "the bottom of the barrel." And the kids had that same response, it was that "I didn't choose to be here; I didn't want to be in here." So many of the students came in with a chip on their shoulder—"I was just assigned here." They would call the school... and it would pain us to hear it,...but you'd hear the kids say, "this is DUMPchester, we were dumped in here," or "DUMBchester High School." And that was very painful. I mean who wants to be part of that, whether you're a student or a teacher? (male teacher)

For Casilli, this meeting became a catalyst. He approached two other teachers at DHS, both of them from the class of '69, one of them a founder of LEAP. These were teachers who had already proved they could create islands of teaching and learning in the midst of school chaos. Casilli proposed that they try again to create a school within the school; his colleagues readily agreed.

This time, though, the little group had support from the outside. One supporter was the zone superintendent himself, who introduced Casilli to innovative urban educators from New York City. The Private Industry Council also came through, providing seed money for the venture. The teachers went to Chicago and New York to see other "schools-with-in-a-school" in action. They held conferences and set up a board to consult with the new academy. The members of that first board represented the Private Industry Council, New England Telephone, UMB and the American Society for Public Administrators—all long time and strong school partners.

In 1992, the Academy of Public Service (APS) opened for business. It started with only thirty students who were recruited out of the ranks of the tenth grade.

We told their teachers, "We don't care where they're at academically. If you see a spark, if you see something in that child's eyes that you feel this program will benefit...tell us about that student and we will take a real good look at them." (Paul Casilli)

The program grew to ninety students in three years, spread out over grades ten, eleven and twelve. Entrance was by application only. Interested students had to fill out an application, secure letters of recommendation, demonstrate good attendance and a positive attitude, and dress up for an interview before a panel of teachers and administrators. As one teacher explained,

> It was a rigorous process. The interview was really a big deal. Kids would dress up and the whole school was involved and it really made the kids feel like they were going to be part of something special. (APS originator)

For DHS students, this was like applying to college and, indeed as time went on, participation in APS was almost a guarantee of going to a real college later. The curriculum was the regular BPS curriculum, plus one course each year in public service administration, study and social skills, and psychology. There were also many "extra" components that distinguished the program and its students: community service projects, summer jobs, a mentoring program, trips to universities, youth conferences, and leadership-building activities.

> We improved the school's grounds; we had kids painting murals on Saturday....The more that we got done around the city, people started coming to us...[asking], 'Do you think your kids would like to be part of this?' One of the best hook-ups was the Summer Search Foundation. We started sending kids abroad to Ghana to build a rural Hospital, Argentina to work in an orphanage, to Northwestern University to study journalism for the summer; to Cornell to study computer science...and the students' eyes just lit up, you know, what kids from Dorchester High are involved in those kinds of activities? That was unheard of for our kids. (Paul Casilli)

APS, like the National Honor Society, which had been slowly dying at the school, was an attempt to create a safe and nurturing space where troubled students might excel within DHS. The academy set high standards and picked students who were motivated to engage with what APS had to offer. Soon, the small academy—it served 90 out of 1000 students—became an oasis of success within the building. For example, on any given day there were about 900 students in attendance at DHS, but there were close to 1500 kids on the enrollment list. Retention was a massive problem in the school. As one teacher pointed out, "we couldn't get our kids to stay from one week to the next." At 75 percent, the school had the lowest attendance rate in the city. The situation was different within APS; in APS the classes were not only full, they were overflowing.

> We got begged. We had thirty-five to thirty-six kids in the classroom. We couldn't get chairs for the extra kids that we took into the program. Other teachers would come from all of the disciplines, from special needs to bilingual, and they would come down to us and plead their case for a particular student. (APS originator)

The academy's success was soon borne out by their graduation rates. While DHS had an overall graduation rate of about 42 percent, the rate for APS graduates was 92 percent.

Outside funders also began to take an interest in the program—notably Pam Trefler, whom Paul Casilli had known only as the student teacher he'd worked with in the early 1990s.

> That is a funny story...Pam was looking to teach English as her student teaching and she came to me and said, "Can I teach one of your English classes?" And I said, "Yeah, I would be glad to work with you," so we did that year and she was very good at it. She went on and about a year later I got a call and actually, my wife said, "Pam Trefler called," and I said, "Oh, that's good, maybe she is checking in to see how we're doing." I think I called her back that night and she said "My husband, I don't know if you heard of Pegasystems," and I said, "You know I've heard of them." "Well, they just went public with the stock and overnight it made 600 million dollars, and we are setting up an educational fund. We want to fund urban high school education. I want you to write up a little proposal because I was really, really impressed when I was there with what you guys were doing with the Academy of Public Service."
>
> Now at that point, I think we had a budget of a couple hundred dollars... I am serious, maybe it was a thousand dollars...So I remember putting a little [proposal] together and I went to John and Frank and our colleagues and I think we asked for $7,500 and we thought that was just being unbelievable, this is so lavish...and I came back and she said, "Is this a joke?" I said, "What, I don't know how much." She said, "Whatever you want." I said, "What?" So I think we still kept it at a reasonable amount. I think I came back and doubled it to $15,000 the second year. (Paul Casilli)

Eventually, Trefler became a member of the APS board, and contributed a significant amount to the academy in the form of college scholarships and academic support for APS students.

> She said she was only going to fund some of these scholarships for a year, well Pam was very, very kind. We said well Pam our kids are having trouble getting passed that first year, they can't stay in. All right, I'll fund the second. Ok, I'll fund the third. By the time we were finished, I think we were up to about $200,000 in full and last dollar scholarships. (Paul Casilli)

Within a few years, Pam Trefler would become a pivotal figure in the middle 1990s resurgence of Dorchester High. But in the meantime, her generosity at APS, coupled with the program's other supporters created hard feelings within the building.

> We had all this help coming to the academy from partners and foundations, and it was great for the academy. But it also led to feelings of resentment, you know..."well you guys get this and you guys get that." (APS teacher)

Some charged APS with exclusivity, elitism and "creaming the crop," but the APS teachers vigorously disputed this.

Dorchester High School [was] the least selected school in the system. So you have the first tier that goes off to Boston Latin School; the second tier is Latin Academy; the third tier is the O'Bryant. Those are the three exam schools. Then you have the next four tiers down: Snowden; the fifth one is West Roxbury High School; and you go right down and Dorchester is at the bottom. Out of fifteen high schools at the time. Yeah, and the Burke. They were the bottom of the bottom, with students who didn't want to be there for the most part...So if that is skimming...? We had special needs students; we had students who were English As A Second Language students....We had students at a fourth and fifth grade level up to twelfth grade level. And we took in thirty-two to thirty-three students per class—Now if that is skimming? The APS classes were loaded, and yet it still worked. (Paul Casilli)

The APS teachers knew that the citywide emphasis on access and inclusion ran counter to their selective admissions process, but they argued that, in practice, inclusion and access really didn't work.

We made no bones about it; we were right up front, so when people called us elitist and whatever, we said, "we will take any student, but we are not going to take that student that day in and day out is disruptive." I'll go to my grave saying there has to be some other alternative. Because even how good the APS was, we couldn't serve all the students there. There were hardcore students that had records this long, that were antisocial, that were hostile to anything that you tried to do....We weren't talking about taking the A kids, the B kids. We had C and D students, and they weren't all angels. The APS kids weren't all angels all the time. We had disciplinary problems, some were suspended at some points and so forth, but by and large, they weren't in that classroom to disrupt day after day. And that's an important component. I haven't seen anyone address that really. You know, they all say, it sounds nice, it looks good, these programs, everybody all for all, and we need to create that kind of environment. Well yes, you need to create that kind of environment for that kind of kid that I just talked about, but maybe it's a year long, two year long outward bound program. Not in this building and not in this program. (Former APS teacher)

But others in the school were bitter about APS's perceived selectivity. Said one administrator, "If I could pick who I wanted to, I'd be very successful, too." Remarks like this greatly angered the APS faculty and staff. As they explained,

Our APS kids were from the same "chaotic families" and violent neighborhoods as the rest of the student population. One story makes this point perfectly clear. In April, our APS students won the "Champion of Change Award" from the United Way of Boston. They won this prestigious award because of the project-based community service projects they had been involved in. I went to the United Way banquet with seven of my APS students in order to see them accept the award. While sitting at the table a conversation arose about families, fathers and dinnertime discussions at home. Seven students out of seven stated that they never had dinner with either their mother or father, and seven out of seven said that they never saw their fathers because they were in jail! This was just a random sample of students.

What are the chances that 100% of any group of teens would have their fathers in jail? This was representative of the types of students we had in the Academy of Public Service.

Unfortunately, some members of the administration only saw the end product of 92% college acceptance, not the extraordinary effort that went into making that happen. Before APS existed, these same students floundered and were never considered the "best and the brightest." They didn't think about continuing on to higher education. For anyone to say that APS served only the "best and the brightest" is ludicrous. It does a disservice to the program and to the great accomplishments of this mixed-ability group of students. (Paul Casilli)

The tensions between APS and the rest of the building spilled over into quarrels about resources, time and space. The teachers had to fight for common planning time.

Common planning time was an unbelievable obstacle. We had a conflict every year with our administrative team about our common planning time vs. doing an administrative period vs. our professional development period. Every single year we had to go up and battle it. I kept trying to tell them that this is one of the most important components. This is where we do our case management. We met about pretty much everyone of our students. What does the student need? Is it mental health services; do they need to see a medical doctor, do they need an internship? We would call the students in during those common planning times. We would call the parents in; we would plan the Project Based curriculum that we would do on a number of occasions. We would plan the field trips everything was done at that time. For some reason it was very hard to get this through to some people. (Former APS teacher)

They had to fight over how their students were assigned and registered for classes.

You'd find kids in APS that never got selected. You'd find kids that did get selected for APS, who would be on someone else's list. You don't know how many fights we were involved in just to make registration successful for the following year. Then you would come back at the end of the summer and get the computer list print outs of all the students that are in APS in grades ten, eleven and twelve, and you'd get your class list and half the kids that were supposed to be in weren't in there, it was a mess. (APS teacher)

At one point, Pam Trefler co-funded a computer writing lab and a writing specialist to run it. When the writing specialist was not staffing the computer lab, she was working in the classroom as a second adult or working with small groups of students on writing skills. Each year, the teachers would remind the administration not to schedule the writing specialist for other building duties.

We would say every year, "now make sure that that computer room is not used for a classroom" because it was not a classroom. It was a computer lab for APS. So don't schedule a math class in there, or whatever. And don't schedule our teacher, but, sure enough, they would schedule her to teach two or three classes to the rest of the student body. I'd have to go in and fight that all the time. I'd tell them, "this is an outside funded position; it's not your position." Of course that's a hard line coming from a teacher and you're telling an administrator that it's not their position. But I'd have to fight that every semester. Most of the time it wouldn't get rectified until November or December, before I'd get that teacher released from those other duties. I mean, you wouldn't mind if you over came an obstacle and then moved on, but the same exact obstacle would occur, as if you never had any discussions about it the previous May or June, and that really was frustrating. (Former APS teacher)

It was a never-ending battle during APS's first five years, but despite the chaos, they held fast to their values and to each other. As one teacher described, many of the students came to think of APS as a family. "Over and over again, over the years, that's what we kept hearing verbally and in writing, that this was my family, not LIKE my family, but it IS my family."

APS was also protected by the successes of their students and by their strong community partnerships. "The partnerships helped because the administration (both in the school and in the district) knew that we were connected." And well connected they were: to the business community, to state and local government, and to various school funders. If we had to, "we would kick it up another notch and have our board members write something or call. It certainly did help, I mean, they knew they couldn't get away with everything." (Paul Casilli)

Despite the tensions in the building, APS would eventually become a model for broader reform at DHS. But that was years away. In the meantime, the program remained an island of order in a sea of chaos. While APS students flourished, many of DHS's other students floundered.

I find myself saying, "Well, who owns these kids? Who is ultimately responsible? I guess in the end it is the parents, but the parents are out working multiple jobs....I would feel a whole lot better if I thought the community owned the kids. That the city owned the kids. That the business community owned them. The university owned them, and felt like these are our kids. They are growing up on our streets in Boston. (Jack Leonard)

But no one stepped forward to help those students who were not in small communities like APS—until the New England Association of Schools and Colleges (NEASC) showed up to review DHS for accreditation, and unleashed a political firestorm downtown.

THE COMMUNITY TAKES ON THE DISTRICT

When the accreditors' team arrived at DHS one morning in 1992, they were shocked. Ten years earlier, they had accredited the school, but left behind a list of seventy-two recommendations for repairs to the building.

Now, they discovered that most of their recommendations had been ignored. The school building was falling apart.

True, Headmaster Cohen had been able to take care some of the most egregious problems in the mid 1980s. But the roof (last repaired in 1968) was leaking everywhere, creating puddles on the third floor on wet days and running down the walls of some classrooms. There was still a critical lack of storage space and substandard faculty rooms, which lacked desks and working equipment for teachers. Most of the clocks did not work and the public address system was faulty. The girls' locker room had no showers and the toilet stalls lacked doors. The science labs had received some repairs but many rooms still lacked proper safety and first aid equipment. The guidance counselors needed private offices and computers. The heating system was 70 years old. Sometimes only one of the three boilers worked; when temperatures dropped below 55 degrees, students were moved to warmer sections of the building.

Then there were the satellites. NEASC had recommended the satellites be closed down in 1982. But they were still in use, and by now had inadequate lighting, roof leaks, chipped paint, and missing clocks. They were also dirty. In fact, the committee noted for the whole school:

> Cleanliness is a problem in the building. All of the lavatories—boys', girls', and faculty—were found to be dirty. A number of classrooms had dirty floors. The stairways and areas around the windows had dust and cobwebs. Areas above the radiators had black sooty deposits.[6]

The evaluators went on to criticize almost every aspect of the school. The library was "totally inadequate". The needs of students outside small learning communities were "neglected." Faculty supervision was "essentially nonexistent." There was no "standard process for establishing... curriculum," and no standardized tests, even for teachers teaching the same subject. There was "a paucity of texts and materials." One student put it more succinctly:

> I mean there's been times when we've run out of paper. Just regular scrap paper or white lined paper...That makes me feel like this school ain't worth anything.

NEASC put the school on warning status. But this time, the frustrated accreditors adopted a new strategy in their report. Rather than blaming the administration of Dorchester High for the problems at the school, as they had done in all previous accreditation visits, they held downtown central administration directly responsible.

They had good reason for blaming the district. By the city's own accounting, there were fourteen Boston high schools with accreditation problems. Four high schools on "probationary" status were in more trouble than DHS, while two more were on "warning" status.[7] Dorchester's other high school lost its accreditation entirely. The district put a good face on the situation. The superintendent appointed a new Accreditation

Task Force. Dorchester High School was targeted for over $4 million in renovations, including a roof, heating system, and electrical repairs. The plan also called for renovation of the girls' locker room and the guidance area, new stage curtain and lighting, repair of intercom and clocks and, of course, library renovation.

But the Boston City Council wasn't satisfied. The Council appointed their own Finance Commission, which issued a report in July 1995, exposing widespread mismanagement and cover-ups emanating from the central office. Specifically, the Council accused the School Department of hiding the accreditation issues from the city, especially the facilities problems. The Council blamed the loss of accreditation at one school and the probationary status of the other high schools on major "shortcomings" in central management.

The Finance Commission pointed out that the mayor had increased funding by $50 million over the last two years and was adding an additional $16 million in the current year. "It seems to the Finance Commission that when $50 million is added to the school budget over a 2 year period, yet students don't have books and schools are losing their accreditation"[8] something is wrong. They also accused the School Department of having "no idea of existing book inventories at the high school level. There is no planning for book purchases and no meaningful dollar allocations to buy textbooks." Last, referring to the two premier public high schools in the city, the Commission pointed out that "funding alone doesn't affect the level of education. Boston Latin School and Boston Latin Academy have the two lowest costs per student at $3,144 and $3,194 respectively. The highest cost is Madison Park, $7,688." (Dorchester High School was third from the top in this list of per pupil expenditures at $4,766.) "There appears to be no correlation between spending and the educational return." The Finance Commission's report ended by questioning why there were no standards for evaluation or professional development of headmasters, given that effective leadership is the key to students' educational gains.

It was now two years since the accrediting team had visited Dorchester High School. Renovations on the building had still not begun despite the sound and fury downtown. In fact, the list of problems had grown: there were not enough textbooks for the students, and there was no handicapped access to the building. In April of 1996, the NEASC notified DHS that its status would be further downgraded from "warning" to "probation." It was the lowest accreditation rating in the history of Dorchester High.

NEW LEADERSHIP

Thomas Menino, the much heralded "education mayor" had been in office for less than two years. The accreditation scandal was deeply embarrassing to him, and he held the school superintendent, Lois Harrison Jones, personally responsible for the debacle. He already had deep disagreements with Jones: She had tried to avoid key provisions of the state's new Educational Reform Act, believing that she, not school headmasters, should have the power to hire and fire teachers. She had even gone over the mayor's head, persuading a state legislator to sponsor an amendment on her behalf—a second embarrassment for a mayor who did not take embarrassment lightly. Harrison Jones was fired in late 1995.

The way was now open for Menino to take full control of the Boston Public Schools. He had inherited the power to appoint a School Committee. Now he was positioned to hire a new superintendent. The man he hired in 1996 proved to be one of the best things that had happened to the Boston Public Schools in a long time.

Thomas Payzant was originally from Boston, and he was savvy to Boston history and politics. He was also a "career superintendent"[9] who had headed large school districts in Oregon, Oklahoma, and San Diego. He was currently serving as Assistant Secretary for Elementary and Secondary Education at the U.S. Department of Education. His leadership of the Boston Schools would last an unprecedented 10 years, a stability that the schools had long needed.

> He has been able to run ten years and get everybody turned around on the purpose of schools, which is to increase academic achievement. It is hard to believe that that is not a given, but it is not a given elsewhere and it never was a given in Boston and that is his legacy. Everything is judged by academic achievement and you need ten years, eleven years to do that 'cause you wouldn't have gotten it with the superintendent shuffle we used to have. (Neil Sullivan)

Within a year Payzant had unveiled a new plan for Dorchester High School. The $3 million plan included many of the renovations already promised by the city two years previously. It also called for a brand new library/media center to be constructed on the first floor where the industrial shops used to be, plus an extensive electrical upgrade of the building in anticipation of more technology in the classrooms. It was now four years since the accreditation team's visit to the school, and renovations were about to begin at last.

THE STARS ALIGN FOR DORCHESTER HIGH

> You want everybody supporting the schools. I mean we need everybody supporting the schools to make progress because most school systems in the country are just contested all the time and nothing ever gets done. We were striving for total alignment, total accountability. (Neil Sullivan)

The arrival of Tom Payzant was not the only sign that things were about to improve for Dorchester High. The economy was picking up, and the business community, heartened by the new mayor and the new School Committee, had signed a new Boston Compact. Many lessons had been learned from the successes and failures of the first Compact, and the new agreement was a far more comprehensive and sophisticated document.

First of all, jobs for kids was a priority. Boston's powerful hospital CEOs had joined the Compact this time around, helping to make the new summer jobs program "the largest private sector effort of its kind in the country." There were also internships and "shadowships," which sent APS students, among others, to work in City Hall and in law offices around the city. The new Compact also led the way for teacher training and professional development for the Boston Public Schools, largely relieving the school district of a job they'd never done that well anyway. After-school programs were funded for the first time, along with an innovative literacy program called ReadBoston. The Compact even committed to the construction of new schools.

The foundation world was so impressed with the new Compact that they, too, began to pledge money for the schools. In 1996, the Annenberg Foundation made a $10 million challenge grant to the city; in short order, the city exceeded the grant's matching requirement with $15 million in additional private donations. The foundation funds were added to the existing Compact funds to create a new initiative called "21st Century Schools." A total of fifty schools, including Dorchester High, were selected to participate in this reform effort. This meant DHS was among those targeted for "whole school change," a combination of financial support and technical guidance for headmasters, teachers, and students.

Then Superintendent Payzant added something else to the groundswell for education, unveiling a five-year plan for reform of the Boston Schools. Called *Focus on Children,* the plan was a direct attack on low academic achievement in the schools, establishing rigorous standards for improvement. The plan closely paralleled the state's new educational reform law, but it went further. Coaches were provided to help teachers and administrators with literacy programs, school change, and mathematics. A twelve-month "transition program" was created for grades three, six, and nine to help students who needed extra time at critical junctures in their schooling. The program offered site-based summer school classes to struggling students. Also, class sizes were reduced to thirty-one students and alternative educational options were expanded for all students. Last, Boston became the "first major city in the country where all schools were wired for Internet access."[10] Best of all, the central administration began a gradual shift from a "command and control center to one that offered guidance, technical assistance, and resources to help schools achieve their goals."[11]

Everything was looking hopeful for the schools in general, and for Dorchester High in particular. The community had expanded, and every member was actively engaged: the Vault, the foundations, the universities, NEASC, the state, the mayor, the superintendent, the City Council, and the newly appointed School Committee. Even the president of the Federal Reserve Bank pronounced herself optimistic. Cathy Minehan, a key player in the Boston Compact, later remarked, "Those of us...often said, the time was ripe—the stars were in alignment—or, if school improvement doesn't happen now, it never will."

Of course, history had already shown that events downtown had a way of bypassing Dorchester High. Too often, the school had been as invisible to the city's powerful as it was to passing drivers in the neighborhood. But Superintendent Payzant did one more good thing for Dorchester High in 1996. He appointed a new headmaster—an administrator and homegrown diplomat who would skillfully welcome the community back into the school.

CHAPTER 7

The Community Returns to Dorchester High School 1996 to 1999

The average person just does not know what it takes to run a school, especially that one. And given all that has happened and the way that it happened, that should never, ever, have to happen to anybody. It's kind of like the Holocaust, it should never take place again....You can be a very, very lonely person, being the principal, especially if you've got a troubled school. (Bobby Belle, Headmaster, Dorchester High School.)

Bobby Belle arrived at Dorchester High at the beginning of the 1996 school year. A career administrator in the Boston Public Schools, Belle turned out to be just what Dorchester High needed. He'd grown up in Boston, and was well known and well liked in the community. Many of DHS's parents already knew him.

Belle had more than the usual number of challenges to contend with that fall: the school had just been put on probation by the accrediting team; Court Street was already pressuring him to produce reforms that would attract more students; and the physical plant was still a mess.

> Every time it rained, the whole darn roof would leak....all we needed was ducks. That's how much water we had up there. The basement was underwater. We threw away over $25,000 worth of supplies that just got water logged. Some of the corridors were so dark, I had to put alarms in the corridors for the little extra light. So when the kids went down there...they would ring, we knew someone was down there." (Bobby Belle)

But the most immediate challenge was the violence.

> In the beginning, out of about 1100 kids, you had about 380 that were either
> court involved, gang involved, or they were doing something that was very,
> very disruptive, or they were overage.... At one point , I had more probation
> officers at my school than I did guidance counselors and teachers. (Bobby
> Belle)

Like Carl Cohen before him, Belle knew that change could not take hold
at Dorchester High unless the violence—and the constant threat of violence—were brought under control.

> Bobby understood right away he needed to get control of the building. When
> he came...I believe between six and eight gangs were active. Within four
> months, those gangs were no longer active inside of the building; nor did
> they ever become active when Bobby was there. In a building like Dorchester
> High School, the disciplinary side of the administration was more important
> than the academic side. (Pam Trefler, Trefler Foundation).

> I had 18-year olds who were only in the 9th grade.... And the kids used to
> say to me, "Mr. Belle, you put me in my right grade, I'll stop acting up." I
> said, "If I put you in your right grade, you'll act up a lot more." They said,
> 'Well, that doesn't make sense, if you put me in my right grade, why would
> I act up?' I'd say, "Because your right grade is the 3rd grade and you're in the
> 9th grade here, you can't read, you can't write, your right grade is back there,
> not up here." (Bobby Belle).

Belle's tough informality worked well with the kids, but some teachers
did not like him. He did not have an academic background, for one thing.
For another, his first task in reforming the school was to weed out the
worst teachers and administrators. Accordingly, his first years were spent
in long battles with the teachers' union. Then there were the long-delayed
renovations. They finally began, but they created new disruptions.

> They did our roof, they put a library on, because they had to, it was man-
> dated by the accreditation people, they were working in our building with
> over 100 contractors every day, while those kids were in those classes. The
> other schools [that were renovated], those kids didn't go to school while
> the construction was taking place, okay?...So all these schools aren't created
> equally. (Bobby Belle).

As he gradually resolved the tremendous nonacademic problems in
the school, Belle was able to turn his attention to educational reform.
The mandate from Court Street was to create more "schools-within-
a-school." Belle already had two of these inside DHS: the Academy
of Public Service was humming along and Health Careers Academy
had started in 1995. The Health Careers Academy was the first pilot
school in Boston. Pilot schools are public schools that enjoy freedom from
union regulations and have more control over their own budgets and
hiring practices. But both of these served students who, with extra help
and support, were motivated to excel. Belle's assignment was to create

"whole school change." That meant that, ideally, the entire student body would eventually be absorbed into one or another small learning community.

Using his two existing academies as models, Belle quickly launched another one. The Economics and Business Academy, later named the Noonan Business Academy, was funded with a grant from one of the newly involved local foundations. After a rocky first year, Belle recruited a teacher he thought could do the job.

> I said, "Ed, listen to me." I said, "here's the deal, bottom line is, we have to create a business academy, I want it up and running in a year, and I want it to be functional." I said, "you tell me, what you want, you tell me what you need, and you tell me the time frame you need it in. It is my job to get that for you, but I'm going to hold you accountable for making this academy run. So, if you can handle that, than I can roll with it, if you can't, we're look-ing for somebody else"...Then it became my job to support him, channel resources into him, so that he could get the academy established. (Bobby Belle)

But things weren't moving fast enough for Court Street. The district was breathing down DHS's neck about being on probation. There was talk of restructuring. One teacher recalls the whole school being in "panic mode" over what would happen if the school lost its accreditation entirely.

WHATEVER IT TAKES FOR AS LONG AS IT TAKES

Then, something entirely unexpected happened. Pam Trefler, by now deeply involved with the Academy of Public Service, offered to donate a large sum of money to help put the school on its feet. Bobby Belle was ini-tially skeptical:

> At some point you have to say to yourself, "Wow, this school is a hell hole all these years, now all of a sudden, [she's] in here, why, what's up with this, why? You know, it's a gift to us, I mean, but what's going on here"? But, you know, in her case, she seriously wanted to make a difference, and she fought hard to get that across.

Specifically, Pam Trefler wanted to replicate the APS model across the entire school, restructuring Dorchester High into small learning com-munities. She'd seen APS work for its students, and she wanted to make the same opportunity available to everyone at DHS.

> It can be pretty intimidating when you're in the 9th grade and 14 years old and you are tossed into a building of 1100 other students. You are all alone, you might well not know anyone, or you might know just a couple of people. You might not ever see the same teacher twice....We believed that the APS model—where relatively small groups of students traveled together for at least half of the day...would work for all the students inside the building.

It would do two things: first, it would let the students in each cohort get to know each other, and second, it would allow the teachers in each of these cohorts to get to know the students. (Pam Trefler)

Bobby Belle was willing to try it. The APS faculty liked the idea. UMB agreed to administer the funds and help plan the new small schools. But there was one more hurdle to overcome: the embattled, distrustful DHS faculty had to be convinced to vote in favor of the restructuring plan. The APS faculty began an informal lobbying campaign.

We would fan out, early in the morning, after school, during our professional development time, even during our free periods, and go door to door to classrooms and start that dialogue. We explained what was going on, "We are going to lose accreditation, this is coming down unless we show that we can really shake up this place. This proposal looks like the best way to really make some systemic changes in the building." A lot of work was done leading up to the vote, a lot of work. I mean, we didn't know everything that was going to happen either and we were trying to be up front as much as possible, acknowledging yeah, some people might not have a position here after we break into these small learning communities. (Former APS teacher)

They were successful; 97 percent of the teachers voted in favor of restructuring the school into small learning communities.

That 97% vote was tectonic. I mean it just shook the ground. People knew that something unique and special was happening at DHS. (Paul Casilli)

With an agreement in place, Pam Trefler announced her grant. It would be $1 million. The city's educators gave a collective gasp.

It was kind of overwhelming, first of all you don't get grants like that in the schools, usually. . . . It certainly gave us a boost, because other people took notice, because we were supposedly the worst school in the city. (Bobby Belle)

Trefler's funding supported two initiatives at the school—the creation of the small learning communities (SLC) and the Teach Next Year Program. There was much fanfare downtown about the grant. The mayor and Court Street administrators promised their support for the small schools effort. Accreditors were impressed, and agreed to take the school off probation and put it back on warning status.

Inside the school—for the first time in decades—school spirit was felt in the hallways of Dorchester High.

There was a huge amount of excitement around the restructuring plan. Dorchester High School got its accreditation back early, like 3–4 weeks after the plan was put in writing and presented. The entire school dressed in matching T-shirts the day they got their accreditation. There was a huge amount of positive energy around the idea of taking this high school that was known as "Dumpchester" and turning it into an institution that people could be proud of. I think that extended to 99.9% of the people who were involved in this. (Pam Trefler)

> We had that big rally and at the time, we had The Crips and The Bloods, and about 9 other gangs in there, and just could not wear another school's colors or another gang's colors. They had on those red Trefler T-shirts, you look out at that audience, if I'm not mistaken, either the commissioner of education or the governor, somebody big was there that day. I mean, I'm on stage and I'm totally awestruck. (Bobby Belle)

Fridays were declared "school spirit day," and for years afterward, veteran teachers wore the red Trefler T-shirts every Friday. Emblazoned across the front of the shirts was the slogan: *"Whatever It Takes For As Long As It Takes."*

When all the celebrations had died down, Belle and the teachers quickly got to work, deciding on the small learning communities that they wanted to create. UMB played a critical role, guiding the planning and budgeting process.

> [Once] all the publicity people, like the mayor and everybody else got through showboating and saying isn't this wonderful, we got down to the business of rolling up our sleeves and working with UMass....A million dollars can get you into a lot of trouble very quickly if you don't really know how to manage it. You know, we stretched that out almost 5 years and we got some pretty good return for what we received. (Bobby Belle)

The school year began in September 1998 without the Health Careers Academy. Because it was a pilot school the Health Careers Academy enjoyed privileges not available to other students and teachers at DHS. The staff worked longer hours and they enjoyed common planning time. Teachers were brought on board without regard to seniority and those who did not work out were simply let go in June, back into the ranks of DHS. Similarly, students who were unruly were removed from the program and sent back into the DHS general population. In 1998, the pilot school outgrew its welcome at DHS and moved to the campus of Northeastern University. However, the new Engineering Technology Academy (ETA) joined APS and The Economics and Business Academy (EBA) in September 1998 as the first SLC to come out of the new restructure plan. Each small learning community began with a cohort of thirty tenth graders and grew out year by year. The SLCs were teacher-created and teacher-driven, meaning that small teams of teachers selected the theme, constructed the three-year sequence of signature courses, and recruited students and teachers from the wider DHS community to participate. With each additional SLC, the competition for students increased during the spring enrollment periods. At the same time, the school grew increasingly frustrated with the "non-SLC students," who floated through the school each year with little attachment or engagement. Slowly, the entire student body in grades ten through twelve was being moved into an SLC, for the school recognized the benefit of the personalization. A Freshmen Academy, along the lines of the old Compact Ventures program, was also added for all incoming ninth graders. In 1999, a

new Performing Arts Academy was added as well as an experimental
SLC in the basement for older, alternative education students called the
Leadership Academy.

Bobby Belle and his administrative team oversaw the whole transition,
working closely with Pam Trefler and her foundation staff as well as
other partners. New England Telephone, now called Verizon, was still
in the school, along with the Private Industry Council representative
and UMB. In addition, there were law enforcement personnel from several agencies, and a variety of nonprofits who worked with teenagers.
Belle found himself becoming something of a diplomat.

> When you have that many partners that come to the table, if you're not
> flexible and if you're not willing to bend an awful lot, it can hurt you, really
> bad. Because you don't want to piss off Verizon, or UMass, or Trefler, or all
> three at the same time. And I think what we did, was we managed to get
> all those people together working on the same plane, so that when we did
> something, we were all at the table together...and we could discuss the pros
> and cons and everybody parked their egos at the door. There was none of
> that, "well Trefler's giving the money, so if it's not this way, it won't go."...
> Headmasters need to know a little about diplomacy....When somebody is
> coming into your house, you know, you've got to be a gracious host. (Bobby
> Belle)

Belle also found that his new partners could be very useful in a conflict
with the district:

> Pam could say things publicly that we couldn't say, or we wouldn't say, and
> she could be a very good advocate for you and for the school, because, I
> never one time, saw her take a stand on anything that wasn't about those
> kids and making something better. So, even if you disagreed with her on a
> lot of things, she was willing to stand up to Payzant and the mayor. Many
> times she said stuff that I wanted to say that I probably would [not have]
> been headmaster, had I said it.

The restructuring of Dorchester High School into small learning communities was repeated in many Boston high schools (Hyde Park, Brighton, Charlestown, English, and East Boston, for example). Meanwhile,
South Boston High School was divided up into three entirely separate
small high schools, each with a new name, new headmaster and separate
budget and staff. Boston was experimenting with competing models for
high school reform and, for several years, Dorchester High staff members
congratulated themselves on the benefits of their own teacher-designed
and teacher-led SLC model.

Shortly after the restructuring plan was in place, Trefler's other initiative, an innovative teacher training program for DHS, called Teach Next
Year (TNY), was getting under way with the help of the Graduate College
of Education at UMB. TNY ended up at the center of Dorchester High's
reform efforts.

DORCHESTER HIGH SCHOOL GETS REINFORCEMENTS

> I think that the Teach Next Year Program is probably the best program and the best bang for their buck that I've ever seen happen in any of the schools ...Cause those kids, they want to make a difference, and they are so committed to what they're doing. I mean, they just want to make change. You find that type of enthusiasm and energy with people that are changing careers in mid-life. I mean, you've got attorneys, you've got people that are in the sciences, that are coming back and want to teach....Trust me, it makes a difference in those classrooms. (Bobby Belle)

Dorchester High had always had its share of conventional student teachers. They came in the spring, taught for a few weeks, and left before the school year was over. Teach Next Year was an entirely different model. Designed as an on-site teacher training program, TNY was the first teacher immersion program in Boston.

> Public schools, for the most part, do not transmit their knowledge base through the literature. They transmit their knowledge through the daily activities of the school environment. So it's the medical school model. You are in my classroom, you learn by experience, you watch, you try, you attempt, we come back and dialogue about it, and that's how the profession keeps evolving and improving upon itself. (Charlie Desmond)

The first ten TNY trainees arrived at Dorchester High in September 1999. They worked alongside mentor teachers during the fall, and in January, took over their own classes. Meanwhile, they studied at UMB in the evenings. By June, they'd earned a Masters degree, eligibility for teacher certification, and in most cases, a job. These new recruits, like those that followed, were primarily career-change professionals, with a specific interest in urban schools like Dorchester High.

> I was a youth worker for four years in Boston, and I came to the conclusion that I wanted to be a teacher, but I actually wasn't that interested in graduate school, I just wanted to be in the classroom and teach. I had no way to pay for graduate school as a youth worker making nothing, and I had tons of undergraduate loans, and I said, "What am I going to do?" I was really in a terrible spot for a long time, and I was really depressed 'cause I knew what I wanted but I just couldn't. And then my friend at work came in one day with this cheesy-looking, xeroxed, tri-folded paper, and everything was due two weeks from that date, and I got it in, threw everything together and lucked out. Here I am, I'm still working with young people every day. (white female TNY intern & DHS science teacher)

TNY was designed to impact the culture of DHS from the inside out. First of all, it was teacher-designed and run.

> TNY is one of the few programs that was truly teacher run and teacher directed. We started it several years ago with two people from UMass/Boston. There was a group of six teachers, and we developed the whole program

based upon other programs and then we recruited the teachers to be part of it. So we started it and kept it going. It's teacher run, and so it does a lot for the morale of the school. And we take a lot of pride in it. (DHS teacher)

DHS teachers also liked the program because it brought them badly needed help—it was a relief just to have ten more adults in the building every day. Teachers had more time to focus on professional and curricular development for the new academies that were coming on line.

TNY really helped build collegiality. Teachers could spend time on a variety of projects including capacity building for the small learning communities. It allowed us to build an infrastructure for academic support systems. (female DHS teacher)

Last, TNY brought teachers a newfound sense of pride. They had the opportunity to teach university courses for the first time; and as they supervised their interns, they began to realize that their expertise in the DHS classrooms was valuable.

Some of us became university faculty. It was quite an eye opener for a lot of us; we had not been in those kinds of roles before. We realized that with TNY and new, young teachers in the building our roles as mentors and veteran teachers were changing as well. (male DHS teacher)

For their part, the TNY interns found themselves grateful for the guidance of the older faculty. Despite their enthusiasm, the interns were unprepared for the reality that greeted them as they began work at Dorchester High.

I came in expecting freshmen, and after the first three weeks...I had them write some essays, and I brought them home and I was like, 'Holy smoke.' Most of them were reading between a second and a fourth grade level, ten to twelve out of 100 were reading at grade level, and some were reading beyond grade level and they are all thrown in one classroom. (white male TNY intern and DHS English teacher)

The thing that amazed me the most—now I'm thinking of two of the neediest kids, they are also the ones that will tend to want to walk [around the room]. I have never seen that....I'm like, "Ted, this is something that by the end of the year you are going to learn to come in here and sit, because usually when you are in a classroom with a lot of students, you can't have everybody walking around." He and another boy do a lot of, it's amazing. I never heard of that. (TNY intern and DHS science teacher).

TNY to me is the ideal teacher preparation program, particularly for urban education. People need to know what they are getting into. A lot of people come in to urban education thinking that commitment and creativity is enough, "I'm devoted, I'm committed, I'm going to do things that those veteran teachers don't' do,...and the students will love me." It's sad but it's not enough, it's not enough. People need stamina, and not to take things personally. You need to understand teenagers and the way they work and that a lot of what they do has nothing to do with you. You need to understand what their lives are like outside of this building and how this is a fraction of what goes on. (white female TNY intern and BPS history teacher).

The Professional Development School model adopted by UMB was the first of its kind in the district. The school system realized its potential, and moved immediately to adopt and adapt it. Four years into the TNY experiment, the district put out a call for proposals from area colleges and universities to design and run more TNY-like programs in the city. They accepted three proposals including TNY, and contributed 300,000 dollars to fund the DHS/UMB partnership for an additional three years. During those three years, Trefler continued funding other aspects of the partnership such as staff positions. Based upon the success of TNY, the BPS partnered with UMB to create its own clinical-based teacher preparation program called the Boston Teacher Residency program. In the program the BPS provides the clinical experience and the students earn a master's degree from the university. This program is now on its way to becoming a national model for district-based teacher licensure programs. Of course, Trefler and UMB still fund TNY. The program is now in its eighth year.

UMB had always been in partnership with DHS, but the Professional Development School model funded by Trefler brought even more support from the university to the school. Dorchester High, said one UMB administrator, "has captivated the imagination of the people in the city. I really do think that a lot of people are very fascinated with Dorchester High School." For several years, UMB professors worked daily in the high school. Lee Teitel collaborated with teachers, heard their concerns, reported to administrators, and provided leadership guidance, feedback, and communication workshops to administrators. June Kuzmeskus guided the nascent Teach Next Year program to maturity. Graduate level classes were offered in the school for both interns and teachers. Other staff traveled to the campus for classes. Other professors, such as Lisa Gonsalves, analyzed MCAS test scores and began to lead workshops with teachers on how to prepare students for the test in English. Academic services from UMB expanded, such as Upward Bound, Urban Scholars, and GearUP, and DHS students began taking college classes in small numbers through the state-funded dual enrollment program.

UMB connected DHS with other academic partners, such as the Northeast and Islands Regional Educational Laboratory at Brown University and the Institute for Student Achievement from New York City.

The last significant event of 1998 came when DHS joined the Annenberg Challenge. In September 1998, early results from the Stanford Nine tests indicated that DHS's entering ninth graders were behind in Math and English. Under the guidance of the new Annenberg coach, administrators and teachers began to learn to analyze data, especially the results of the Stanford Nine and the MCAS. They examined test-item analysis reports and shared test-taking strategies. Based upon this analysis, the decision was made that freshmen would receive double period instruction in both these subjects. (The rest of their six-period day was Science and History). With a six period day, the new schedule left no room for electives or study halls.

Understandably, the schedule was not popular with incoming students. In the spring, the school purchased the new Boys Town *Reading is FAME* remedial reading program and sent several English teachers off for training. This would be the "safety net" strategy for underperforming readers for several years.

Sadly, after a year of remedial work and emphasis on the standardized tests, the students who took the Massachusetts Comprehensive Assessment System exams (MCAS) in May 1999 did terribly. The failure rate in math jumped up to an unbelievable 97 percent and in English to 88 percent, much worse than the previous year. This was the first MCAS that "counted"; that is, students who failed it could not graduate. The dismal results, which became public in fall 1999, set off alarm bells at the district level and brought an "Intervention Team" to find out what was wrong with the school in spring 2000.

This was the first of several major inspections, which wearied the staff, undermined respect for the administrative team, and failed to move the school forward. The staff at DHS attributed the terrible test results to the departure of Health Careers Academy, which moved to another location the previous year, and the loss of thirty top tenth graders who would otherwise have taken the test through DHS, but this fact was lost on the district.

Despite the new school structure, the extra funding, the expanded support from the Boston Compact and school partners and the Professional Development Relationship with UMB, DHS was never able to develop firm footing on the way toward reform. The school continued to stumble along from 1999 to 2003 often feeling like the school was in a rapid race through countless reform initiatives. Much of the reform effort was focused on restructuring with less effort going toward teaching and learning or toward attempts to re-culture the school. There were many positive steps taken during these years. However, certain factors undermined significant progress. There were almost too many community partners and too many competing plans for improvement. The school leadership team was unable to unite around a compelling vision for school improvement. They met weekly, but they were not united in philosophy or style. Central administration was so anxious for accountability that hundreds of hours were spent preparing reports and getting ready for inspections. School leadership tended toward compliance, rather than creativity. As a result, they were more successful in leading the school in large-scale restructuring than in reforms related to teaching and learning or a collaborative school culture. Thus DHS entered the twenty-first century still uncertain in what direction she was ultimately headed.

CHAPTER 8

Bruises and Betrayals: The Last Years of Dorchester High School 1999 to 2003

The 1999–2000 school year looked at first like it would be a good one. The building renovations mandated by the accreditors had been completed over the summer. The new library/media center was the showcase of the building, with greatly expanded study space, sixteen computer stations, numerous TVs, VCRs, video-editing equipment, digital cameras, scanners, computer projection equipment, plus two small conference rooms. In addition, there was new paint throughout the building, another new computer lab where the old girls' locker room used to be, new exterior doors, ramps and accessible elevator for wheelchair use, and landscaping around the entrance of the school.

But the renovations did not solve the educational issues still plaguing the school. The DHS administrators summarized the problems in a report to the accreditors early in the school year:

> School year 1999–2000 began with an influx of 200 extra unanticipated students which severely challenged our capacity, resulted in 85 overenrolled classes, and compromised the advantages of the fledgling SLCs. Desperate efforts to schedule all of the new students and relieve faculty grievances broke down the barriers between the SLCs and resulted in the loss of common planning time. There was a very strong feeling in the building that we had taken two steps forward, only to take one back. At the same time, there was a growing conviction that we must take control of our own program.[1]

The overcrowding brought predictable results: a return to the violence and mayhem of previous years. In October, a ninth grader was stabbed on the playing field in front of the school at the end of the day.[2] A few weeks later, another student was shot on the front steps and ran into the school bleeding. Finally, the gruesome story emerged that several DHS students were connected with the live burial and murder of a pregnant teen at the nearby Boston State Hospital grounds.[3] The school community was reeling:

> In October 1999, our staff was already exhausted and demoralized. The 200 additional students undermined our best efforts at restructuring and left the hallways a bedlam of disorder, false fire alarms, and frightened teachers and students. (DHS teacher)

Two students summed up their feelings:

> I was afraid that people were just gonna come up to me and try to start a fight out of nowhere. Just people that just instigate and try to start a fight because you are quiet or because they know that you are not gonna do anything if they talk trash and stuff. This happened to other people, I've seen it done to other people, that's why I was like apprehensive, like I hope they are not gonna do it to me, if they done it to somebody else they are bound to do it to me. (DHS student)

> I feel like I don't want to come because just the things that been happening. Sometimes you just can't concentrate in this school because they are always pulling the fire alarms or there's like somebody yelling in the door while you are trying to take a test or something, or the class won't quiet down when the teacher is trying to teach. (DHS student)

The administrative team struggled to respond. One thing the headmaster and his veteran team did know was that there were too many troubled students in the school—court-appointed youth and kids released from the Department of Youth Services, students in the Department of Social Services system, students who had no ownership in the school, and students who did not report to school. Headmaster Belle repeatedly warned the district that the building was entertaining an inordinate share of "bad" kids, but without the comparative statistics to back up his claim, little was done.

> I said to the deputy superintendent, here's the statistics. You have ninety kids here, who are nineteen or older, you've got fifteen kids here, thirty kids over there, these kids came from the Burke, South Boston, they came from DYS, they threw them out, we got them. We were the school that they were assigned to because everybody else doesn't know what to do with them. (Bobby Belle)

Pam Trefler, too, was concerned about this problem. When she'd begun working with the school several years earlier, she had won an agreement from Court Street to stop the indiscriminate dumping of "hardcore" students into Dorchester High. Initially, Court Street honored this agreement.

> We had asked that the number of Department of Youth Services students be limited, and that request was honored in the beginning and then that request was taken away. That was actually in the original restructuring plan, and it was agreed to by Central Administration and then ignored. There were a large number of things in the original restructuring plan that were agreed to and ignored. Tom Payzant said to me, "Pam, I will do whatever is in my power to make this work." Then, the very next year we received [a large number of] students from DYS. (Pam Trefler)

Special needs students were another issue. Trefler and Headmaster Belle knew they would need help from Court Street to integrate special needs kids into the new small learning community's (SLCs). Again, initial promises of support from downtown were not honored.

> The superintendent promised that the special needs students if they were to be incorporated into the various SLCs would be sent along with the appropriate resources, meaning an extra teacher in the classroom, appropriate help outside the class. That promise was blatantly ignored....In a number of meetings down at Court Street we were basically told, "Yes we promised that, but technically we can get around that, and we're just not going to do it." (Pam Trefler)

An administrator from Court Street later provided a window into the world of the Boston Public Schools' downtown bureaucracy.

> I don't think they get it. It is not part of their work. I believe there are two reasons why Central Office people don't get it. Number one, they don't understand it, or two, they do understand it and they don't want to do it. That is at least my experience. I think it is more that the SPED department is just lazy. They don't want to be pulled in, and it is just as easy to keep the kids there. (Central Office Administrator)

TOO MANY COOKS IN THE COMMUNITY

The "dumping" of DYS and special education students was only one problem. The school was also beginning to experience "reform overload": it was being pulled in too many different directions by its various partners and reform initiatives. For example, during all of this confusion, DHS acquired two new partners in 1999, the Northeast and Islands Regional Education Laboratory at Brown University (LAB) and the Institute for Student Achievement (ISA) from New York City. The LAB was introduced to the school through UMB. Soon DHS was recruited into a five-year project based on *Breaking Ranks*, the new publication of the National Association of Secondary School Principals, which summarized the latest thinking on high school reform. Unfortunately, the addition of the LAB created some embarrassing duplication of effort, as it exemplified the notion of "too many cooks stirring the pot." The high school now found itself caught between two powerful and competing reform models (the Six Essentials and *Breaking Ranks*) and two influential parties for change (the district and UMB/Trefler/LAB). For example, under the direction of the LAB, the school began an intensive effort to align its curriculum with the Massachusetts state standards. After several months, the district's Director of Curriculum and Instruction put an end to this project with the stern reminder that central administration had already aligned the citywide curriculum several years earlier and mandated its use in all schools.

In the end, the LAB project fizzled and fell short. First, the research team was simply unable to get data expeditiously out of Court Street. As a result, they were unable to track the school's progress in a timely fashion. Second, the research team was located in the next state, and eventually came to realize that they could not effectively compete with the unrelenting pressure from Court Street.

The Institute for Student Achievement was a unique attempt to direct at-risk students toward college through an intense, on-campus academic investment. The leaders came to DHS, recruited sixty promising ninth graders, and hired two teachers to work with them for four years. The high school provided space in the satellites where they set up offices and classroom space, complete with their own computers. A local director visited periodically to check on progress. The program was entirely funded for four years, in advance, with monies collected out-of-state. The targeted students spent many afternoons with the ISA teachers, as well as summers, and often visited the site during the day. Unfortunately, the ISA program was undermined by two problems. The high rate of student turnover at DHS prohibited tracking a solid cohort of sixty students for four years. There were many dropouts, transfers, and new additions. Secondly, the ISA teachers failed to really communicate with the rest of the school. DHS teachers were unimpressed with the results and often viewed the ISA site as a "hangout" where students could skip classes. The final results, after four years, were unimpressive.

There were simply too many competing agendas in the school. In an early "mapping project," the LAB surveyed the recent history of DHS and tallied up 92 different "initiatives" which had floated through the school in the past seven years. In their place, the LAB offered the eighty-two recommendations of *Breaking Ranks*. In truth, the LAB helped DHS identify the confusing plethora of initiatives, but then added to the confusion. The city offered the Six Essentials of Whole School change, as well as the Ten Key Practices of a Restructuring High School. Plus, Dorchester High was responsible for the most recent recommendations of the NEASC committee.

In the end, Robert Belle made accreditation the priority, so the NEASC recommendations rose to the top of the heap. Any one plan seemed

incomplete, however. The NEASC outline ignored the work the school
was doing in inclusion, the strengthening of the Code of Discipline, and
the school-wide focus on literacy. No one plan encompassed all the fronts
on which the school was struggling.

As part of Payzant's plan for reform (Focus on Children and the Six
Essentials of Whole School Change), a team of teachers, administrators,
and community partners, called the Instructional Leadership Team, was
created and began meeting monthly to address the problems at DHS.
Members of the team included the headmaster and key administrative
leaders, the teacher-leaders of the SLCs, plus representatives from DHS's
business and university partners, UMB, Verizon (formerly New England
Telephone), and the Trefler Foundation. The leadership team began meeting in earnest at DHS in 1999. It was the first and only forum where all the
players came together.

The accreditors were scheduled to make a return visit in fall 2000 and
during the 1999–2000 year the school was racing to get ready. Headmaster Belle sent several letters to the superintendent, requesting help
in the face of extreme overcrowding. The letters asked that the superintendent maintain his promise of capping enrollments at 850 (they had
already climbed to 1,139 students) and funding additional replacement
textbooks. (NEASC had already reported that many textbooks were lost
each year, victims of the 37 percent mobility rate and the 23 percent dropout rate.)[4] The headmaster also asked, again, for the satellites to be retired
(which would also mean a smaller overall school population). The science
labs were all being renovated in preparation for the NEASC visit, so there
was even less classroom space than normal and more crowding. There
were also six SLCs to deal with in 1999 including APS, the Economics
and Business Academy, the Engineering and Technology Academy, the
new Performing Arts Academy, the new Leadership Academy, plus the
Freshmen Academy.

The administrative team also had to deal with about six other initiatives while preparing for the NEASC visit. First, they were taken out of
the building in staggered teams for advanced training in supervision
and evaluation with the Lexington-based Research for Better Teaching.
The Annenberg Challenge brought math and literacy coaches into the
school, who worked alongside teachers to improve instruction. A new
Vanguard grant provided funds to move the special education students
toward greater inclusion, so consultants from UMB met regularly with
DHS teachers to consider how to bring this about.

Meanwhile, Court Street rolled out new science and history textbooks
and curricula for the district, prompting extensive professional development for those teachers. The school was also implementing the new Boys
Town reading curriculum. In addition, the Teach Next Year interns
required mentoring, and several administrators helped teach the TNY
graduate classes at night. UMB professors were still on board several

days a week to help guide the restructuring. There was a new Data Management Team of teachers, which was assembled to analyze the voluminous data which were arriving at the school: from the Stanford 9 exams,
the MCAS, and the thrice-annual Scholastic Reading Inventory; from
spontaneous writing prompts and the biannual math assessments. With
the LAB looking over its shoulder, the school was swimming in data
and data analyses, but making little progress.

By this time, author Jack Leonard was assistant headmaster at DHS. As
a new administrator, Leonard had to quickly become acquainted with the
myriad procedures and policies put in place by the district. There were
numerous reports and documents to be assembled for NEASC, all of
which were in response to suggestions, consultations, mandates, and
models from the District and the various partners of the school.

But Leonard found that getting answers was not easy. For years, Court
Street issued policy decisions in "Superintendent Memoranda" which
were distributed to schools and filed in large binders in chronological
order. Without indexing, the memoranda were soon buried and people
operated from their memory of the policy. For a newcomer, the lack of
codified, easily accessible policy was frustrating. Many times Leonard
sought written definitions regarding one policy or another in the school,
but was unable to find an authoritative answer. Everyone had an opinion
about what the policy for such and such was, but there appeared to be no
written definitions, no concrete piece of paper that spelled things out.
Eventually, Court Street shifted to a computer-based economy and the
various policies were indexed and made available online.

Given all this activity, the school had an air of vitality and success that
belied the underlying problems. Thanks to the involvement with the
LAB, DHS was becoming known across the country as a model of high
school restructuring. Increasingly, visiting teams from Chicago, Seattle,
and London, as well as parts of New England came to observe the small
learning communities (SLCs) and interview the leaders and teachers of
DHS. For those on the inside, there was an uncomfortable conflict
between the national attention and the intransigent problems with absenteeism, low test scores, and dropouts.

GRIDLOCK IN THE SMALL LEARNING COMMUNITIES

The addition of four small learning communities by the 1999–2000
school year brought the growing realization that there were some fundamental problems with the schedule and structure of the school. First, the
six-period day simply did not give students sufficient opportunity to
complete the high school graduation requirements. The nineteen different credits required for the BPS diploma plus the additional period of
math and English required for all ninth graders, and the three signature
courses required in most SLCs added up to twenty-four different classes,

equal to the twenty-four slots available in a four-year sequence. Add in an MCAS or SAT prep class, or just the need to repeat a failed class (a common experience at DHS) and students were faced with an impossible load of requirements. The leadership team visited other high schools to see how others had succeeded in scheduling their SLCs, but the visits did not lead to any tangible improvements. Finally, the team recommended a seven-period day for the following year.

In addition, the Instructional Leadership Team was beginning to realize that there were really more than six SLCs in the building. If an SLC is defined as a distinct cohort of students taught by a designated group of teachers with some common planning time, then it became apparent that there were nine SLCs in the high school:

- Freshmen Academy
- Academy of Public Service
- Economics and Business Academy
- Engineering/Technology Academy
- Performing Arts Academy
- Leadership Academy
- Haitian creole bilingual program
- Spanish bilingual program
- The Occupational Skills Development Center program
- The Learning and Adaptive Behavior Cluster

Each of these operated somewhat independently of the other SLCs. In some cases, especially the bilingual and special education programs, there was complete interaction between the teachers within the cluster and minimal interaction between clusters. They were truly distinct. This meant the students had separate schedules, of course, and common sense dictates that it is far more difficult to schedule students in a small program than in a large school where there are multiple course options each period. The registrar was faced with trying to successfully schedule about 1100 students into nine SLCs each summer, where students from one SLC did not take math or science or history with students from another SLC. Needless to say, this was an impossible challenge. As a result, the regular education SLCs were not "pure," while the bilingual and special education SLCs often were.

Each fall, the faculty returned to find a disastrous schedule, which required numerous adjustments and prompted many grievances. Students repeated classes they had already passed, missed classes they needed for graduation, and often lost up to one month of valuable instructional time as the fall adjustments and corrections were made.

I had freshmen this year for the most part, and I had to do a lot of explaining to the freshmen from last year who are now in the 10th grade—because for a month, at least, they were even in the wrong grade, never mind in the wrong class—these kids were placed, if they were special ed, they were put in regular ed, regular ed kids were put in special ed classes. It was just a mess. (DHS teacher)

The students themselves were understandably upset by the confusion. Some were also unhappy with the new SLC structure itself. There was a sense in the building that some SLC's were better than others.

The way they split us up like APS, ETA, and EBA, I don't like that because it's like they put, I mean it's not APS students' fault, I mean, it's just how the teachers are sometimes, they put them on the pedestal. Why can't we have teachers like that, that feel like we should be high and mighty? Other academies, they just don't seem like they put us high standards like that... they don't put us on the pedestal, they just want to get us out. (DHS Student).

The LAB [the Learning and Adaptive Behavior cluster], which I am in, is about learning behavior. We can't learn in a big class because we get distracted too quickly. It's maybe no more than thirteen kids, you know, some classes have two teachers, some have one, it's a better learning environment for us, so we can get our work done. Most of the time we are to ourselves, we stay within the LAB cluster....We are the down people, everybody looks down on us, when something goes wrong, it's the LAB kids just because we have a history of learning behavior. They really look down on us. (DHS student)

The troubles with the SLCs happened right under the noses of the district administrators (who strongly encouraged the school to move toward SLCs), the UMB consultants and the LAB research team. The LAB invited DHS participants to seminars with other New England high schools and lauded the personalization possibilities of the small learning communities. UMB worked to reduce the tensions and distrust between the administration and the faculty and strongly supported the Teach Next Year interns. Court Street came to visit in spring 2000 and mandated additional forward movement on SLCs until every student was given the opportunity to participate.

But despite all the praise for SLCs, no one had the expertise or foresight to warn DHS that a school of 1100 students could not support nine SLCs. Instead, the school struggled to address the problems, which were only dimly understood in the beginning and then increasingly appreciated as year after year followed with inoperable schedules. The impasse with restructuring and scheduling meant that for too long, attention was diverted from teaching and learning.

Even though the district worked very hard to promote collegiality—the Six Essentials instructed the school to participate in "Looking at Student Work" and the new curricula rolled out by Court Street was accompanied with lots of new professional development—the faculty was too demoralized by the overcrowding, the threats of violence, and the unmanageable schedules to truly take advantage of these opportunities.

Even the premier Academy of Public Service, which had enjoyed such success for years in moving students on to college, was exhausted and frustrated. First, they were no longer the "only show in town" since other SLCs now offered competing programs and reached out to the same pool of tenth graders.

Second, the superintendent's emphasis on high standards for all students pushed DHS to eliminate basic level classes as well as elective classes (such as the specialized courses which made up the APS program) in favor of mixed-ability grouping and mainstreaming. APS teachers were faced with teaching the "hardcore" kids with behavioral issues that the program had always refused.

> So we fought and fought that and we lost. Ok, we are going to take them in. We did for at least the first four or five months, we exposed them to everything everybody else had in the academy. If they wanted a mentor, they could have a mentor. If they wanted to go on some enrichment field trip, they could go on the field trip. There were certain steps all of our kids had to go through if you were going to get a summer job and all that. It was miserable. All I can say is it was an incorrigible group of students. They never bought in. We did the same build up, you are part of something special. If you do x, y and z, you can maybe go overseas this summer, leadership things. All of the things. They were so incorrigible and so nasty, the crew that came out of there, that we never made inroads with that group. (APS teacher)

> We would fix them up with a mentor and sometimes they would blow off the mentor. Now this is one of those things you build for years, you know, there aren't thousands of mentors out there. Adults in kids' lives who want to come to [Dorchester] High once a month. The mentor program adults would come once per month at the school, and we would have this breakfast, and we would do some kind of team building things in the cafeteria. Then we asked them to call their mentor or mentee once a week and they would ask to see them one time a month outside of the school at their job placement, take them to a Red Sox game, take them to Alvin Ailey, whatever, do something and follow them about their college stuff. These students blew off a number of the mentors. I was just losing it. They didn't want to do anything. (Paul Casilli)

In time, the power of the APS program declined. The small faculty deeply resented the DHS administration that seemed intent on jeopardizing rather than supporting their program. The administration, for their part, grew increasingly impatient with the Academy's complaints. The stand-off was not well negotiated.

COURT STREET INTERVENES

In the spring of 2000, the long-dreaded intervention from Court Street began. In March, Superintendent Payzant sent intervention teams into the three Boston high schools with the lowest MCAS scores in the city— Dorchester being one of the them—taking advantage of a previously

unused provision in the 1989 teachers' union contract that empowered
the superintendent to send evaluation teams into failing schools. The recommendations of the intervention teams could empower the superintendent to make drastic changes without a union vote. The 2000
intervention team was a mix of Court Street administrators and teachers'
union members, and they spent two weeks combing through the school,
observing classes and records and interviewing teachers, students, and
parents.[5] Intervention was humiliating and disruptive. The school was
working hard toward full accreditation and the process raised serious
doubts about that work and delayed full accreditation.

> I mean, come on, you don't go up for accreditation, and just before you get to
> go out to get fully accredited, the School Department tells you, "we're inter-
> vening."...I mean, that's not the way you do business, but that's the way it
> was done. (Bobby Belle)

The school felt unfairly targeted; the declining MCAS scores were
attributable to the departure of the Health Careers Academy, and the
renewed violence was easily connected to the overcrowding and prepon-
derance of court-involved youth. Teachers felt that more than low standardized test scores should have prompted the Intervention. One glaring
statistic was the rising dropout rates at the school. Dorchester High
School had enormous student turnover from 1993 to 2000; many of these
students dropped out of school altogether. Of course, each dropout left
an empty seat that was filled with yet another student who came on board
midyear with little investment or ownership in the school. The school
regularly processed 1,500 students each year, although the daily attendance never rose above 1,000. Students ran through the school "like
water."

> My turnover rate was so tremendous, I mean, I would have on an average
> daily attendance, I was missing 360 kids, ok? A lot of those kids were in jail,
> a lot of them never came to school, some of them got caught up in the neigh-
> borhood violence and were dead or hospitalized. (Bobby Belle)

From 1996 to 2000, the school had the highest dropout rate of any comprehensive high school in Boston.[6] And state figures indicated that the dropout rate at DHS was the worst for any major high school in the
commonwealth in 2000. Dorchester High School's dropout rates were
higher than any other of the high schools in the major urban districts of
Massachusetts. In addition, the promotion rates at the school were falling,
especially for Spanish-speaking students.

The report of the DHS intervention team came out in May 2000. It
called for the replacement of the entire middle management team—
everyone between the headmaster and the faculty. Newspaper headlines
crowed, "Reform ax may cut Hub school managers."[7] For a month, the
assistant headmasters and program directors worried anxiously about
their future while teachers quietly rejoiced that for once they had not been

the scapegoats. The intervention report also called for radical restructuring of all the failing high schools into small learning communities, a process nearly completed already at DHS.

One significant recommendation of the intervention report was the creation of a new position—the Chief Academic Officer—to replace the Assistant Headmaster for Curriculum and Instruction. This beefed-up management position reported "directly to the superintendent" and no longer belonged to the administrators' union. After a month of wondering about his future as part of the panned middle management team at DHS, Jack Leonard was asked to fill the role of the CAO.

The new position was an affront to Headmaster Belle, who recognized this end-run around his leadership. After the intervention report, Court Street had three choices for Belle: invest in him with professional development, replace him, or supplant him with a competing position, which was directly reportable downtown. Court Street chose the last.

> I've always had a vision, I always knew what I wanted to do, I always knew where I wanted to go. It's kind of like, if you're trying to build something and you don't have the tools, you can still build it, but it might not be as strong and as nice as esthetically appealing as you'd want it to be, and the building that I had to do with Dorchester High School was from the ground up. And you know, it never got recognized, and that's ok, but you say what you want to say, in the midst of all that madness and craziness that was going on over there, a lot of kids did get an education, a lot of programs did come together, they did get fully accredited. (Bobby Belle)

The position of Chief Academic Officer was a vaguely defined and uncomfortable one at DHS. In some respects, the new position strengthened the school. Leonard had a listening ear at Court Street now. Certain grant monies, for books and professional development, for example, were funneled directly through his office, allowing him to work more easily with the faculty. He was regularly included in communications from Court Street, which also helped in keeping the building attuned to central objectives. Like any new arrangement, there were some at Court Street who worked closely with Leonard and others who were not aware of his role at all, so implementation of the model was uneven.

In other ways, the arrangement was irritating. While the responsibilities were high, the new position was not vested with clearly defined authority. Job descriptions were vague. Since Belle continued to write the evaluations of the administrative staff, they tended to follow his lead when there was a conflict in work to be done. Similarly, Belle often placed the other assistant headmaster (for operations) in charge of the building in his absence, recognizing her greater familiarity in dealing with dangerous situations. As a result, other administrators and teachers were often unsure of who was in charge. The DHS business partners expressed consternation at an administrative structure with two heads. The two leaders adjusted however, made the best of the situation, and tried to keep the kids in focus.

SCRAMBLED MESSAGES FROM THE DISTRICT

DHS began the 2000–01 year as an "Intervention School." This meant that the school received much more attention from central administrators—a circumstance that didn't turn out to be all bad. The Director of Curriculum and Instruction brought his entire team of senior program directors (math, English, science, history, art, and world languages) to the school to observe classrooms, syllabi, and lesson plans and measure the degree of conformity with the citywide learning standards. On the whole, many of the program directors were warm and supportive, while they pushed the school to standardize course syllabi and assessments across similar classes in regular, special, and bilingual education. The team left the school with their report and a new measuring tool, the Indicators of Teacher Effectiveness, a two-page rubric designed to help administrators evaluate teaching performance.

The rubric did not sit well with teachers; it was cumbersome and teachers found it impossible to adequately meet all the standards in one observation.

> I feel that sometimes things are stated downtown, like—you got to have an MCAS question on the board—and yet I need to have my learning outcomes, my warm-ups, you know, so—they are telling me that I need to have like five to ten different things on the board at one time and then I have to keep the kids engaged and it just seems like overwhelming....We got a mandate for literacy across the content areas...we got this new curriculum. We got all this stuff...so it just seems like whoa, I'm not God. (DHS math teacher)

Numerous meetings of the DHS Instructional Leadership Team were devoted to discussing and redesigning the document. Sadly, it exacerbated the contentious climate in the school. One teacher asked, "How can we move the building toward a culture of collaboration instead of adversarial positions? These visits from Court Street are only antagonizing teachers."

The year brought new grants and new reform plans. Dorchester won a Comprehensive School Reform project grant, and signed up for a new set of meetings, trainings, and reports. The school was also drawn into a new federal grant with UMB that supported collaborations between seven Massachusetts universities and public schools. Though it was announced with great fanfare, in the end, the grant produced a relatively small amount of financial support, but required an additional slate of monthly team meetings, rubrics, reports, and write-ups. School administrators, notably CAO Jack Leonard, were loath to turn down any opportunity, but increasingly the troubles and tensions inside the school were causing the staff to look more critically at the many partnering opportunities.

Some, such as the LAB and the federal grant, were distant and hard to explain to the faculty.

The leadership problems at DHS were not solved with the new CAO position. Headmaster Belle was becoming ill; the long hours in the first few years had seriously endangered his health. He had heard through the grapevine that the school was about to be fully accredited at last. He should have been proud; accreditation had been his number one goal and he had led the school in its accomplishment. But the impending success went unrecognized by the superintendent. The combination of this neglect and the insult of the tag-along CAO were tiresome, and in February, 2001, he left the school for health reasons and did not return for almost two months. No one knew how long he would be out and the school drifted, disjointedly, in the interim, with unclear leadership.

The confusion over leadership was symptomatic of the whole school by 2001. The Accelerated Academy—a new SLC recommended by the intervention team—began with great fanfare, but from the start struggled to define its leadership; was it the headmaster's administrative team, the program director for English who helped design the school, or the Diploma Plus consultants? A similar conflict appeared in the SLCs, which had always been teacher-led. However, while the "Academy Heads" (as they were known) could recruit students and design the curriculum, they could not evaluate teaching and learning for they were union members themselves. Because of this, teacher supervision had always been done by department; the math program director evaluated all the math teachers, regardless of SLC affiliation and the history program director evaluated all the history teachers and so on.

With its new push for SLCs however, the District ordered the school to follow the pure SLC design and assign one program director to each SLC to evaluate all the teachers in that SLC. This was fine for the program director of bilingual education or the one for special education, but it did not work for the regular education SLCs. Instead, the arrangement meant that the math program director was evaluating English teachers and the English program director (who was struggling to get the Accelerated Academy going) was called upon to evaluate math instruction. So, they collaborated on evaluations instead.

This confusion in leadership led to similar confusion over who was responsible for discipline. The academy heads could only handle the simplest student discipline cases and relied upon the program directors to handle suspension or expulsion hearings. Both students and teachers complained that school discipline was disintegrating—a serious issue for a school with a history of violence.

> People get in with weapons and stuff. Why do you have metal detectors if you really don't use them? And they make you go home for all the wrong reasons. Like if there are too many fire alarms, you are free to go home...
> but like when people bring weapons into the building or something major

happens...they want you to stay here, so it doesn't feel safe at all. (DHS
student)

We do not have the power to put kids out of the building, we don't have the
power to discipline them, we have no power—the students have the power
as to whether or not they are going to follow the rules...they know that if I
send them out of the room, nothing is going to happen to them. (DHS
teacher)

Somehow, the MCAS scores continued to improve anyway (as they did
all over the city). Data management uncovered other successes:

As we have grown in our ability to disaggregate the data at DHS, we have
been in a position to "crow" about our successes more convincingly. For
example, last year we discovered that our average scaled score on the MCAS
placed us among the top seven public high schools in the city. This year, we
have disaggregated the Stanford Nine data and discovered that out of nineteen high schools, we were number four in improvement on our math scores
and number six in improvement on the reading test. This is encouraging
news for the school.[8]

The school was still under scrutiny, however, and so there were still
many reports to be filed. A progress report was sent to NEASC in January
2001, outlining the results of the curriculum audit and the response to
Intervention. After brief hesitation in light of the intervention team,
NEASC decided to fully accredit the high school. There were in fact substantial improvements in the school. Four hundred thousand dollars
worth of science lab renovations had been completed the previous
summer. The notorious satellite classrooms had finally been closed—the
intervention team had insisted on this as well. Dorchester High had not
looked this good in many years.

In April 2001, NEASC informed the school that a recommendation was
being made to the Board of Trustees for full accreditation for Dorchester
High School, eight years after the original warning. Again the disjointed-
ness of events bewildered the faculty: the intervention team had publicly
vilified the high school while NEASC had approved it. Despite the years
of effort to meet the accreditation standards, there was no celebration.

2001 TO 2002: DECLINE

The 2001–02 school year showed the same disjointed mix of awards
and recognition on the one hand and troubling indicators on the other.
For example, the staff took pride in the school's accreditation and the
emerging success of new programs that came out of the last few years of
grant-funded hard work. The Accelerated Academy—which had been
designed especially for older students who had been repeatedly kept
back—was running smoothly. The program was also developing strong
connections to the Building Trades Union, which opened up doors for

summer jobs and postgraduation employment. The academy was a model for what one school could do for its alternative learners. Visitors were coming to examine and, hopefully, duplicate the work.

The Teach Next Year program had also been a resounding success; this year, six of the graduates were employed as new teachers at DHS. Building on the success of TNY, the Trefler Foundation was interested in supporting more model university-high school partnerships across the city and they provided funds to award $100,000 to successful models. Dorchester High won the first professional development school partnership grant. The school, said Pam Trefler, "was an incubator and testing ground for initiatives later adopted system-wide."

Recognition also came to Ed Noonan, the academy head for the Economics and Business Academy, who won the Milken Family Award for teaching in recognition of his innovative efforts at inclusion. The award brought national recognition and some nice articles in the local newspapers. Finally, state figures show that the dropout rate declined to 13 percent—still the highest for any large high school in the Boston—but way down from a high of 25 percent just three years previously.

The school was struggling, however. Student enrollments had diminished; there were 929 students in the school in June 2002, which made for a safer school, but 54 percent of the students were boys and they were not doing well. Even more troubling, 62 percent of the incoming ninth graders were male (a percentage inflated by the high number of males who failed classes and repeated the year), while 55 percent of the seniors were girls. Clearly, the boys were having a hard time negotiating four years of education at DHS. In addition, approximately 60 percent of the incoming ninth graders had failed two or more core academic subjects in middle school (English, math, science, or social studies). In short, they were unprepared for high school (BPS policies allowed only one retention between grades one and eight; even failing students were moved along into high school).

Even though overall enrollment figures were down, bilingual enrollments had increased from 17 to 22 percent, and special education assignments to substantially separate classrooms had also mushroomed from 13 to 18 percent of the total. Some faculty members, noting the alternative education program that also functioned inside the school, lamented the relative scarcity of well-prepared regular education students.

"A FIGHT SCHOOL"

The school climate was not good. A dead body was discovered in the parking lot in front of the school one May morning; the death was unrelated to the school but added to the dangerous reputation of the neighborhood. A few weeks later, a DHS student was beaten to death with a baseball bat. The beating took place outside of school, but stemmed directly from an altercation among some girls inside the school.

Perhaps because of these problems, fewer and fewer students chose to come to DHS. One teacher remarked that in 2001–02 "Dorchester High had fourteen kids who wanted to come and fill 300 seats." Unfortunately, most of the students knew that their fellow classmates did not choose the school, causing further damage to their own sense of self worth. As this one student explained, "I didn't want to come here. They said it was like a fight school. All these bad stuff happen there." In terms of student behavior and student engagement, Dorchester High hit bottom in 2001–02. This really damaged the overall school culture and led to other problems for students and teachers that were very difficult to overcome.

One problem was that students had real trouble making friends at the school. One female student talked about making friends at DHS:

> The only thing that kept me from totally dreading going to Dorchester was knowing that I was gonna be with my friend. I had only like one really good friend in the whole school. It seemed like everyone [else] that I knew in that school just had that kind of ignorant kind of attitude, so I didn't make as many friends as I really wanted to because I don't really hang out with people like that. I wasn't really comfortable in that type of environment.

This student ended up transferring out of DHS one year later. A 17-year-old boy talked about friendships at DHS this way:

> I don't have a lot of friends here. This year has been filled with drama for me, people trying to steal my stuff, steal my clothes, steal my hat, steal my sneakers, that type of thing, try to rob you. I have friends that go to other schools. I was thinking about getting transferred.

The lack of real friendship among students seemed to breed dread and fear of the other, unknown peers that students encountered in the hallways. One student explained:

> I did not like my ninth grade year. I don't think anybody liked their ninth grade year. I mean I think the kids who bullied other kids had an okay year because they don't have people bothering them basically, but for a person like me getting picked on in ninth grade, I didn't like it. It's just the type of situation where they talk about you—not necessarily pushing you around or slapping you upside your head—it's just basically talking about you.

The school was so chaotic in 2001–02 that it was easy for students and teachers to imagine that anything could happen not only in the building, but also in the classroom. There were just enough troubled kids in the school to make it very difficult for teachers to control the classroom. One teacher described it like this:

> In a class of 28 kids you maybe have 6 that just don't want to be there and are disruptive, you have 12 that could go either way, and then you have 3 or 4 that really want to be students, so you got the 6 involved, that infects the 12, now you got 18 disruptive kids.

Perhaps students' overall negative attitudes about each other came from witnessing this kind of behavior among their peers. As one student said, "the people that come here, the way they act—childish, immature, and rude. They don't have respect for anybody else." Other students attributed the problems to a poor upbringing. "These kids here are unruly. Some of them come from bad homes. Some of them come from no homes." "I think a lot of kids were like that before they came to Dorchester, I mean you must get it from your parents or your environment because you don't just, you are not just born ignorant. The students, their background is kind of messed up."

Sadly, one student blamed the whole African American race for why the students at DHS couldn't get along. She said, "not to say this in a racist way, but you can't put black people in the same place for more than an hour. Because it's like say for instance the Caribbean festival, we can't even have that without anything happening bad, like violence. We just can't get along. We should not be in the same place."

The teachers struggled to contain these behaviors. Some lost control of their classrooms.

> They stand up; they smack the guy next to them; they walk around; they're disruptive. So you maybe isolate them and you can work on them, but if you have six or seven that are like that, that are super frustrated, and infect the whole class, and you don't have recourse discipline-wise to either get them out of class or to understand that that kind of behavior is not acceptable, then that's where your job becomes beyond your means. (DHS English teacher)

The students often blamed teachers for the chaos. Many of them were unprepared to teach in urban schools.

> We got a teacher and she just left like when she couldn't deal with it, we went through like so many teachers, and they are saying we ran her out, but . . . basically what she did is she gave up on us. (DHS student)

Unfortunately, many of the teachers at DHS began falling back on using worksheets as a "kind of measure when chaos is reigning," as one teacher put it.

> Because they have been so horrible this week, I gave an assignment, and this works every time, but I have to use it sparingly like once a month. This is all rote work. I said "if you get to page 23, you get an A for the day, page 21, a B", you know. It's very simple. Cause and effect, and it works like a charm. They were silent all period long, and I can do that with grammar. As long it's something they can do. They just want that A for the day. Now if I walk around and say write three pages on this topic. They can't do that; they just can't do three pages. I mean I don't know how to get them to write three pages in one day.
>
> It's like [The students need to] see that something is done by the end of the period, that they've accomplished something. If they don't see something complete, they don't think they did anything that day. So I have a worksheet.

They see at the end of the day, "oh, I got this done. This is what I learned to-day. This is what I did today." Whereas I could do that same thing without a worksheet, and they might still get the concept, but not think that they accomplished anything. I create worksheets to go along with activities to give them a sense of accomplishment.

Teachers found that students had a low tolerance for the "wrong" answer. They often appeared very uncomfortable with ambiguity in the classroom, making it difficult for those teachers who wanted the kids to learn by exploring their own thinking. One science teacher explained:

The right answer, they want the right answer. "Tell me the right answer." They are very uncomfortable with not having the answer. In fact one girl that does well in my upper level class, I had asked a question about a problem they did, and I said, 'What do you think?' She came up and said, 'Oh is this right?' This is a girl that wants to have an A+ all year. I said 'Do not change that answer, and we will talk about it.' It was the wrong answer, but I thought she made a good observation and that was important. I did not mark it wrong because it was a good observation and that's all I want them to do. They don't want to be wrong, but I guess we have to tell them it's okay if you think.

These student and teacher observations were collected in a report at the beginning of 2002 that was widely read both inside the school and across the district, fixing in print the fundamental flaws with the school.[9] The report attempted to explain why the school lacked a culture of achievement. One reason was the poor academic preparation students received in middle and elementary school. Teachers credited the students' frustration in high school to "never having had a successful school experience." And this did appear to be the case, with many incoming freshmen at DHS lacking core middle school classes.

As teacher comments reveal, this created a real challenge for teachers. Many were committed to creating classroom environments where the students could have a successful educational experience. But the kids were so far behind that the teachers felt it was beyond their means to help them catch up—without extra adult assistance in the classroom. Teachers were also acutely aware of their students' troubled home lives.

I do have a number of students who when you ask them what their home is, it's a little unclear. They might be homeless; they might be moving between family members, friends; their family might be in another country they're staying with an aunt or uncle. Foster care—I have a number of students who moved from homes within the foster care system. And then, a lot of our students work or have children or children that they take care of.

The report chronicled the feelings of hopelessness among many DHS teachers. Like the APS teachers, they believed that disruptive, "hardcore" students should be removed from the school and placed in special programs. They pointed out that the school system had mandated the inclusion of these students, without providing the school with adequate supports for the task. Teen Empowerment, a city organization once known for mediating gang disputes, was working inside DHS and trying to negotiate a new set of codes for student behavior. However, teachers were not heartened by their presence; they believed it essentially represented Court Street's indifference to the discipline problems. This left the school, and the teachers, with little choice but to deal with the students themselves on a day-to-day basis.

> You have a few people you can go to, but basically you gotta do it [yourself], and...if you can't handle it yourself, more or less, you are not going to make it, whether it means taking "fuck you" or whatever. You want to give them a detention, you give them the detention, but if they don't come, don't think you can get somebody else to make them do it. (DHS teacher)

> The school police fraternize with the kids. My classroom is adjacent to the cafeteria and is very isolated from the rest of the school, and a couple of times I have had to run out—I mean serious fights, and I don't know if somebody has a weapon on them, or how something will escalate—and the school police look at you and they don't even bother to come. (DHS Teacher)

DEATH KNELL FOR DORCHESTER HIGH

While the school continued to hobble along, Superintendent Payzant was readying a new set of mandates for the Boston Public Schools. *Focus on Children II*, his follow-up five-year plan, focused on "maintaining high standards, accelerating the rate of improvement, holding schools accountable for results, developing leadership at the school level, focusing on family and community engagement, and cultivating external partnerships."[10] Among other reforms, Focus on Children II required the restructuring of all of Boston's "comprehensive" high schools (i.e., those that were not elite exam schools). In essence, the superintendent ordered that all of the big high schools be broken down into either small learning communities, or separate small schools. Ironically, just as Dorchester High was foundering, its reforms were adopted system-wide. Both the Carnegie and Gates foundations funded the restructuring effort, as the Trefler Foundation had at DHS.

The Dorchester High experiment also inspired another system-wide reform. Teach Next Year, which had received so much attention, had one glaring problem: often, the TNY interns could not get jobs in the Boston Public Schools after they had finished their training. It was not because they weren't wanted. The problem lay in arcane practices inside the school district's human resources department, which often failed to hire new teachers until August. By then, the TNY interns had usually accepted jobs outside Boston, a fact that was not lost on Superintendent Payzant. The human resources department was overhauled so that teachers could be hired by May.

Other reforms recognized the need to strengthen early childhood education, to better prepare Boston kids for elementary, middle, and high school work; and provided Boston teachers and administrators with more sustained and comprehensive leadership training.

The last of Payzant's reforms had an immediate and devastating impact on Dorchester High: the so-called In Depth Review, a new process for evaluating the Boston Public Schools. Each of the district's schools was now required to undergo a thorough investigation every four years. The schools were expected to prepare an extensive self-study, similar to the accreditation process, followed by an on-site visit. One of the first on the list for review was Dorchester High.

Once again, the staff spent hundreds of hours gathering documents, addressing the Six Essentials and assembling a portfolio to show the school in the best light. Following on the heels of the intervention team report and the NEASC self-study—both of which had been completed only two years earlier—the process was exhausting. The inspection required countless hours of preparation and writing, but did little to improve the school.

After months of preparation, DHS was visited and evaluated in January and February 2002; the final rating, on a scale of one to four, was just above a two. The In Depth Review report contained recommendations addressing each of the Six Essentials. Most demanded compliance with district initiatives: implementation of the "Reader's Workshop" model, adherence to the math curriculum and the Looking At Student Work protocols, initiation of an all-funds budget review, clarification of professional development guidelines, and so on.

Again, the blame was squarely placed on the leadership team. There was a strong feeling in the building that the visit was designed to "build a case" against the school for possible reconstitution in the future. The superintendent had already uttered the dreaded word "reconstitution" once during a school visit. Added to the intervention, the In Depth Review only strengthened the conviction that no matter what the administrators, teachers, or partners did, the school was just unable to highlight its strong suits.

But the report identified some real issues at the school. It outlined, for the first time, the intractable problem of scheduling students into nine SLCs. The school leadership team knew that there was no way to succeed without a reduction in the number of SLCs. They presented this very problem to the faculty in November 2001, but with little hope of a solution. No one had the heart to kill off any one of the teacher-led SLCs, and the school had no authority to eliminate the SLCs in bilingual or special education. Only a higher authority could step in and make the hard decisions to simplify the programmatic offerings.

In addition to the In Depth Review report, complaints were mounting from several other sources. University faculty, nearing the end of the four-year Trefler funded partnership, privately expressed their frustration at the adversarial relationships between faculty and administration and their inability to move the school forward. A literacy coach fired off an E-mail message, which was highly circulated at the district level, outlining the lack of respect and support for her work and, more importantly, the Boston Public Schools "workshop" initiatives.

Finally, one other disgruntled voice being heard downtown was the Academy of Public Service. The competition with other SLCs, the pressure for inclusion, and the constant invasion of Court Street mandates were all taking a toll. Pam Trefler, who still strongly supported and defended the program, strenuously complained about what appeared to be the disregard for APS inside the school, while Paul Casilli, the academy head, protested to Court Street in defense of his work. APS was highly favored downtown. The program had been the brightest light at Dorchester for many years. But in reality, other factors were threatening the program. As Neil Sullivan, executive director of the Boston Private Industry Council put it,

> For the past 80 years high schools were judged based on the success of the top quarter of the class, those who went to good colleges....the Massachusetts Comprehensive Assessment System has turned that upside down. Now schools are judged based on how well they do with the bottom quarter of the class, students who were often ignored or overlooked.[11]

As a result, DHS was throwing its attention and resources into the Accelerated Academy and the Freshmen Academy, as well as inclusion strategies. APS was increasingly taken for granted. The central administration only vaguely understood the problem. Nevertheless, the threat to the program was more cause for concern in the superintendent's office.

THE END COMES FOR DORCHESTER HIGH SCHOOL

In November 2002, the superintendent returned with his team to DHS for one more visit. The one-day walk-through brought a scathing verbal analysis that noted, among other things, some teachers reading newspapers during class and other teachers providing flatly wrong information to students. Not more than two weeks later, the superintendent announced his decision to recommend to the School Committee the dissolution of Dorchester High as of July 1, 2003. In its place, three separate and distinct small high schools would operate in the building.

The new plan cut through the Gordian knot of SLCs. The two best SLCs would be preserved—the Academy of Public Service and the Economics and Business Academy—and would be reconstituted as small independent schools. The Engineering and Technology Academy and the Freshmen Academy would exist no longer. The Accelerated Academy would be phased out after one year. Bilingual education would be removed forever (this decision came in concert with the new state initiative to eliminate the 30-year bilingual education program and move toward a full-immersion model). Special education students would be gradually reduced in number.

In addition, the overall school population for APS and the Economics and Business Academy would be reduced to 600 students, making room for the importation of Tech Boston Academy. The new advanced technology school had started the previous year in Brighton with a large Gates grant, and was now the darling of the mayor and the public. The hope was that Tech Boston would bring much-needed cachet to the building and make the combination—now known as the Dorchester Education Complex—far more attractive. In one fell swoop, the problems with leadership, scheduling, improper restructuring, and reputation were addressed. The district also promised—once again—to reduce the number of court-appointed youth and the ratio of special education students.

Understandably, the superintendent's decision raised a lot of questions. Teachers wondered which school they would work for the following year and how they would be assigned—or if they would even be working at all. The Academy Heads, Paul Casilli and Ed Noonan, were concerned about student recruitment for the following year. For Casilli, this meant a clear end to the ten-year tradition of recruiting and interviewing students for the program. DHS administrators, too, were concerned about where they stood in the new arrangement. The answers soon came as the district entered the season for budgets and personnel selection. The administrators were all told, with the exception of Robert Belle, to look for another job, preferably outside the district. (Belle was a special case. He was one of the few remaining black male headmasters in the city, and he was popular with the community.) All the DHS teachers were officially excessed (put up for hire). This was logical, technically; the school to which they had been assigned no longer existed. But it was incredibly insulting to the faculty.

The community—including the school's university and philanthropic partners—was of two minds about the reconstitution. On the one hand, the school's partners welcomed an end to the chaos in scheduling and discipline. On the other hand, some of them felt that Court Street itself was ultimately to blame for the failure of the Dorchester High experiment—an experiment that had sparked so much excitement less than ten years earlier.

> They could have totally turned around Dorchester High by not doing harmful things...[like] dumping such large numbers of troubled and difficult students into the school...The question is, why did they dump? It wasn't one person you could point to. It was a whole way of doing business....I think the actual underlying problem was fairly simple. Jealousy is a very ugly thing, and we were actually told point blank in a private conversation, "You gave Dorchester High School a million dollars. You brought in all these other people to help them; therefore we don't feel like we owe the school

anything." We were told this by one of the top two people in central administration. It actually was discussed in open meetings, when the school was applying for a Carnegie grant. It was stated that Dorchester High School, East Boston High and Madison Park, all of which had received money from the Trefler Foundation, would be given less money than the other schools if the grant were obtained. In effect, I believed very strongly that Dorchester High School, since it got the most attention, was ultimately penalized because of the extra resources that were brought in. (Pam Trefler)

Our work caused central administration to have to deal with the fact that they had low expectations for the school—that they wrote the kids off. We changed the outcomes they could expect from Dorchester High....That really disrupted the status quo. It changed the way they had to think about the school....Just because the school was black, it didn't mean you shouldn't have high expectations. It didn't mean you shouldn't put in resources.... Ultimately, they couldn't let the standard of excellence for the school system come out of Dorchester High. It would have exposed the mismanagement in all of the other schools. (Charlie Desmond)

So ended Dorchester High; a school that had graduated the likes of Rose Kennedy no longer existed. Now, three small schools were expected to rise from the ashes—to carve new identities from the remains of an institution that had once proclaimed, "Whatever it takes, for as long as it takes."

CHAPTER 9

Learning How to Educate Together: The Hope and Promise of Small High Schools 2003 to 2006

ROCKY BEGINNINGS: THE DESIGN TEAMS

Design teams made up of teachers, school leaders, business and university partners, and central administrators were assembled for the two new small schools—Academy of Public Service (APS) and the Economics and Business Academy (EBA)—two months after the superintendent's announcement. Building the teams was not easy. Of course the business and university partners were thrilled to be part of the design teams. They had been working with DHS for years and felt that this was their chance to effect real change at the school. It was a different story for school personnel, however. The school leaders were not invested, for they knew they had no future in the small schools. The teachers were outraged at being excessed[1] and having no guarantee of a job in the following year. The central administrators were looked upon with suspicion and derision, as if they were there to ensure that the district's agenda for each school become reality. Despite these tensions, the work progressed.

Almost immediately, distinct differences between the two teams developed. The EBA team was led by a soon-to-retire administrator from the Office of Instructional Technology in the district. She was a good listener and easy to trust. She was also the mother of a new young teacher in the building. Academy Head Ed Noonan was excited to see his program singled out and promoted to full-school status. As a result the meetings started off cordially and were productive, despite apprehensions about the uncertainties of the future. The team wrote a new mission statement and began making decisions about schedules and curriculum for the following year.

The APS planning team was not nearly as productive. First, the team facilitator was entirely different. He had a long history of fighting for educational reform in Boston and was known as an advocate for pilot schools. He was also a representative for small schools all over New England. He was condescending toward the non-pilot schools in Boston, so he was not well received by the APS staff. His overly confident nature could be abrasive. Second, the academy head of APS, Paul Casilli, and the veteran teachers who helped build the program were far more threatened by the transition to a small school and the prospect of losing control over their program. One of the big sticking points for both schools was the question of special education (SPED) students and how many each school would be forced to take. EBA had somewhat of an advantage here because they had already taken the lead on including special education students in the curriculum. APS was concerned about the SPED numbers as well because they knew that too many students with special needs would hurt the unique APS culture. As a result, the team meetings were tense and little progress was made.

Things changed as the year ended however; now, tensions were running high on both teams (albeit for different reasons) and the planning process was halting. The EBA team met weekly to plan the new Economics and Business Academy. On the surface, the meetings were courteous and productive, but underneath there was tension between the teachers and business/university partners. The partners were excited to create a new school that took advantage of the latest research on what works for small schools. They envisioned bold, new organizational structures and innovative approaches to scheduling and curriculum. Their visions matched with those of the district personnel who were also urging that the school implement more favored reforms such as block scheduling, student advisories, and humanities (a combining of history and English curricula in one class), but the EBA teachers would have none of it. Unfortunately, they took a more cautious approach. They were in no mood to draw bold and creative plans for a new small school. The teachers were worried about their own jobs, who the next school leader would be, and what else the district might spring on them.

Ed Noonan, who carried some weight as a successful SLC leader, counseled small steps. As a result, they stuck to the familiar six-period day with no advisories and no humanities and the same course offerings and business activities as the previous year. This left the business/university partners wondering for whom the teachers were designing the school, the students or themselves. Eventually, the group hit an impasse that the facilitator was unable to negotiate. Out of frustration, one of the outside partners shared this information with the district, bringing the head of High School Renewal to the table. She used the meeting to layout what the district would and would not accept. "The superintendent will not accept a model that includes a headmaster and assistant headmaster. ...Any converted high school will do a humanities instructional block within three years....There will be some form of block scheduling." To which one of the teachers asked, " what if the teachers in the building don't want block scheduling." The answer – "the superintendent will come back and say you need to do a block schedule."[2]

Meanwhile, the Academy of Public Service meetings were just as bitter and contentious at the end of the year as they were at the beginning. The APS teachers were still angry over the forced conformity of the new school model that they believed violated the original APS charter. They were further antagonized by the abrasive approach of the planning team leader. The anger of the APS team aroused teachers all over the district. In truth, teachers everywhere knew that their school might be next and were reacting to the precipitous process of high school restructuring. The Boston Teachers Union leaders visited Dorchester High on several occasions and shared with teachers their concerns with restructuring across the city. The teachers at Dorchester were just beginning this journey. They had been excessed; they were angry and fearful for their own future. With union encouragement, the teachers, under Casilli and his team, led a citywide protest. The result: no union members across the city would apply for any of the new teaching positions available at the new small schools unless the Dorchester veterans were promised a first option on the jobs. Furthermore, the same veterans would have rights to positions in the building, across both schools, for the next 16 years, so that if a program was cut in one school, the teacher would have seniority bumping rights in the other school as well. Of course this arrangement was frustrating for the new headmasters who would be hobbled in their attempts to build their own staff and school cultures, but they had to walk a fine line lest they begin the new year at odds with the teachers.

Finally in April, the district suspended the design team meetings indefinitely, most likely due to the union action. This angered the powerful school partners, especially those from the Trefler foundation, which had supported DHS, and especially APS, all those years. The president of the foundation expressed dismay over this turn of events in an email to the schools partners. "I am deeply concerned about what is happening to the school—once again by outside forces. As long time partners and investors in DHS, we all have an interest in seeing this school succeed.... It is difficult to stand by and watch as the school is being so severely impacted."[3]

The teachers in both schools, as well as the union leadership, were criticized by the media and by central administrators for blocking and not supporting high school reform. The fears of the teachers were not, however, unusual or unsubstantiated. An early analysis of high school restructuring in Boston by Education Matters[4] revealed widespread teacher dissatisfaction with the process.

> Teachers who worked in [the new] small schools reported that they were quite alienated and frustrated by the process of reorganizing their schools as well as the resulting organizational structures. The sentiments they reported were a result of their having had little or no voice in the reorganization of their schools, [of how] the resulting organization isolated them from colleagues, and, in some cases, of the requirement that they teach courses out of their area of competence in order for the school to "cover" those courses.[5]

The APS teachers were shocked when, in June, Casilli and another of the founding APS teachers decided to put in for early retirement. They walked away from the school. Even as late as September 2003, tensions with the union impeded the planning work. Unfortunately, the district was in the middle of contract negotiations for the next three-year contract with the bargaining unit. With a contract agreement still not reached in September, the union membership voted for a "work-to-rule" stance for the opening months of school in fall 2003. This worked against the new schools by taking away the extra time needed for teachers to plan collaboratively on school structures.

The disbanding of the design teams did not halt all planning for the new schools. The major impact it had was to remove the outside partners from the discussions. Those within the schools still had to plan since there was no reversing the superintendent's decision. Both schools were required to select a headmaster for 2003–04. By March 2003, Leonard was reconsidered and invited to apply for the positions and he joined 20 other applicants. The interview teams included deputy superintendents, business and university partners, parents, and teachers. Leonard was selected for the EBA headmaster position, while APS selected an outsider with no prior history with APS or the Boston Public School system. This decision turned out to make a world of difference over the next two years.

Several other decisions were made in spring 2003. With the arrival of Tech Boston Academy (TBA) the building had to be carved up among the three schools. TBA, which strenuously resisted the move to Dorchester, was promised the first floor of the building so their students could enter and leave relatively untouched by the other schools. EBA won the second floor and APS the third and then considerable time was spent negotiating the distribution of the science labs (which were all on the third floor) and sharing arrangements for the library, cafeteria, auditorium, and two gymnasiums. As the schedules for the following year began to take shape, the tensions over "real estate" in the building increased.

Another decision concerned the fate of the Accelerated Academy, which served overage students. The district wanted to continue the program for one more year, allowing the program to use the full five years of federal grant money, and so students could graduate on time. Initially, Tech Boston Academy was asked to oversee the program, but they had no interest or investment in the students. No one really wanted the added challenge of overseeing an alternative education program for eighty troubled students on top of starting a new small school. Everyone knew that the Accelerated Academy students would count toward year-end averages on the state's high stakes assessment and on attendance, and dropout rates and would make the school look bad. In the end, Leonard agreed to take on the program, for he knew the students and teachers well, plus his own new assistant headmaster had been an English teacher in that Academy.

With summer approaching, a core of teachers from EBA agreed to meet with Leonard and Noonan during July and August to hammer out plans for the coming year. Again, EBA had an advantage, for the core teachers had been meeting every summer for four years anyway. The teachers had two major concerns. One was the need to create a schedule that really worked for students and would not require major revisions in the fall, and the other was to get on top of discipline. The team spent all summer hammering out rules, while Leonard worked with a smaller team on the schedule. The EBA team also spent some time communicating with the leaders of APS and Tech Boston to ensure some building-wide rules that would govern travel in the school, use of the cafeteria, entering and leaving the building, and use of cell phones and other electronic equipment. There was a determination that behavioral expectations for students should be largely the same in all three schools, to reduce comparisons and tensions. EBA was well prepared for opening day.

The new APS leader did not have the luxury of ample planning time. The new APS team had not met during the summer; and by this point, most of the original team members had retired. She assembled a small crew in August to begin creating the master schedule and to get ready for opening day. However, much more time was spent in just developing relationships, communicating, and, for someone new to the system, learning about the Boston Public Schools and the school building. They completed an initial plan for student discipline, but the new headmaster was still meeting many members of her faculty, just one day before the opening of school. When school did open, APS had a schedule, but it was created on a software program that did not communicate with all the other online BPS software. This left them without the capacity to produce report cards in November causing frustration for teachers and students. It took another six months for the school to completely convert to the BPS systems.

All the headmasters were determined to establish a distinct identity for their school and they all wanted to distance themselves from the old image of Dorchester High School. For Tech Boston, this meant to stay as separate and isolated from the rest of the building as possible. For EBA, it meant strict rules about tardiness, cell phones, walkmans, headwear, being in the hallways, and classroom behavior, plus consistent enforcement of the discipline-based rules. The headmaster of APS was the "new kid" in Boston, and she didn't want to just follow everyone else. In order to distinguish her school, she decided that APS would start ten minutes later each day. She also allowed her students to wear hats in the cafeteria and to listen to music during lunch, a seemingly small decision that opened the door to widespread disregard for the rules on the third floor.

The three schools were largely assigned to one floor each, but they shared many spaces, including the cafeteria, gymnasium, auditorium, library, the front lobby, and the stairwells. Students from APS and EBA, who had been close friends the year before, resented that they were no longer allowed to meet during the day. Not that they didn't have opportunities to get together. Students could gather together during sporting events, (either as team members or spectators for the games), and they also planned dances and shows to bring everyone together. The seniors petitioned for a joint graduation so they could see their friends walk across the stage; in the end, the two schools agreed to hold side-by-side, but separate, graduations in rented space at UMB. For school leaders, the emphasis was still on carving out a distinct identity for each institution.

In September 2003, students returned to a "new" building. Over the summer, each floor was painted with a theme color on the lockers and doors: green for EBA, blue for APS, and maroon for Tech Boston. Hallways, stairwells, and the lobby were similarly painted, so the building looked fresh and promising to entering students. There were new signs on the exterior of the school. The new look boded well for a new school experience. In addition, there were metal detectors at the door, signaling that students would be searched and weapons, as well as walkmans and other electronic gear, would be confiscated. There were new, additional surveillance cameras on every floor, so there were very few places to hide. Safety was the watchword.

In EBA, the small school structure had an immediate effect on school climate. Students soon learned that they could not avoid classes by hiding on another floor. Administrators and teachers soon came to recognize who were their students and who were not; it was easy to spot an unfamiliar face in the hallway or cafeteria and the consequence for trespassing was a suspension. In no time at all, students settled down and began going to class. In the first year, there were several false fire alarms until December and then nearly a full year passed before the next one, a remarkable improvement after years of weekly fire alarms. In the first two years of EBA, the number of suspensions annually went from eighty to twenty-eight. The incident reports with the school police declined from seventy-eight to less than fifty in the second year. The number of fights diminished; in the third year, staff members wondered why it was almost November and no students had yet been involved in a fight.

> My observation was that the "chip" came off the shoulder. For several years, at DHS, I noticed that every encounter I had with a new student in the hallway began with distrust, suspicion, and fear, which created a tense standoff. Only after a few encounters did students relax and relationships develop. Now, however, everyone seemed more relaxed. The initial distrust was largely gone. For me, it meant that my students were more approachable. They were "kids" and not "thugs." I noticed that they did more things suitable to their age; they laughed, they joked and played, and were more likely to reach out in conversation. (Jack Leonard, Headmaster of EBA)

One exception was the Accelerated Academy in the basement, where older students struggled to attend and complete course requirements. This alternative program was marked by poor attendance and poor attitudes. Both students and teachers struggled. Out of the sixty-five original enrollees, six had graduated by the end of the first year. Many others were transferred to alternative education sites in the city in anticipation that the program would end in one year. Many of the students dropped out. The annual dropout rate in EBA was twenty-six percent in 2003–04, with 95 students of the enrolled 365 students dropping out, over twice the rate of other district high schools. In APS, the rate for the first year was 12.6 percent with 38 students of the 302 students dropping out. (The following year, 2004–05, the EBA dropout rate declined to a comparable 14.6 percent while the APS rate increased to 17.7 percent.)

THE SCHOOL YEAR BEGINS: THE ECONOMICS AND BUSINESS ACADEMY

The first year at EBA was a race to invent all the systems, procedures, and protocols that would be necessary in a new school: how to monitor bathrooms, how to handle late students, how to handle attendance and schedule changes and records without a registrar and on and on and on. There was a new wireless network to set up and the utilization of thirty laptop computers. Teachers and leaders made decisions about how to recognize and award academic excellence, how to build the culture of the school, how to develop youth leaders and enhance the student voice, how to market and promote the school, and how to work with community partners.

The academic climate improved as well in EBA. With the scheduling problems solved and safety and security under control, the school began to aggressively shift the focus to academics. Many students agreed with what one girl told the *Boston Globe*: "I'm doing much more work this year, because it's harder to fool around." Teachers worked together on higher standards for writing, homework, promotion, and graduation. Report card grades improved slightly in the ninth grade and SAT scores eased upward. The state's assessment scores showed improvement in English while math scores were inconsistent.

While everyone enjoyed the improved climate and better relationships the new small school afforded, they also discovered some of the drawbacks. The guidance staff found that it was much harder to schedule students who had unusual scheduling needs (because they had failed a class or came into EBA from another school). There were just not enough sections of algebra or biology, for example, to accommodate all the needs. The teachers found that they had to wear multiple hats. No one had the luxury of a single "prep"; everyone had to teach two or even three different courses and everyone needed to assume extra duties to coach the sports, or monitor the cafeteria and hallways.

In addition, the teachers quickly realized that there was a smaller pool of colleagues with whom to hang out. When there are only two regular education math teachers, for example, it matters if they can get along together, for there are no other options for sharing practices or materials. At least one very good teacher left EBA before it opened because she foresaw conflict with her counterpart. This has become a prominent factor in the selection of new staff; the silent question being, "Will this person be able to get along well with his or her counterpart in that department?"

The administrative team also discovered unexpected consequences of the new small school design. While there were far fewer students and a much smaller staff, many of the same reporting requirements and centrally driven tasks remained, and there were fewer administrators to do them. Dorchester High School enjoyed a team of ten administrators for 1,000 students while EBA and APS combined had six for a little over 600 students. The ratios were fair, but many aspects of the workload did not decrease. For example, the whole school improvement plan still had to be written; grants had to be pursued and then later reported on; tests had to be administered and the resulting data disaggregated, interpreted, and shared with the faculty; professional development activities still had to be planned and delivered; and myriad requests for information and reports from central administration had to be honored. Likewise, the number of meetings did not diminish, with English and math teachers for common planning time, the Instructional Leadership Team, the School Site Council, the Parents Council, the cluster meeting and monthly meetings with the Director of Curriculum and Instruction.

Some of these responsibilities reflected the incomplete conversion of Court Street to the small school model. Headmasters were often expected to answer to the traditional model of high school leadership—such as attending to all the subject area department meetings—while also answering to the small school requirements, such as attending monthly meetings for small school leaders. The headmaster was often pulled in two directions by these directives and could not afford to ignore either one. Another pull on the leadership schedule, however, was the greatest strength of small schools: the personalization. The headmaster and his team came to know the students better, for there were not so many of them. Students knocked on their doors, asked for time, for attention, and for favors. Even though the headmasters relished these closer relationships with students, they were conscious of the changed dynamic and the demands upon their schedules. In the small school, layers of administrators no longer shielded the headmaster.

The dynamic between teacher and headmaster also shifted within the small school structure. The small size meant that the headmaster was much more available to observe classroom practice and to see things that were previously unnoticed by a headmaster. Teachers came under greater scrutiny. Since in a small school most students will have the same teacher twice in nearly every subject, it matters that the instruction is the best possible. Teachers who could previously get away with being only acceptable now experienced more pressure to improve. The small school size created opportunities for more interactions, more conversations, greater collaboration, improved trust and personal relationships, but it also meant more inspection and pressure for some individuals.

> As the headmaster, I did numerous evaluations; some were tough and, of course, the news got around. One teacher was evaluated out of a job, one teacher retired on threat of a negative performance review, another voluntarily transferred, and another did not have his contract renewed. I had to keep a close eye on the delicate balance of school culture; tense relationships with a few teachers, who in my estimation needed to improve, could easily sour the entire staff. (Jack Leonard)

Beginning in fall 2004, EBA used their Gates grant money to lengthen the school day for ninth graders on Tuesdays and Thursdays by seventy-five minutes. The added time was used for advisory-type activities (relationship building, goal setting, self-assessments) as well as homework completion. The school also used 30 mobile laptops with wireless connectivity to bring technology to the classrooms. The first year showed a small improvement in report card grades. In the second year, state money was used to include tenth graders in the extended day plan.

EBA also continued to expand its business program. The school extended the business curriculum to include grades nine through twelve and added a business teacher to replace Ed Noonan, who passed away at the end of EBA's first year. The school's relationship with business partner TJX Corporation continued to develop. Students took elaborate field trips to the headquarters to participate in business workshops and they visited the stores and the distribution warehouses. Corporate leaders came to the school and taught leadership classes to the tenth graders. They sat on the board of advisors for the school and helped judge the annual spring business student plan presentations. They donated thousands of dollars toward college scholarships and set up campus tours with Bunker Hill Community College and Northeastern University and accompanied the students when they visited. At the same time, EBA worked to move the business themes into the rest of the school curriculum. In this way, students at EBA received rich exposure to the business world and had ample opportunity to interact with business leaders.

THE SCHOOL YEAR BEGINS: THE ACADEMY OF PUBLIC SERVICE

The first two years in the Academy of Public Service were different. First, the dissatisfaction and departure of the Academy founders cast a pall over the entire school. The two remaining teachers who had been steeped in APS culture, and who knew best the APS curriculum and design, were also gone by the end of the first year; one left on a sabbatical never to return, and the other was laid off by the new headmaster. These departures were unsettling to the rest of the staff who were less familiar with the APS theme. The new headmaster came with a vision and leadership style that did not fit well with the culture and value system of the old APS. In her prior position, she was the assistant principal in a suburban high school, and it was evident that she wanted to reconstruct elements of that experience. However, her vision for an elite core of college-ready students who traveled to Florida for their senior class trip was not realistic. When the school was reconstituted, all the students in the other nine small learning communities were placed haphazardly into either EBA or APS, diluting the number of engaged and motivated students left in APS. These new students were not as well prepared and needed much remedial instruction. As one teacher expressed it, the new headmaster's "mission was not driven by public service.... This was only the Academy of Public Service by name.... We didn't have a unique sense of ourselves."[6]

She rejected her assistant headmaster, a DHS administrator who was assigned to her at the eleventh hour, and wasted much of the first year maneuvering to get rid of him. By the end of the second year, the man she recruited from the second floor to be her assistant was ready to quit as well. She targeted certain teachers and worked for their dismissal, barely hiding her conviction that students needed more African American teachers. Key members of the guidance staff were replaced. For a staff that had just been excessed the year before, the experience was unnerving. She did not work well with the other building administrators, and she began to lose their support. The one man with real experience who had ample time to help her, Bobby Belle, was largely ignored. (Belle had become the building overseer, responsible for building-wide operations). As he often said, "She won't listen to anyone." In the rush to secure employees that were acceptable to the new headmaster, there was little opportunity to carve out the systems, protocols, procedures, and structures that would carry the school through the second year. As a result, for two years in a row, the school struggled with poorly defined disciplinary standards and expectations, an uncoordinated effort to move students on to college and a makeshift schedule which did not initially meet the needs of students.

The school did not fare well and the traditional excellence of the APS name began to vanish. Select seniors who had benefited from three years of prior APS investments still applied to four-year colleges and won scholarships, but the younger students suffered. Things were especially hard on the sophomores and juniors who had been accepted into the old APS. They were used to being shielded from the more homogeneous population that had occupied the rest of the building. Now there were fights and suspensions and expulsions among APS's own members. Now, APS was the "ugly duckling" in the building. The students felt like they had fallen from the pinnacle of the school to the basement, and they began to complain loudly; they did not like how things were deteriorating. They knew their reputation was not good and that their education was suffering. The state's standardized assessment scores attested to APS's decline. As with EBA, the first year showed modest improvements but the second year showed drastic declines in math achievement. In both years, however, the overall results were far below the district averages.

As the first school year progressed, an unintended "pecking order" began to develop in the building. The schools on the second floor (EBA) and third floor (APS) believed without a doubt that Tech Boston had favored status. They had the convenience of the first floor location, and the administrators made it clear they did not appreciate students or staff from the other floors cutting through their territory to reach the library, cafeteria, or gymnasiums. Students and staff in Tech Boston could hardly hide their disdain for the disruptive students upstairs, so the schools were assigned separate entrances in an attempt to keep the students apart. Tech Boston won the main entrance to the school, while EBA was assigned a side door entrance near the corner of the building. APS was relegated to a rear entrance, which only served to reinforce how far the school had fallen. Tech Boston had a longer school day, so their schedule seemed more relaxed and productive. They had very few special education students. Their clientele were focused and serious about education. Their parents were highly involved, and they were livid that the school had moved to this new location in Dorchester, which they viewed as dangerous. The parents rallied city support and won a bus to transport their children away from the school and over to the train station at 4:00. All this was insulting to the students and staff on the second and third floors, most of whom had to walk the half mile to and from the train station. They wondered why no one ever worried about their safety and why they were not wanted in areas of the building that they had called their own the year before. Of course, the common explanation was that pilot schools were not "equal"; they were allowed to pick and choose their students (which was not true) and they were not expected to deal with severe special needs and clusters of learning and adaptive behavior students (which was true).

Tech Boston requested and received many building improvements, including a $500,000 upgrade of the old satellites into an attached wing of modern classrooms. This only solidified the conviction of a building pecking order, further souring relationships both within the building and with central administration. Bobby Belle recalled the days of Dorchester High and compared it to the current situation:

> We asked for this, this and this [in facilities improvements], and there was never any money, and all of a sudden Tech Boston comes into that building. I said for years, "Put lights in this building; this building is dark." They said, "What?" I said, "We can't see down the corridor." ...Their [part of the] building got painted; they got upholstered furniture. We still had our broken chairs and...stuff like that. The element of pilot school, that was funded by Gates...makes a big difference in terms of how that place looks now. You go out back, look at the [satellites]; we asked them to do that nine years ago. Nope, no money....So all these schools aren't created equally. (Bobby Belle)

Unfortunately, a silent pecking order emerged between EBA and APS as well. EBA had the experienced headmaster who knew how to navigate through district policies. EBA still had the support of its academy head and its original teachers. EBA had all the office space (for in the original building, all the office space for administration and guidance was located on the second floor). EBA had the added advantage of having the former headmaster (Bobby Belle) located on its floor, so his experience and assistance were right at hand. In the eyes of one APS teacher, EBA somehow managed to scoop up all the technology (which had unfortunately been stored in a large pile in a basement room during the restructuring renovations in the summer of 2003). The computer lab that formerly existed on the third floor was not reassembled. Students struggled for two years with little access to technology, except through the library. Last, the 30 laptops APS inherited from Dorchester High were mysteriously lost. For this reason, APS had no computers. (But this was only partially true.)

The assistant headmasters for both schools met it the fall of 2003 to divide up the pile of computers and equipment in the basement. However, the EBA administrator was knowledgeable in technology, so he moved quickly to utilize the equipment; the APS administrator was less confident, unsupported by his headmaster, and unable to apprehend what belonged to the school. Some equipment was stolen, such as the laptops, and some just became outdated as it sat on the basement floor. Finally, there was a belief that EBA had more "real estate" in the building. Because the original design of Dorchester had all six science labs on the

third floor, three were assigned to EBA and three to APS. The perception
on the third floor was that Tech Boston was sprawled all over the first
floor, taking the basement and the outlying satellite buildings as well,
while EBA had the entire second floor and hogged a corner of the third
floor. (A counter-argument was that EBA had much less real classroom
space on the second floor, due to the abundant offices as well as the
space occupied by the auditorium and gymnasiums). Nevertheless,
APS students and staff were cramped in the remaining classrooms of
the third floor with limited office space and no storage room. Resent-
ments followed. Teachers in APS were not impressed with the small
school jargon:

> This is a small space; it's not a small school. The ratio is the same [students/
> teachers were the same as when the school was larger]. So when people put
> down on paperwork that this is a small school, it's not. It's not. It's not a
> small school. You talk about this physical space; it's ridiculous. This physical
> space is not at all conducive to a school.[7]

The three headmasters met regularly in the first year to discuss
building-wide issues. The meetings were mandated by the superintendent's office and were largely devoted to hammering out rules to keep
the students separate and in line. However, the meetings were often
tense, and when they were no longer mandated, they ceased altogether.
Instead, Belle met with the assistant headmasters weekly to discuss security issues, and these meetings were far more productive. The assistant
headmasters got along together because they shared common challenges,
and they had less to defend.

Slowly, the ice thawed and respect and trust grew between the schools
over the two years of operation. The students were brought together by
sports, and they came to know and respect each other in this way. The
games brought everyone together. There were school-wide pep rallies,
Friday evening dances, and fund-raisers. The students began to get along.
The science teachers began to collaborate and share equipment because
they were all located in the same corner of the building and they needed
help. Even the administrators began to come together, aided partly by
university partner UMB who brought them together through a Nellie
Mae foundation grant that required all three to meet once a month.
Slowly, trust grew within the building.

Trust may have been improving building-wide, but within APS the
new headmaster was unable to connect with her staff or lead them in a
productive direction. She held numerous weekly meetings, but staff
members emerged feeling tired. They complained that their time had
been wasted and they had not been heard. One teacher remembered,
"We spent ten weeks on data analysis, but it never went anywhere. We
didn't do anything with the results." Under these conditions, there was
little collaboration or planning between teachers, unless it was surrepti-
tious or irrelevant to the headmaster. For example, the special education

programs continued to meet as they always did to plan activities for their students. The headmaster laid off many of her provisional teachers and began searching for minority replacements, under a conviction that her students would be better served. She pursued several veteran teachers with the evaluation process and, as mentioned above, managed to lose the only teachers who knew the core signature courses for the school. After two years, many teachers were prepared to leave. "There was a lot of retreating into classrooms. The floor was demoralized." Finally, Paul Casilli, even though he had retired, had had enough. Near the end of APS's first year, he wrote a letter to Superintendent Payzant asking him to retire the Academy of Public Service name. The letter was widely circulated to the school's community, business, and university partners, many of whom felt torn by the request. In the end, the notion of renaming the school slowly died; it just still wasn't clear to anyone how "APS-like" the new school would end up being.

One of the new leader's biggest mistakes was to alienate her business and university partners, including members of the Trefler Foundation which had amply supported APS for years. Increasingly, the members of APS's board of advisors took a standoff approach and simply waited for her departure. When graduation came in June 2005, there was little in scholarship donations to distribute to the graduates, a sad state of affairs when one remembers the nearly one million in scholarships that had been awarded over the previous ten years. Meanwhile, having maintained its business, university, and community partners, EBA was handing out almost $100,000 in senior scholarships at the first graduation. In late spring 2005, there were mounting signs that this leader would be replaced. She accepted a job in another state, and her position was quickly filled by the assistant headmaster from EBA, Zachary Robbins. He was familiar with the building, the history of DHS, the Boston school culture, and the students whom he had coached on the track team for two years. Students and teachers welcomed his arrival.

APS REBOUNDS

Under Robbins' leadership, APS began to rebuild its vision, staff ownership, and community connections. He presented a vision that combined a clear instructional focus with very high expectations for student learning. Since APS had lost all of its "founding" teachers, Robbins inherited a young and inexperienced staff. They were not indebted to the APS history, and they were ready to try anything. Robbins also reached out to the traditional APS partners and rebuilt the board of advisors. Soon, they were meeting again, although the scholarship support—which once meant hundreds of thousands of dollars to college-bound graduates—was not restored as quickly.

Robbins, of course, had close relationships with Belle and Leonard on the second floor. He often commented that, despite two years under the first headmaster, there were almost no structures on the third floor – the kind of protocols and procedures that would guide annual school affairs, such as scheduling, orientation, assessments, grades, teacher collaboration, professional development, and graduation. He pulled together a small energetic team that met daily to brainstorm those structures. He then gathered a team of dedicated teachers who were willing to work with him as the Instructional Leadership Team.

These developments yielded many positive accomplishments at APS in year three. They resurrected the core APS classes (Public Service, Public Administration, and Strategies for Success) and began teaching them seriously again. With the help of the Teach Next Year interns, Robbins personally launched a Debating Club, by recruiting a faculty sponsor, purchasing team sweaters, and helping to train them for some early competitions (which they were soon winning). He worked hard to steer select seniors into four-year colleges to ensure the academic reputation of the school. With strong support from his deputy superintendent, he pioneered a credit-recovery program designed to help his failing students make up missing course credits so they could graduate on time. Finally, at year's end, he led his faculty in the exploration of some new scheduling options that would make further room for the credit recovery program in the following year, as well as student advisories for the ninth graders. The proposal was passed overwhelmingly by the staff—a sure sign of the positive feeling that was growing in APS.

EBA FALLS BACK

In October 2005, the EBA name was changed to Noonan Business Academy to honor the founder, but the honor soured as the school ran into troubles. Three things happened that might have contributed to the decline: Zac Robbins, an African American male upon whom teachers relied to oversee student discipline, left to become headmaster of APS; the entering freshmen class was very difficult and unruly; and, finally, NBA teachers did not get along with Headmaster Leonard's small schools coach who often ran the professional development meetings. They felt that she was indifferent to their concerns, and they objected to her "single" focus on student advisories. Leonard, unfortunately, did not become aware of the animosity between his coach and the teachers.

Partly due to these three difficulties, the entire year at NBA was filled with bad news and threats. The spring 2005 state standardized assessment results came back with sobering news; NBA students had the worst math scores seen at Dorchester for the past six years and almost the worst in the city. (The scores from APS were worse, but expectations had not been high in that school for obvious reasons.) This resulted in a second year of not making Adequate Yearly Progress according to the Federal No Child Left Behind guidelines, spelling more trouble for the school's reputation and recruitment efforts.

In December, there were severe cuts in the 2006–07 budget, based upon a projected decline in enrollments. Both Leonard and Robbins learned that their schools were among the least selected in the city (along with the other Dorchester Public High School two miles away). After two years of hard work trying to put a new public face on the high school, this news hurt. Discipline was a constant challenge throughout the year. Boston was experiencing a new surge of violence in the streets, especially those surrounding the high school, which could be felt in the school as well. There were more fights, thefts, and drugs, and in May, a student was apprehended with a knife in his possession and a sawed-off shotgun in his locker. The media broadcast this news all over the city, only confirming the long-standing convictions that Dorchester was not safe. Leonard expelled fourteen students, far beyond the two expulsions of the previous year. Teachers and administrators openly expressed their fear that the "old Dorchester" was returning.

Still, Leonard continued to work with outside partners to build a new image of the school. The TJX Companies put their marketing department on the image problem and provided beautiful, professional brochures and banners, as well as hundreds of photographs and a DVD showcasing the school. The headmaster worked with the Private Industry Council to build real-life business experiences into the school year. In February, they sent 40 sophomores out on a one-day "shadowship" where they trailed a business professional. In May, 12 juniors went out on a pilot two-week internship, working in all the departments of a local bank, which was a huge success, but which frustrated the teachers, who felt that the students should not have missed two weeks of school so close to finals.

In an attempt to make the school more attractive to students, Leonard put most of his energy behind creating the beginnings of an "early-college" program at NBA. Unfortunately, his efforts only contributed to the wall of resentment building up between him and his teachers. Leonard began by having juniors and seniors take the college placement tests for both UMB and Bunker Hill Community College. He then sent students over to UMB to take college classes in the afternoons and evenings, and he secured a promise from Bunker Hill Community College to offer 20 free classes per year to NBA students. Leonard's goal in all of this was to promote the unique advantages of the school for prospective students who might be interested in business and college. However, nearly every student failed both the placement exams and the college courses, indicating that, once they enrolled in college, they would have to pay for remedial courses. These courses would provide no credit toward graduation. The news was depressing and undermined both the students' and the schools' confidence and the lofty goal of sending high school students off to take college classes. At the same time, the extended day program, which seemed so promising the first year, failed to achieve

Progress the first year simply because the overage substantially separate special needs students were counted as seniors. These students never take the standardized assessments and they never graduate. They stay with the school year after year, listed as seniors over and over again, until they age out at 22. Eventually, NBA realized the error in the calculation of Adequate Yearly Progress and found itself having to instruct the district on the problem.

Another problem that plagued the old Dorchester High and that has never been solved by the district is the abundance of empty seats now at NBA and APS that results from under-selection and the high dropout rate. As a result, far too many students are arbitrarily assigned to the school. These students have little buy-in and tend to have a high rate of problems both socially and academically. The under-selection of the school is based, in part, on the dangers associated in the public mind with the neighborhood and not just the school. When 50 percent of the students at NBA have to walk through some of the most dangerous streets of the city, one can anticipate a higher rate of absenteeism and weapons violations (students carry knives and guns to feel safe), and a higher dropout rate.

> They [the district] know about the dangers of Codman Square and Grove hall. One thing they could do is make sure there is transportation from the train station to the door for every single kid. Do they really want kids walking through neighborhoods where they are being held-up? They would never do this with their own kids! (NBA teacher)

Despite the bad news, there were small victories at NBA during year three, including the sophomore shadowships, the junior internships, the success again in securing a letter of acceptance to a two- or four-year college for every senior and the $80,000 in scholarship monies raised during the year for graduates.

The superintendent was preparing to leave at the end of June, even as he was meeting with the high school reform team and listening to the case study on NBA. The words "intervention" and "reconstitution" were mentioned as possibilities for the coming year. Sixty years of history and three years into the most aggressive reform work ever performed at DHS and these words were still distinct possibilities. Reform was still not accomplished.

SMALL SCHOOLS: SUCCESS OR FAILURE?

Overall, the verdict is still out on the conversion to small schools at Dorchester. The hallways were safer and the academic climate improved, even if unevenly across the two schools. The major community partners assessed the situation and decided to forge relationships with each small school, just as they had done with Dorchester High in the past. The Trefler Foundation looked for ways to support each small school. The

Verizon Foundation provided support, in smaller amounts, to each school. UMB continued to send Teach Next Year interns to work in the building each fall. In addition, the university used its five-year Nellie Mae grant to measure and improve college preparation and college retention programs vigorously with all three schools.

By the standards of the Gates Foundation the conversion to small schools was a mixed bag. The annual reports on the Carnegie and Gates Foundation grants, performed by outside evaluators, spelled out the slow progress of high school reform. While the reports summarize district experiences, the information reflects what was happening at "Dorchester High School." In many respects, NBA and APS still looked like the old Dorchester High with the same schedule, same teachers, same curriculum, and often the same teaching methodology. Again, Dorchester was not alone, for the challenge to improve instruction was everywhere in the high schools:

> Classroom instruction has not yet undergone a revolution. Ambitious instruction is not yet the norm. Teachers still appear to work harder than most students and a great deal of classroom instruction is teacher directed. Students are not yet the "workers" that Ted Sizer envisioned in *Horace's Compromise.* Many students are absent in body or mind much of the time. Students arrive late, take their seats, and, often, nothing is mentioned other than a reference to the page the class is reading. Teachers still accept a wide range of behavior from students—from passivity to deep engagement, from adherence to the rules to wild flouting of them.[9]

The Office of High School Restructuring placed a "capacity coach" in both NBA and APS to support the conversion and guide the school toward reform. The coach made it evident that reform meant a block schedule, student advisories, and a humanities course to replace English and history. Teachers at Dorchester, however, were reluctant to experiment. The restructuring was traumatic enough, and they were not convinced that these new innovations would strengthen the school. NBA rejected a block schedule all three years, and APS only considered a new schedule in the third year, finally approving very modest changes. Leaders from the Office of High School Renewal reminded the small schools over and over again that small schools were not just "big schools in drag." They wanted to see substantial change, but school staff felt they were looking through a very narrow lens. Instead, the innovations went in other directions such as credit recovery programs, internships and shadowships and dual enrollment programs.

On the first floor of Dorchester High was Tech Boston Academy and it was apparent they were benefiting from a longer school day and a profusion of laptops. Not far away, the Codman Academy Charter School was gaining strong media attention because of their high standardized assessment scores and graduation rates. The school ran ten hours each day and Saturday mornings. This was the local competition.

Overall though, high school conversion was not as simple as many were led to believe. Again, this was a district-wide problem in all the high school conversions. For example, the professional development goals of the district based on coaching and collaboration between teachers within and across disciplines did not match well with the new small school size. The evaluation reports pointed out that all the small schools and small learning communities were struggling with the promises of smallness. They listed several sticking points that were important to teachers:

> Teachers in the same content area and/or grade level did not always have common planning periods in which they could participate in a coaching cycle.
>
> Small schools and cross-grade small learning communities often had only one core content area teacher at a grade level. This made it impossible for coaches to create grade-level, content-focused Collaborative Coaching and Learning cycles.[10] The Collaborative Coaching and Learning groups that were constructed in the small schools and cross-grade learning communities, in particular, included teachers from multiple subject areas. Not surprisingly, it was difficult for coaches to create cycles that met all of the teachers' learning needs.[11]

There was progress, no doubt, but the progress was not nearly as fast or far as everyone hoped. Sometimes, the progress was more visible when one looked back twenty years instead of one or two. For example, professional development was profoundly different:

> There are differences between the schools in our current sample and the high schools observed twenty years ago that represent an enormous, positive change. Twenty years ago, for the most part, teachers valued their planning periods as their personal time to use as they preferred. They went to professional development sessions off-site as individuals and returned to their schools to use or not use what they learned. Often, what they learned had only slight relevance to their students and curriculum or was too complicated to implement without further assistance. School-based professional development was not yet part of the equation of teacher learning. Teachers did not, as a rule, have formal opportunities in which to plan together or discuss students' progress as part of case management teams. Largely absent from the normal school day were discussions among teachers about how to improve teaching practice. Certainly, teachers were not working together with school-based instructional coaches. When this context of teaching, professional culture and professional development is considered, it is clear that Boston's small high schools, cross-grade learning communities, and grade-level learning communities represent a dramatic change in the organization and culture of high schools across the district. Our data reveal that teachers in Boston's small high schools and small learning communities work or seek to work in schools that are more collaborative and instructionally-focused than those of twenty years ago.[12]

Nevertheless, teachers who were focused on the immediate challenges "felt that the advantages of small schools had been oversold."[13] They questioned the thinking of central administrators.

For many of the teachers in the small schools and cross-grade learning communities, the mandates and subsequent decisions about the smaller units have
left them thinking that no one in the district has fully thought through the
redesign of high schools and, instead, the district is responding to the desires
of outside funders whose resources come with their own set of mandates.[14]

Teachers also began to question the district commitment to small schools.
In NBA, some teachers openly evoked the "pendulum theory," claiming
that the next superintendent would merge the small schools into large
schools once again. The evaluators also alluded to the emotional trauma
of abrupt conversions. Only on rare occasions is the emotional impact of
sweeping changes discussed, but in Boston, there is a history of this activity, and it has left educators raw:

> Indeed, for some staff members, the mandate to become small was a reprise
> of an earlier mandate to desegregate. The depth of negative feelings aroused
> by the mandates should not be underestimated or discounted.[15]

For APS and NBA the conversion to small schools is still very much in
process. There is not a lot of trust toward the district or the other occu-
pants of the building. NBA had several successes, but progress was slow.
The small school structure makes possible levels of teamwork and collaboration that have not been deeply explored by the school. A small core
of teachers in NBA met for summer planning two years in a row, which
was very productive. A similar core took several weekend retreats to create ways to integrate business themes into science, English, and history
classes, but the plans were only partly implemented later. At the same
time, the special education teachers continued to function independently
from everyone else, largely because their students were still substantially
separate. The school still feels splintered, with cliques of special education teachers and regular education teachers. The science teachers work
closely together but the main reason for that is that they are located side
by side. Some, but not all, of the English and math teachers meet for
common planning time each week. Another cluster of teachers meets
regularly as the ILT, but they are not yet ready to really lead. Everyone
knows that they live in a district where central mandates could interrupt
their life at any point. They know they are still expected to follow the pacing guides ("racing guides" as one teacher called them) in math and
adhere to Readers and Writers Workshop in English. The climate among
the staff is warm and cooperative, but guarded. As one teacher put it,
referring to the adversarial relationships in both APS and NBA, "There
has to be something done about the 'us-versus-them' mentality." In these
respects, the small school conversions were still incomplete by the end of
year three.

At the same time, Court Street keeps looking for additional angles to
bring real, substantial reform to the district high schools—and they keep
looking to the local schools to come up with the new angles. One obvious
block on this route to reform was the Boston Teachers Union. In

December 2004, two years after the momentous decision to restructure Dorchester High, Payzant issued another sweeping idea: all Boston Public Schools were invited to seek pilot school status. Funding from the Boston Foundation was made available to support the initial planning and proposal. Fifteen applications would be accepted and pursued. Pilot school status would allow the winning schools to avoid union rules and immediately pursue change strategies around the "big five" untouchable areas of governance, curriculum, schedules, budgets, and staffing. The idea fell short, however, when the union president announced that he would not sign off on any pilot school applications until the compensation question was addressed. Pilot school teachers who worked extra hours should get extra pay. It was easy to blame the teachers union for blocking reform, which the media did. Only later did the conviction grow that some real blockages to reform were central, not local.

When they restructured South Boston High School in 2001, school leaders had the summer to plan the conversion. Mistakes were made and the Office of High School Renewal realized that more time was needed for planning and "reculturing." As a result, a full eight months were allotted for the conversion at Dorchester High. Again, mistakes were made and lessons were learned. The mandated process of restructuring, with few choices, alienated teachers. As a result, teachers were unwilling to move beyond what was required in structural changes. No one ventured to experiment with block scheduling, student advisories, or integrated curriculum in the first year. In addition, the reculturing did not go well, if it happened at all.

In spring 2004, the superintendent decided to restructure Hyde Park High School and West Roxbury High School into seven small schools. This time, a full year was devoted to the planning. An additional difference was that the superintendent called for proposals from each school community for the design of the new small schools. Any number of proposals was welcome, but the initial call spelled out clearly what kinds of innovations would be favored, including, of course, block scheduling alternatives and student advisories as well as any other personalizing strategies. A competition was established which worked in a healthy way to stimulate creativity and push teachers out of their comfort zones. In the end, there were twelve solid proposals and seven were selected for implementation. Each one met the reform goals of the Gates and Carnegie grants. So, in this manner, central administration learned to lead the task of high school restructuring more effectively.

Deep high school reform is difficult work, however, certainly more difficult than restructuring. We hypothesized in the beginning that structural change would be easier than curricular change and all would be easier than cultural change. In 2004, the evaluation report noted that, so far, high school reform work in Boston had accomplished the first step and was only poised for the next:

Put simply, Boston has set the stage for instructional reform in the high schools by its efforts to create small, instructionally focused, collegial cultures for teachers. Teachers want to work in those cultures. The district now needs to develop policies and practices that better support this teacher culture in the schools, a culture in which teachers have the opportunity to fully address their students' instructional needs.[16]

Without the cultural changes that will make the new small high schools true communities, the district has a long way to go in addressing the root problems of alienation and poor literacy.

CONCLUSION

Ten years of high school restructuring have yielded some incredible dividends and, for this reason, the superintendent and his team must be commended for great boldness, risk-taking, and determination. Most of the district high schools are showing demonstrable progress, and, without a doubt, conditions are better at the more challenging "Dorchester High School" than they were ten years ago. However, enormous challenges remain and some fundamental problems, which are unique to Dorchester, still have not been addressed. One of the biggest really dates back to the 1960s.

Dorchester is still considered one of the most dangerous neighborhoods of the city. We saw that in the late 1960s, the neighborhood demographics changed and the student population became increasingly poor and black. To this day, Dorchester, along with Roxbury and Mattapan, are considered relatively dangerous and undesirable. In NBA, 50 percent of the students live within two miles of the school and must walk to school (or buy their own bus tickets or hook a ride with a parent). Eighty-nine percent of the student body lives in Roxbury, Dorchester, or Mattapan. In 2005, the murder rate was rising again in Boston and the bulk of the 75 annual murders were committed in these three boroughs. After two years, APS and NBA remain among the least selected high schools in the city (along with Dorchester's other high school). It appears that students will not opt to go to school in these neighborhoods unless there are compelling reasons, such as the clear benefits of being in a pilot school where every student gets a laptop (Tech Boston) or an exam school (Boston Latin Academy). Otherwise, with over 15 small schools from which to pick, NBA and APS remain very low on the list. This is a function of poverty and associated crime. Being under-selected brings the same string of complications that it did 20 years ago: less student buy-in, more student turnover, more alternative education and at-risk students, more court-appointed students, and so on.

In this respect, the restructuring of Dorchester High has not solved some fundamental problems. We are reminded of the local newspaper article of December 2002, when the superintendent announced the reconstitution of DHS:

Nine of Boston's 12 non-exam high schools have created several small learning communities within their buildings, but with varying degrees of success.
Dorchester High is still struggling to carve out a successful identity as its reputation for violence and low test scores has persisted. "One of the things that
didn't change at Dorchester was some of the external forces," Payzant said of
the school's reputation. "When everything else was filled and students have
to be placed, they go there."[17]

Sadly, APS and Bobby Belle claimed for ten years that the students at
Dorchester were different, but without the statistics, few believed them.
However, the feeling persists. One insightful guidance counselor, who
moved to East Boston High School called to say how much she missed
the "kids" at Dorchester, but she made no bones about how students really were different at her new school. They were respectful; they took
off their hats when asked; they cleared the halls; they did not swear at
teachers. An administrator who left to lead a new small school at West
Roxbury reported the same: more respectful, more likely to obey, less
ready to leap to anger and rebellion.

There is still so much we do not know about our children. We know the
students who have Department of Youth Services connections (and those
numbers have been more equalized among the high schools) but we do
not know the numbers of students whose lives are complicated because
they are involved with the court system, the Department of Social Services or the Department of Mental Health. According to Bill Walzcak at
the Codman Square Health Center,

> Out of all areas in Boston, the 02124 zip code [the health center's service area]
> has the highest number of families receiving Department of Social Services,
> Department of Mental Health, and Department of Youth Services service,
> and the highest truancy rates in Boston.[18]

Again, half of the students at APS and NBA live in proximity to this area.

Tech Boston Academy has proven that parents will send their children
to Dorchester if there are compelling reasons. Tech Boston is still one of
the most highly selected schools in the district, as is the Boston Latin
Academy, an exam high school that is also located in Dorchester. However, Tech Boston has lost families because of the neighborhood assaults
and the school leaders have talked of moving. NBA and APS, to date,
have not been able to provide the "compelling reason" to draw students
in the face of prevailing danger. More importantly, one can question
whether it is healthy or ethical to lure children into dangerous sections
of the city with compelling school programs. The problem of poverty is
larger than the school and the school cannot be expected to solve it. In
fact, in the end, it could be said that poverty also claimed Dorchester
High School. Whether APS and NBA survive remains to be seen.

Lessons Learned for Urban Education

Introduction

THE LESSONS LEARNED FROM THE HISTORY OF DORCHESTER HIGH SCHOOL FOR URBAN EDUCATION IN GENERAL

We wanted to tell the story of Dorchester High School because we believe this story has a lot to teach us about educational reform in the context of our most embattled and entrenched urban high schools. As a nation, we have come a long way in terms of designing and implementing educational reforms that work for urban children. Yet we continue to see more failure than success in about 18 percent of high schools nationwide.[1] These high schools are concentrated in urban areas and tend to stubbornly defy reforms that have proven successful in other schools. When reforms do work in these schools, they do so for short periods of time, becoming easily defeated at the slightest setback, such as the loss of a key promoter or a downturn in the economy. Some of the lessons described in this section are unique; others extend our thinking about educational reform initiatives that have been debated by educational researchers over the years. Each lesson is presented from the perspective of interacting ecological systems and how they impact schools. This ecological systems approach allows us to reframe educational reform in relational terms, and returns us to the concept of community.

SUMMARY OF THE ECOLOGICAL SYSTEMS MODEL

To review the model, an ecological systems approach to educational reform focuses on the primary settings of the developing individual, in our case, students, teachers, and school leaders. These are the settings in which the school's constituents have direct, face-to-face relationships with each other and with those individuals who are working on their behalf to ensure optimal growth and development. These settings are referred to as microsystems and they include the school, the home, the workplace, and the individual's social affiliations such as the church or the peer group. An ecological systems model also considers the relationships between these settings and other sectors of the society, such as the business community, higher education, government, and community organizations. These sectors of society are referred to as the exosystem. In most cases, the developing person does not participate in direct, face-to-face relations within the settings that make up the exosystem. However, the decisions made by individuals from the exosystem do influence schools. These partners can either impact the school from afar, never interacting directly with school constituents, or they can work directly with students, teachers, and/or school leaders. When they relate directly with school constituents, they help to create a network that connects their particular segment of society, be it business, higher education, or government, to the school and the individuals who make up the school community. These networks act as a web of connections that provide support for students, teachers, and school leaders. The lessons gleaned from the story of DHS demonstrate that educational reforms are more successful when these networks are strong and firmly rooted within the school community.

CHAPTER 10

A Conceptual Framework for Enacting Cultural Reform in Struggling Urban High Schools: Re-engaging the Community

In our struggle to make sense of the educational reforms visited upon Dorchester High School over 60 years, we kept noticing how often the school was buffeted by outside forces like an anchorless ship adrift on the waves. The only time between 1945 and 2005 when the school appeared immune to outside forces was in the first 15 years. We wondered why this was so. After 1960, outside forces began overwhelming the school. These forces, initiated by various social and institutional changes, impacted the school in a number of very different ways. As the history illustrated, changes in one sector of society, no matter how far removed from the idea of schooling, ended up having a tremendous impact on this one urban high school. The impacts of these changes were either slow and subtle or swift enough to alter the life force of the school and its constituents. As we saw, many sectors of society were involved in influencing the school both consciously and unconsciously. These societal settings, sometimes as a single setting and sometimes in concert with other settings, had tremendous influence on the school. Given the power of outside forces, we developed a framework that extends beyond the school to the wider community in which students live their lives. This chapter explains this framework and provides an alternative model for approaching urban educational reform.

The most telling observation that emerged from our examination of the 60 years of reform efforts visited upon one urban high school was how little things had changed in terms of student achievement. The school never really experienced sustained improvement at the student level. In fact, student outcomes steadily declined over time. When student achievement did rise, it did so in small pockets made up of teachers and students who worked together in isolated "micro" communities within the building while the rest of the students languished in boring and unengaging classes. These micro communities differed from the school as a whole in several ways. Although isolated within the building, they developed strong ties to individuals, organizations, and institutions outside of the building. The students served by these communities had higher achievement levels than those in the rest of the building. Relationships between teachers, students, and parents were strong, and there was a cohesive culture to which the adults and students adhered. Overall, these micro communities enhanced student achievement when the adults who created them were able to maintain a culture that put the optimal growth and development of the student at the center of their day-to-day efforts.

EXPLORING AN ECOLOGICAL SYSTEMS APPROACH TO EDUCATIONAL REFORM

These observations led us to an ecological systems model of school reform. An ecological systems approach to educational reform allows us to focus on the relational conditions necessary to create and maintain a healthy school culture while also keeping the need for optimal growth and development of each school constituent, i.e., teachers, students, and school leaders, at the forefront of the reform agenda. This cultural/developmental approach provides us with a deeper understanding of the ways in which cultures combine within the school context to impact relations, either positively or negatively. Developmental psychologist Urie Bronfenbrenner's ecology of human development brings the developmental focus that we believe is crucial to an ecological systems approach to school reform. Bronfenbrenner focuses on optimal human development *at all age* levels. This means that in the context of the school, optimal growth and development would be the ultimate goal for all constituents. All other reform efforts, the tightening of educational standards, the strengthening of school partnerships, the overhaul of curriculum, and the restructuring of school communities would be in service toward this end. Thus, in our efforts to reform whole schools the spotlight would shine on teachers, students, and school leaders at various times. We begin by laying out how this looks when the spotlight shines on the student.

WHAT DOES IT MEAN TO PLACE THE STUDENT AT THE CENTER OF SCHOOL REFORM?

Placing the student at the center of school reform efforts means first and foremost that the primary goal of the school is the optimal growth and development of the urban adolescent. We believe in and support the primary role of schooling—to provide students with an academic education, one that focuses on the acquisition of critical thinking skills and subject matter content knowledge.[1] However, as students become increasingly stressed and disengaged from school, urban high schools have been forced to ask of themselves "what can we do to ensure that our students are able and willing to participate in acquiring the academic skills and knowledge we have to offer?" We believe that focusing on the optimal growth and development of each student will enable urban schools to better answer this question.

Our focus on ecological systems puts new emphasis on the student's total environment. That environment consists of all the settings in which the student engages in direct, face-to-face relationships with others, as well as those settings that impact the student but in which the student him or herself does not participate. Bronfenbrenner views these settings "as a nested arrangement of concentric structures, each contained within the next."[2] The settings closest to the student—those in which the student has the most face-to-face contact—include the student's school, home, neighborhood, and workplace, as well as any social affiliations the student has, such as with the church, after school programs, health care centers, the courts, or gang membership. Bronfenbrenner calls these face-to-face or primary settings the student's microsystem. Those settings furthest from the student—those in which she has only indirect contact—include the School Committee, school partners, the parent's workplace, etc. Bronfenbrenner calls those settings that indirectly impact students the student's exosystem (see Figure 10.1).

Working within the context of the school then, an ecological systems model encourages us to ask with whom the student has face-to-face contact. In most cases, the student has direct relationships with peers, parents, teachers, and guidance counselors. Students may also have face-to-face contact with tutors, employers, and other support personnel working within the school. These individuals have the potential to create a network of relationships around the student. Bronfenbrenner calls this network the student's mesosystem.

In this model, all of the student's face-to-face relationships and primary settings become potential contexts for development. A critical component for optimal student development is relationships—both within the primary settings and across the nested structures of the ecological environment. For example, the capacity of each one of the student's face-to-face relationships and primary settings for fostering optimal development is enhanced if there are strong interconnections within and between each setting, if there is effective communication between the adults in each setting, and if each setting has accurate and up-to-date knowledge about the other settings. In other words, when the adults within and across settings who are responsible for the student's well-being engage in informed,

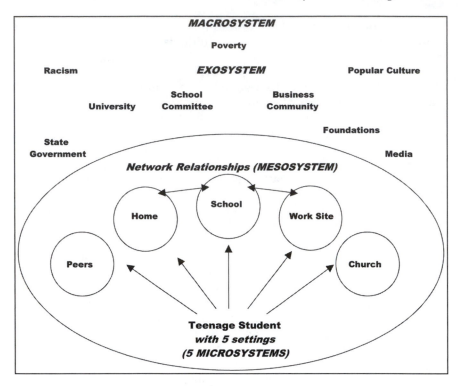

Figure 10.1   The student at the center of the ecological system.
(Adapted from Bronfenbrenner 1979.)

open, face-to-face interactions with each other, then the student's chances for well-rounded, healthy development increase. These social relationships form a network around the student. This network can be tightly woven, with few gaps and strong threads that support and promote the student, or it can be loosely woven, with wide gaps and broken threads that allow the student to fall through. Strong links between the student's primary settings—home and school, school and neighborhood, workplace and school—enhance development; weak, unsupportive links delay development.

The quality of direct relationships in the student's primary settings is only part of the story, however. Students, as well as the adults in their network of direct contact, are also impacted by decisions made in settings outside of that network. Thus, when the school system makes a decision about student assignments or when the state legislature passes educational reform laws or when an employer changes a parent's working hours, these decisions directly impact the quality of the relationships between students and adults within some of their face-to-face settings. Even though the student is not involved in these settings as a direct participant, events and decisions made in these settings influence and affect what happens in the other primary settings in which the child is involved. Thus the forces that impact the adults who interact with a particular child influence that child as well.

Turning again to the context of the school, we see that today's high school is surrounded by networks whose members often do not have direct, face-to-face contact with students. For example, school administrators, district personnel, business and university partners, school boards, and unions most likely have direct relations with teachers, school leaders, tutors, and guidance counselors, but not with students. In most cases, the individuals and organizations that make up this second level network are once removed from students. The strength of the interconnections between the teachers and the members of this network either enhances or inhibits the ability of the teachers, tutors, and guidance counselors to do their job in the service of students. The same thing applies to what might be called a third level network operating in the service of schools. This network involves the local and state government, school funders, and the media. The individuals in this network often have direct relations with the district and business and university partners working with the school, but not with the teachers or school administrators. Strong interconnections between this third level network enhances or inhibits the ability of the second level network to do their job in service to the school, and so on. Thus, an ecological systems model of educational reform allows us to shine the spotlight on any set of individuals, or networks, working with in or being served by the school, as well as on the school itself.

This leads to what we believe is the most important question for those working with schools—on whom is the spotlight focused? We have made the point that for optimal growth and development the student and those that he has direct relationships with must be the ultimate focus; however, in order to realize optimal student development, sometimes the spotlight must be on teachers or school leaders. When business, university and community partners, school districts, and state and federal governments work with schools, it is important to view school personnel as developing persons and to view schools as developing institutions. For example, teachers are developing in many ways in their role as teachers and research has shown that teachers benefit when their roles are expanded and when they gain more responsibility over their working lives. The same is true for administrators and especially for school leaders who are developing in their capacities to lead diverse individuals in a challenging setting.

When we focus the spotlight on a particular individual within the context of the school, we end up working with a different network of individuals within different settings. For example, when the student is in the reformer's spotlight, it becomes necessary to focus also on the settings and individuals with whom the student has direct relationships, i.e., her teachers, parents, employers, peers, tutors, etc. These individuals make up the student's primary network. We maintain that when outside partners, for example, want to work directly with students, they must also work within, and become a part of, this network. Other educational reformers may choose to work closely with teachers, thus putting those teachers in the spotlight. In this case, it becomes necessary to also focus on those settings and individuals with whom the teacher has direct relationships, i.e., her students, school leaders, union representatives, student support personnel, etc. Last, some educational reformers choose to work with school leaders. Again, for optimal growth and development of the school leader, this entails working also with district personnel who have direct relationships with the principle, with teachers, with school partners and with accrediting institutions, etc.

The framework not only helps us understand and create optimal environments for all school constituents as developing people, it also helps us understand and create optimal environments for developing institutions. Urban high schools, by virtue of the intense focus and effort by many sectors in society to reform them, are developing institutions. Consequently, educational reformers, and business, university, and community partners, can enhance the overall growth and development of the school as an institution if they approach the school from an ecological perspective. Relationships between the school and its partners ought to be as reciprocal as possible, with a "mutuality of positive feeling and a gradual shift of the balance of power in favor of the developing" institution.[3] We propose that those who work with schools be mindful of the developmental needs of school personnel and of the developmental needs of the school as a developing institution.

Finally, development is impacted by the ideological and cultural belief systems that shape the behaviors and actions of those who occupy particular settings. Every environment or setting operates within a sea of unstated values, norms, assumptions, and expectations. For example, the various environments that urban students have to navigate, such as the school, the neighborhood, and their homes and workplaces, are often shaped by different or even conflicting cultures. Those who have strong interconnections between their primary settings—between their home and school or school and workplace—can more successfully navigate the transitions between settings that operate according to different cultural rules.[4]

CULTURAL REFORM AND THE ECOLOGICAL SYSTEMS MODEL

Thus we have established the need for cultural reform. Creating and maintaining school cultures that provide optimal opportunities for growth and development of all constituents is a very complex task. It is complex because it requires reflection, introspection, and change on the part of all stakeholders both within and outside of the schoolhouse walls. For us, to focus on cultural reform in schools is to focus on understanding and perhaps changing the relationships, beliefs, behaviors, and expectations of all school stakeholders. If culture is defined as the unstated values, norms, assumptions, and expectations that shape beliefs and guide behavior over time, then reforming the often toxic cultures found in troubled and challenging urban high schools entails *explicitly* helping all school constituents uncover and transform the values, norms, and expectations that guide student and adult behavior and that shape relationships both within and outside of the schoolhouse walls.[5]

Culture is always local. For example, in each setting in which the student participates, there is a prevailing culture—a culture which can be supportive or encouraging or achievement-oriented or neglectful or toxic. When there is cultural consistency across the student's primary settings, i.e., when the cultures are positive and complementary, we can expect that the student will prosper; when the cultures are conflicting, then healthy development is undermined. Furthermore, the world of the student is embedded in a larger sea of cultural forces, cultures that predominate in central administration, the School Committee, or community partners, for example. Each of these, in turn, operates in the sphere of American values and belief systems that predominate in society and are heralded in the media. What is important for the student's welfare is that the clash or complement of cultures has an impact on development. For example, it is easy to see that positive results will be limited when a school is working to consistently communicate high expectations to students, but the district has low expectations for the school and secretly uses it as a dumping ground. For these reasons, it is important for educational reformers to be cognizant of the networks that surround those on whom they have chosen to shine the spotlight as well as the cultural environment or environments in which those individuals operate.

Understanding only the internal culture of one school is not sufficient to explain the lack of student engagement and the failure of effective high school reform. Instead, we must also understand the many cultural settings that influence the student, directly and indirectly, and consider the relationship between these cultural settings. As Bronfenbrenner says, the "key to the enhanced effectiveness of public education lies not within the school itself but in its interconnections with other settings in the society."[6] For this reason, we adopt an ecological approach to educational reform, for ecology focuses on the big picture of relationships between organisms and their various environments. An ecologist, for example, may study a field, noting the ecological niches where various birds, mammals, and reptiles live and how the niches are arranged and interact with one another. We study the school in the same way. An ecological approach delivers us from fixating on one local culture and helps us capture the relationships between cultures.

Thus, an ecological systems approach to educational reform, with its additional emphasis on human development and cultural cohesion, can be distinguished from many other known approaches to urban school reform. Current educational reform efforts take a number of different approaches to "fixing" urban schools. Some focus solely on curriculum and instruction,[7] or on relationships within the school,[8] or on the student context apart from the school,[9] or on making the school more like a community center, where parents and social service providers work inside the school with teachers and administrators; (this approach brings social service agencies and parents into the school to collaborate with teachers and administrators),[10] or last, on the wider influences that impact the school from without.[11] For example, Michael Fullan appreciates the "plethora" of partners and forces impacting the school and he offers a useful model to understand the relationship between the school and these forces.[12] However, his analysis does not focus back on the student. Furthermore, he does not distinguish between the direct relationships, indirect relationships, and the various networks of stakeholders described above. The ecological model of school reform posited here rests on the premise that we cannot keep our focus on the school setting alone. Reforms focused inward, on curriculum, instruction, and in-school relations, and reforms that link the school with external supporters are crucial, but educational reform also needs to extend outward to include all the institutions that impact the student's other primary settings. Most importantly, the ecological systems model of school reform adds and prioritizes the connections between the school and the student's other primary settings.

AN ECOLOGICAL SYSTEMS APPROACH IN ACTION

Based upon what we saw over 60 years, we have identified five relational factors, in addition to the importance of school culture discussed in the introduction, that greatly impact the ability of teachers and administrators to cultivate and maintain student success. They are student engagement, relational trust, role expectations, parent involvement, and the influence of school neighborhoods. Engagement, relationships, and location represent the ecological elements that impact schools. We believe that until the problems they present are addressed, our most troubled urban schools will never be able to sustain mandated educational reforms. This history demonstrates that the problems that result from these five factors have been building up in failing urban schools since the late 1960s. We need to bring these problems into the light in order to restore health to our most troubled urban high schools.

Nothing will Happen until we Re-Engage the Students

Earlier, we discussed how curricular and structural approaches to educational reform attempt to raise academic performance and expectations without leaving certain groups of students behind. However, a relatively recent phenomenon has blunted the effectiveness of the curricular/structural approach—the lack of student engagement. Since the mid 1980s there have been numerous studies on the high levels of student disengagement from school, particularly from the academic activities required for school success.[13] In 2001, the Boston School district, which contains DHS, applied for a Carnegie Corporation planning grant to address "the profound alienation"[14] of the district's high school students. The district turned to Carnegie because despite several years of intense high school reform work the students themselves seemed alienated from school. The problem of student disengagement is an especially serious matter in those schools located in, and which serve students from, poor, urban neighborhoods. In one of the largest and best known of these studies, Lawrence Steinberg found in 1996 that at least 40 percent of high school students were "just going through the motions"[15] when it came to academic engagement. Unfortunately, Steinberg deliberately chose not to study student disengagement in poor, urban populations. The reasons why are worth quoting:

> We felt that the problems associated with the most severe poverty are so devastating and multifaceted that it is simply impossible to consider schools in these communities along side their counterparts in more advantaged neighborhoods. Understanding the problem of low achievement is difficult enough; trying to understand it in the context of environmental deprivation, crime, teen pregnancy, malnutrition, poor housing, violence and parental unemployment is a different matter altogether.[16]

Tellingly, this is precisely the population that DHS serves. Even though Steinberg did not include students from poor, urban neighborhoods in his study, his research did uncover some important information about the impact of neighborhoods on families and on the school performance of youth. These findings, which we outline below, have implications for the cultural reforms we advocate for in this book. Steinberg argues that schools will not be able to re-engage students until the other forces that impact them outside of the schoolhouse walls are dealt with. The major question is how many of those other forces schools can realistically impact. This history demonstrates that instituting curricular and structural reforms alone won't do it, but combining these reforms with cultural reforms can go a long way toward improving urban schools and re-engaging students.

The good news is that many of the recent structural reforms put in place have recognized the need to focus on the student. This is evident in the small schools movement, the push for block scheduling and advisories, and in whole school improvement plans that include goals to engage parents and the community in support of student learning. The major purpose of these innovations is to structure the school for optimal relationship building—small schools and advisories allow for more meaningful contact between the adults in the building and the students. Block schedules provide more time for learning and for creating a community of learners in the classroom. Goals for parent and community involvement are being included because we know that authentic parent involvement improves student achievement.[17] These structures allow the adults in the building—teachers, administrators, and school leaders —to interact with students in ways that form tighter bonds between the two. Schools often turn to these types of structural reforms in an effort to change the school culture, but this history demonstrates why structural reforms alone are not enough.

Many of the leading advocates for educational reform recognize the importance of cultivating relationships among all stakeholders in the school building. Bryk and Schneider in 2002[18] developed the concept of "relational trust" and demonstrate through case studies that the higher the level of trust between the adults in a school setting, the more likely it is for reforms to take hold in that setting. Fullan points out that the single most important factor in successful school change is improved relationships. He cites both structural and cultural barriers as the major impediments to relationship building within schools. Other researchers focus on the relationship between the school and the broader school district. Again, the better the relationship, the more likely successful reforms will take hold within the school.[19] This research and the types of relational reform it suggests are crucial steps for improving highly dysfunctional schools. We maintain that without a focus on school culture and relationships, it will be next to impossible to accomplish the twin tasks of reforming urban schools that are located in poor, crime-ridden, and violent neighborhoods while also re-engaging the students from such neighborhoods in authentic school work.[20]

Building Quality Relationships: Relational Trust

The concept of relational trust helps us begin to think about the dynamics of forming relationships both within schools and between schools and the homes and neighborhoods where students live their lives. Schools function better for students and adults when there are strong relationships among and between all stakeholders. However, the work of schools is dependent upon various sets of interpersonal exchanges between individuals who are "mutually dependent" upon each other. For example, teachers depend upon parents to ensure that students will complete homework and be prepared to participate in school each day. Parents depend upon teachers to properly educate and care for their children. Teachers depend upon other teachers to uphold the rules of the school, and teachers depend upon administrators and school leaders to enact and maintain school policies that enable them to successfully fulfill their roles as teachers.

These structural dependencies create feelings of vulnerability for the individuals involved. This vulnerability is especially salient in the context of asymmetric power relations, such as those between poor parents and local school professionals. A recognition of this vulnerability by the superordinate party (local school professionals) and a conscious commitment on their part to relieve the uncertainty and unease of the other (poor parents) can create a ...meaningful social bond among the parties.[21]

The Impact of Role Expectations on Relationships

A sense of relational trust is needed in order for the stakeholders in a school community to successfully overcome the vulnerabilities set up by their "mutual dependencies." In the ecology of the school each of the stakeholder groups—teachers, parents, students, administrators, and school leaders—have their own understandings of the roles that others are supposed to play. These understandings are accompanied by expectations about how those who hold a particular role are supposed to behave, and of how others are supposed to act toward them. Roles themselves, especially those as established as "teacher," "principal," and "parent," are imbued with societal, cultural, and historical meaning.[22] These larger contextual meanings also influence the activities engaged in and the relationships established with other stakeholders while the role is enacted.[23] A sense of relational trust is cultivated when the role expectancies each party has of the other are reciprocated. We maintain that cultivating relational trust is a first step toward establishing quality relationships among all school stakeholders, especially parents.

Unfortunately, the most challenging urban schools face many obstacles to achieving the kind of role reciprocity that cultivates relational trust. Bryk and Schneider studied the conditions that either foster or inhibit relational trust between various stakeholders in schools. They found that it was more difficult to establish relational trust between teachers and parents in schools that had a high rate of mobility. When school populations are stable, parents and teachers have more opportunities to interact over time. It is more difficult to establish relational trust between teachers and parents in schools that have a history of academic failure. Parents are more likely to see teachers as professionals when there are outside indicators of school-wide achievement. Schools with racial and ethnic tension have more difficulty establishing relational trust between all stakeholders, with schools that serve predominantly African American students reporting the lowest levels of relational trust. Other researchers have confirmed this last sad finding.[24] Last, Bryk and Schneider found that it is easier to establish relational trust in smaller schools where there are fewer people and more opportunities to communicate.

Students bring role expectations with them when they make the transition from middle to high school. These role expectations influence how students behave, the kinds of activities they choose to engage in and how they act in relation to their peers, to their teachers, and to the other adults in the school context. Teachers also have expectations about how high school students ought to behave, about the kinds of activities they ought to engage in, and about how they ought to act in relation to the teacher and the other adults in the building. Last, the transition from middle to high school also alters the parent's role in relation to the child and to the teacher. All too often, in the most challenging urban schools students and teachers have expectations about each other's roles that differ from actual behavior. Parents and teachers get caught in this same trap. If too many teachers and parents experience role deviation in their relations with each other, this contributes to the stream of negative knowledge exchanged between the two systems. This in turn sours communication and weakens the connections between home and school. Unfulfilled role expectations also hurt student-to-student relations, causing division and dissention among the student body. Eventually, too much deviation from role expectations breeds anger among all stakeholders, poisoning the school culture.

Frustration, disappointment, and outright anger over unfulfilled role expectations are, unfortunately, a very common occurrence in the most troubled urban high schools. It is nearly impossible for curricular reforms to tackle this problem. Structural reforms can help, but without explicit support in untangling these frustrations it would be very difficult for school stakeholders to see their way out of this kind of relational trouble. We maintain that focused cultural reform, reform that explicitly targets the norms, beliefs, and expectations embedded within the school community, is the only way to help schools combat this kind of difficulty.

Why Aren't more Parents Involved at the High School Level?

Parent involvement improves student outcomes—Period! But parent involvement takes many different forms, some closer to the workings of school than others. Furthest from the school context are parents who get involved by creating home environments that support their children's schoolwork. Next are parents who make themselves available to talk with the school as needed. Closer to the school are those parents who actually participate in school activities or serve as teaching assistants in the classroom and on the local PTA. Closest to the school are parents who become partners in decision-making and problem solving.[25] Some refer to these types of parent involvement activities as being "schoolcentric" because schools, rather than parents, tend to define the levels and types of involvement open to parents.[26] Even so, children whose parents are involved in schoolcentric ways tend to have overall higher academic achievement than children whose parents are not involved at all.

The types of parent involvement described above tend to vary depending upon the parents' ethnicity, race, and social class. Schools that serve children from low-income neighborhoods tend to have either "minimal, sporadic or altogether nonexistent" schoolcentric parent involvement.[27] However, this does not mean that parents from low-income neighborhoods are not involved in their children's education. When one talks to low-income African American parents[28] a different definition of parent involvement emerges. This definition is intricately linked to the neighborhood in which the parents live. For example, many parents from impoverished urban neighborhoods are acutely aware that drugs and violence plague their community. They are therefore, very concerned for the safety of their children, especially before and after school when the children are often left alone due to their parents' employment. These parents see the school hours as the only hours in the day when they know their children will be safe. Parent involvement under these conditions means creating the conditions that allow their children to attend school in the first place. This differs from the school's vision of parent involvement where parents are responsible for creating an educationally supportive environment in the home.

Parental awareness of the hazards of their neighborhood colors their perceptions of how the school views their children.

> Parents believe that drugs, violence, and other environmental hazards have created a school environment that is centered on suspicion and fear. In fact, many [low income] parents believe that the school is not only wary of the potentially harmful environmental conditions [of the neighborhood] but scared of the children as well.[29]

For low-income parents trapped in crime-ridden and violent neighborhoods, the neighborhood itself mediates parental relations with and beliefs about the local school. Teachers, on the other hand, tend not to factor neighborhood influence, or the impact of race and class, into their explanations about the lack of parent involvement. Rather, teachers tend to have two conceptions of parent involvement, neither of which extends beyond the school-home dynamic. They see parent involvement as "school-based" and "home-based." Those parents who participate in school activities or who serve as teacher aids are seen as engaging in school-based parent involvement. Parents who volunteer at the school are there on the school's terms, either to aid student learning or to help students conform to classroom procedures and school rules thereby facilitating student success. Teachers perceive home-based parent involvement as serving a more ideological purpose. They see it as the means through which parents impart the value of education to their children. In other words, if parents value education enough to stress its importance in the home by encouraging and helping children with their homework, then children will come to value education as well and this will be evident in the child's classroom behavior and work ethic. Unfortunately, teachers tend to perceive children who do not exhibit these behaviors as having parents who do not stress education in the home. All to often, this leads many teachers to conclude that the parents are not acting responsibly toward their children. This in turn frustrates and infuriates parents.[30]

Regrettably, parent involvement is much more common at the elementary school level. Some of the reasons for this are structural;[31] multiple high school classes and teachers provide fewer opportunities for parent-teacher interaction. Other reasons are developmental;[32] many parents believe that as their children get older, it is better to keep some distance in order to prepare them for adult roles and responsibilities. There is also a tendency for school personnel and parents to believe that parent involvement is not as crucial to school success at the high school level.[33] However, it turns out that the prevailing beliefs about parent involvement during the high school years might not be accurate.[34] There is a type of parent involvement that makes a difference in terms of student engagement and achievement at the high school level—parental presence in the school. When parents spend time in the school, for teacher-student conferences or to attend school activities and programs, their teenage children achieve at higher levels. Steinberg cites two reasons for this. It sends a message to the teenager about the school-home connection, making the school a part of family life. Second, teachers are more likely to attend to students whose parents spend more time at the school, and parents find it easier to talk with teachers when problems arise if they have met the teacher in person beforehand.

Although home-based parent involvement may be helpful at the elementary school level, it makes very little, if any, difference in achievement at the high school level. One possible reason for this is that parents of adolescents mainly attempt to monitor their children's schoolwork when the student is having trouble. This often causes tension in the home. Rather than reach out to the school for help, parents tend to get more strict and rigid, leading to typical adolescent rebellion. The children of those parents who do turn to the school system for help perform better. Steinberg refers to this as "system-work" versus "home-work." System-work is more successful because most parents of high school children simply do not know enough to help their children with academic difficulties. Teenagers' schoolwork suffers for a number of different reasons. Often the parent's solution, telling the child to work harder, is the least helpful. When parents are able to work with the system on their child's behalf, they avail themselves of the special expertise that teachers and counselors have. Parents who are able to "work the system" in these ways have students who are more engaged and who achieve at higher levels. Sadly, high schools do not tend to encourage this type of parent involvement. Also, engaging with "the system" often feels very threatening to many poor, urban parents.

Neighborhoods Matter

It is unfortunate that the vast majority of parents pull back when their children reach high school age, not only because of declining achievement, but also because it is during the early adolescent years that outside forces have the greatest influence on teenage behavior. We return now to a discussion of the impact of the neighborhood. Not only does the neighborhood mediate parent responses and reactions to the local school, it also shapes adolescent behavior in unexpected ways. In terms of school outcomes, neighborhoods matter. They matter for children who live in more affluent neighborhoods and for children who live in low-income neighborhoods. However, the overall consequences of neighborhood influence are graver for adolescents who attend neighborhood schools when those schools are located in low-income neighborhoods with high levels of drug abuse, crime, and violence.

There are many dimensions to neighborhood influence. First of all, adolescents tend to become friends with other teenagers who live in their immediate neighborhoods. These friendships often have greater influence over teenage behavior than their home environments. For example, it is true that the home is where most children are initially introduced to drugs and alcohol use, and teenagers may experiment with these substances based upon what they see in the home. However, if those same teenagers end up hanging out with friends who tend not to abuse drugs and alcohol, they have a much greater chance of escaping any real trouble with substance abuse.[35] The same principle applies for school engagement. If teenagers end up within a peer group that values school work, they will be more likely to value education and engage with school even if their parents have not stressed educational attainment.

There are two dimensions of parenting that influence student achievement, parenting style and participation in school activities. The teenagers of parents who have an authoritative parenting style, as opposed to an authoritarian or permissive parenting style, have better school outcomes. Also, as explained above, the children of parents who participate in school activities have better school outcomes. Steinberg surveyed and interviewed over 500 sets of white, African American, Latino and Asian parents. He found that when one compares Asian American and African American parents on these two dimensions, African American parents come out ahead on both, regardless of socioeconomic and family status (single or two parent families).

> Black parents, on average, are more involved in their children's schooling than are Asian parents—at least in terms of overt participation in school activities—and black parents are more likely than Asian parents to be authoritative.[36]

Based upon this extensive data set, Steinberg and others have concluded that it is the peer group that undermines the efforts of black parents in terms of school achievement. And it is in the neighborhood where the peer group is formed. The longer students live in unhealthy neighborhoods the greater the effect.[37]

Therefore peers tend to have the most detrimental impact on children from the poorest urban neighborhoods. Elijah Anderson chronicled the ways in which the poorest neighborhoods shape children. Respect on the street, or in the public arena, is a highly valued quality in neighborhoods characterized by high levels of poverty, crime, and violence. Anderson surmises that whereas middle and upper class youth have many more opportunities to engage in activities that demonstrate their self-worth, respect on the street is one of the only avenues available to low-income urban youngsters, particularly boys, for attaining self-esteem and a sense of self-worth. Having respect on the street not only enhances one's self-esteem, it also keeps one safe, and possibly extends one's life. In this sense gaining respect on the street is often tied to violence. Anderson points out,

> In the wider society, particularly among the middle class, people may not feel required to retaliate physically after an attack....They are much more likely than street oriented youth to feel that they can walk away from a possible altercation with their self-esteem intact....In impoverished inner-city black communities...such flight would be extremely difficult. To run away would likely leave one's self-esteem in tatters, while inviting further disrespect. Therefore, youth often feel constrained not only to stand up and at least attempt to resist during an assault, but also to seek revenge....Through these various conflicts the connection between actually being respected and the need for physical control become internalized.[38]

The need to gain respect through physicality is not new or unique to inner-city, black communities. Anderson points out that similar behavior is seen in working class urban Irish, Italian, and other communities. However, the level of persistent poverty experienced in some inner city neighborhoods, coupled with racism, creates a sense of isolation and alienation from mainstream society that exacerbates the tremendous need for respect that will give meaning to young people's lives within the peer culture.

Many of these confrontations—what Anderson would describe as "campaigns of respect" for the young people involved—take place in particular neighborhood hangouts. Anderson identified three types of hangouts: the local liquor store, the local business strip, and concerts or skating rinks. It is through the number and type of hangouts it has that neighborhoods gain reputations as being associated with a street or gang culture. This reputation taints other neighborhood institutions.

> The reputation of the neighborhood affects the reputation of the school.... The school's reputation is shaped by its history...the achievements of its students, the levels of violence and of entrenched and persistent poverty associated with the areas and the number of [hangouts] in and around it.[39]

Eventually, the high school itself becomes a "hangout" for street oriented youth. This is especially true for high schools that are racially segregated and located in neighborhoods where crime, violence, and drug abuse are widespread. When these schools double as neighborhood schools, it then becomes very easy for the street culture to find its way into the classroom. For those who work in these types of high schools every day, it's very easy to recognize these students. They are the ones who appear ready to fight at the drop of a hat; they are constantly trying to pull one over on the teacher and test teacher authority; they spend most of their time in the halls rather than in class; and their confrontations with other students and teachers take on the same tenseness and intensity experienced during street fights. In this situation many of the other children learn how to code switch—not because they emulate the street culture, but so they can get through the day without being bullied, challenged or having to fight. It is this atmosphere that leads some children to adopt "gang" clothing and to hide their books when walking to and from school.

DEVELOPING INDIVIDUALS AND DEVELOPING INSTITUTIONS

At the most fundamental level, an ecological approach to school reform allows educational reformers to shine the spotlight on any of the networks operating within or in service to the school. We maintain that, ultimately, the spotlight must be on the student lighting the way toward his or her needs. Toward this end, however, it is crucial to examine and highlight the interconnections and relationships at all levels, i.e., the networks that comprise the students' primary settings, the networks that support teachers and school leaders, and the networks at the upper echelons of society that support school districts and set school policy. What the spotlight does is enable school reformers to understand who has face-to-face relations with whom; this in turn allows us to understand what types of networks are operating to serve the student and most importantly, whether or not those networks have relationships with each other.

The conceptual framework grew out of our realization that despite 60 years of educational reform efforts aimed at one urban high school, student outcomes never really improved, and when they did improve, they did so only in small pockets within the school. As we examined what was special about those pockets of success, we saw relationships, we saw connections and we saw a cohesive culture to which the adults and students living in those pockets adhered. In most cases, it wasn't the mandated reforms coming from outside the building that created those pockets. This history of Dorchester High School has demonstrated that as a country, we have steadily improved in our efforts to reform urban high schools; we know more about what's needed; we have learned a lot from

our mistakes, and we have grown more reflective about our limited successes. However, true, system-wide student achievement has eluded us,
especially in the poorest schools in our urban districts. We believe this is
because we have shied away from a focus on building relationships, on
maintaining connections, and on creating healthy cultures within schools.
We have forgotten about the community, and how central the community
is to the optimal growth and development of our neediest neighborhoods
and students.

CHAPTER 11

School Culture and School Partnerships

THE FIRST LESSON: THE FUNDAMENTAL ROLE OF SCHOOL CULTURE

It has been demonstrated that a strong, internal school culture, where the teachers, staff, and school leaders share norms, assumptions, and expectations for students, is necessary for sustained student success. Success is even more likely in those schools where the internal school culture mirrors the norms, assumptions, and expectations of the student's home and of the wider community in which the students and teachers live. Fortunately, many schools in America do share their internal cultural norms with their students' families and the surrounding community. For those schools that have toxic or broken cultures, certain educational reforms, such as the recent small schools movement, are aimed at strengthening the internal school culture. However, as appears to be the case with DHS, the verdict is still out on the success of this approach to reform in our most challenging urban high schools. "The challenges of transforming an existing school culture and organization within the same building and with largely the same population of teachers and students are often very different from those faced by the new school teams." These differences "risk preventing the paradigm shifts often required to instill a culture of high academic expectations for all students."[1]

This led us to ask ourselves the following question: If a school does not have a strong internal culture or if there is a mismatch between the culture of the school and the culture of the home and wider community then what can we do? What can take the place of a strong, internal school culture in ensuring student success? The history of DHS provides us with some clues as to where we might look for an answer.

THE DESTRUCTION OF SCHOOL CULTURE

One thing that stands out about the first decade in the history of DHS is the shared culture. The adults and students shared a set of norms, values, beliefs, and expectations about students and schooling. This shared culture helped hold the school community together. Formality between constituents was the rule; there was little need for overt, spoken rules governing the behavior and interactions of all constituents. Both students and teachers knew how to "act" in relation to those above them in the school's hierarchy. Teachers never openly questioned the headmaster's actions and decisions, and students knew not to cross the line in terms of in-school behavior.

The shared culture allowed the adults in the school to be more fluid; they were better able to make decisions and to move as one unit when the need arose. This happened after the passage of the National Defense Act of 1957. DHS was able to meet the challenge rather painlessly by expanding the academic offerings and experiences for students. The DHS of the early 1960s looked more like the suburban high schools of today. There were abundant activities and events for students; the school was dealing with increasing levels of diversity, but that diversity did not threaten to overwhelm the homogenous majority, and most important, there was a strong internal culture that was shared between and among students, teachers, parents, and school leaders. Suburban schools, even though they have opposed the most recent wave of standardization required by No Child Left Behind, have not struggled as much with implementing those standards, just as the DHS of the 1950s did not struggle as much with the reform mandates of the day. They were able to tinker and adjust here and there to meet the mandates of the National Defense Act, without upsetting their overall methods of operation.

As you may recall, 1957–69 were the best years ever at DHS in terms of academic achievement for students. We maintain that these somewhat rapid curricular reforms were possible because of the shared culture that held the school community together. We are not saying that the prevailing culture at the time was desirable or just. What is significant however is that it was *shared*, not only within the school building, but across the surrounding neighborhood and wider community as well. We know that the culture of a school impacts student achievement.[2] "The bedrock of cultural vitality and stability lies in the mission, purpose, values, beliefs, assumptions and norms that people *share*."[3] The more stable a school's culture, the more easily the school itself can withstand change. Unfortunately, this goes both ways. A school can have a very stable toxic culture, one where a majority of constituents work to keep the culture unhealthy.

When we examine the changes that took place within DHS after 1969 simply in terms of culture, we see that the shared culture within and around the urban high school began to splinter into distinct pieces. First, the neighborhood surrounding the high school changed rapidly, interrupting the cultural cohesion between the school and its surroundings. No longer did teachers and a majority of the students feel "at home" in the neighborhood. Despite these changes, DHS remained a neighborhood school. This in turn impacted the relationships within the building. The first relationships affected were those between teacher and student. After 1968, enrollments at DHS jumped from 960 to 1,579; the students were younger, poorer, racially different, and politically aware. (Many of them had participated in the black student boycotts and freedom schools in 1963 and 1964.) The teachers were still operating under the norms of formality. They expected students to follow the unspoken rules and behavioral norms of the high school. Some students were simply too young and unfamiliar with the norms of high school in general. More of the students were very poor and brought the concomitant problems of poverty to school with them. Other students were politicized and no longer willing to simply "accept" the social mores of the dominant society that schools and teachers represented.

Despite these changes in the surrounding neighborhood and the student population, the teachers were able to remain focused on academic reforms and behavior so long as they shared a common set of norms, expectations, and values among themselves. Maintaining this shared culture became severely challenged in 1969, however, when the teacher population nearly doubled in size from 63 teachers in 1967 to 106 teachers by 1969. Many of these new teachers were forged in the hotbed of college activism roiling the nation. They were young, idealistic, and motivated toward political change in the service of a more equitable society. They took this activism into the schools that hired them. First, they fought and won union representation. Second, they tended to support the students in their increasing calls for less formality between themselves and the adults. The values and norms of this new set of teachers were almost incomprehensible to those who had been working in the building prior to 1969. Almost overnight, relations between teachers and students became more relaxed and those between the adults in the building, between teachers and teachers and between teachers and administrators, more strained. These tensions wiped out any cultural cohesion that existed in the building.[4]

Now, not withstanding all of the other setbacks the school faced—the overcrowding, the deteriorating facilities, the racial strife, the legislative mandates—we are left with a school that has lost its shared vision, its shared culture. Almost overnight, the school lost its historical moorings, its traditions, and its values. This happened in urban schools all over the country. It should not be a surprise to anybody that in 2002, six of the ten urban high schools with the highest dropout rates[5] (dropouts being an indicator of failing schools) are in states that endured difficult court-ordered desegregation battles. We maintain that these struggles over desegregation, struggles that destroyed internal school cultures and separated the school from the community, are one of the main reasons why some urban schools seem impossible to reform. This loss of cultural cohesion happened so rapidly that there was no help available when the dust settled. Not only was the country totally unprepared at that time to fix broken school cultures, they actually mistook the cause of the damage as being curricular and structural, when in reality it was a cultural problem that needed a cultural solution, one that we are only just now, over 60 years later, beginning to realize.

It took six more years for Dorchester High School to hit bottom in terms of student achievement. By 1975, the students and the school itself were failing on all indicators. First, the district tried to improve the situation through school leadership. Because they misconstrued the school's problem as being a discipline problem, the leaders tended to be physical education instructors rather than community builders. Second, the state legislature got involved. However, throughout the 1970s the legislature was still rightly focused on access. This led to the addition of bilingual and special education students. A noble and just move, but one that served to fill the school with even more difference, making it even harder to develop *shared* understandings among staff and students. The addition of bilingual and SPED students caused more division among teachers. General education teachers became too distracted by the issues special education students brought into the classroom, and those who were trained to work with these students did not know the content—causing them to focus too much on the affective components of a high school education. Evidently, those responsible for urban high school reform—staff and students within the schools and the districts and local and state governments outside of the schools—wandered in this wilderness of school-wide failure for the remainder of the 1970s. Luckily, as we saw, the courts and the business community were making progress.

Lesson Learned for troubled urban schools:

Schools cannot successfully operate without cultural cohesion. The cohesive cultures of some urban high schools were so severely and utterly destroyed that it was and is impossible for them to fix themselves. We have a human problem here that we keep attempting to fix with technical solutions. Curricular standards and academic rigor alone will never help urban schools fix their broken cultures.

PARTNERS (THE EXOSYSTEM) TO THE RESCUE

Like many urban high schools, DHS as a whole never regained the cultural cohesion that was present in the 1950s and 1960s, nor have the levels of student achievement improved since then. Human beings cannot survive for long without a sense of community. By 1982, up to ten years after the culture fell apart, some teachers, fed up with the isolation and divisiveness, began working together to create small pockets of shared values, goals, and expectations within the school. These pockets grew into small in-school communities that operated as safe havens for the teachers and students who had the good fortune to be part of them. Ironically, the chaotic atmosphere of the school is what helped sustain these isolated communities. Between 1982 and 1998, seventeen small communities of teachers and students were formed at DHS. All of the successes in terms of student achievement during this period were connected with one or another of these small communities, rather than with the school as a whole. In the end, only six of them survived. Their survival provides us with some valuable information about the relationship between cultural cohesion and school partners.

The six that survived had two characteristics: First, they were developed by a group of teachers who shared a set of values, norms, and expectations about themselves and students. This shared culture held them together. Second, they managed to connect to some part of the exosystem. Thus the successful SLCs had strong networks both within and outside of the schoolhouse walls working for the optimal growth and development of students. The small communities that did not survive had one of these two characteristics but not both. For example, the teachers who created LEAP were united by a shared vision and culture, but in the beginning they lacked partnership support. This caused LEAP to stagnate, unable to make a large impact on student outcomes. It wasn't until LEAP became the Academy of Public Service ten years later, with the support of outside partners, that this small community was finally able to make a difference in terms of student outcomes.

This points to the power of partnerships as a catalyst for improved student outcomes. As we have seen throughout this history, when it came to making a real difference in terms of student achievement, the outside partners had to be involved with the school. However, the involvement of partners was made possible through their connection to a cohesive in-school community thus creating a strong network of support for teachers and students. This history shows us that for failing urban high schools both partnerships and a cohesive culture are necessary for student success, but partnerships are essential. We believe this was necessary because the cohesive culture was not school-wide. Had the whole school shared a strong, cohesive culture that mirrored the culture of the students' homes, then we believe that partnership participation would not have been a crucial factor in terms of student success. At DHS, the history shows that after 1968 nothing was happening in terms of student achievement until the exosystem—made up of the business and higher education

communities, the local and state government, the media and the School
Committee—got themselves together and on the same page. Once key
members of the exosystem became organized for student achievement,
they were able to work with the teacher-led, in-school communities
already in place at DHS. This created a strong network of support for both
teachers and students in those communities.

THE ACTION FOR CHANGE BEGINS WITHIN THE MICROSYSTEM

We have seen that once the internal school culture began to fragment
through the loss of shared understandings among staff and between staff
and students, there really wasn't anything else in place that could play
the role of school unifier. The old systems for regulating behavior and
interaction between people in schools had broken down and new systems
had not yet been developed. At some point in the early 1980s both those
inside the school, mainly teachers, and those outside of the school, starting with the business community, realized that some new form of organization was needed. The teachers took the route of banding together with
like-minded colleagues with whom they could create a community for
learning and teaching. The business community took a similar route.
They reached out to like-minded colleagues in other sectors of the exosystem to form a network of institutions who could fight for real change in
schools.

While the internal cultures of urban high schools throughout the city
were crumbling, the business community was making progress toward
their version of school reform by working first within their own microsystem. They then branched out to other microsystems within their network
of relations. For example, the business leaders began meeting with the
superintendent and with the School Committee in 1974, creating a strong
connection between business and the schools just when the situation in
schools began to hit bottom. Leaders from the higher education community began meeting within their microsystem the following year. Their
next move was to invite high school leaders to meet with them, in order
to set up the partnerships called for in Phase II of Judge Garrity's order.
This move created a new connection between higher education and the
city's high schools.

By 1979, the business community began to realize that a more direct
link to the actual schools was needed. They created the Private Industry
Council (PIC) whose main responsibility was to help local businesses
partner with area high schools. In time, the PIC placed paid staff into each
high school in order to facilitate the mentoring and hiring of more Boston
graduates. This shift moved the high schools into the business community's network giving them more of a sense of what actually happened in
schools. It also made one segment of the business community a part of

each high school's network since there was now a business representative talking with teachers and students on a day-to-day basis. These moves strengthened the connections between the business community and the schools in terms of job creation.

Once the Boston Compact was signed, the business community created the Boston Plan for Excellence (BPE), an education fund for the Boston Public Schools. BPE staff also worked directly in schools; this time the focus was on providing professional development for teachers. This created another direct connection between the business community and teachers, further embedding schools in the business community's network and vice versa. In addition to the Boston Plan for Excellence and the Private Industry Council staff, some businesses and higher education institutions, like New England Telephone and the University of Massachusetts Boston, assigned a school liaison to work directly in the schools. Again, this brought DHS and its business and higher education partners into each other's networks. Now teachers, school counselors, and some students had direct, face-to-face relations with a member of the business and higher education communities.

While some members of the business community were moving forward through direct involvement with schools, other members of the same business organizations were working to effect change in school governance by working through the state legislature, another member of the business community's network. However, all the settings within a particular network do not exercise equal power or have equal influence within that network. When the business community first set out to change how schools were governed in Boston, they began working directly with the superintendent. Failing to get anywhere, they moved to the School Committee. This failed too; the business community then called on their connections in the legislature where they finally met with some success. In the end, the legislation they believed would fix the governance problems was not followed, in effect constituting another failure. Throughout these efforts, the business community had been working separately to effect change. They would set up meetings between a business community representative and the superintendent or School Committee president. Once these efforts failed they tried a new tactic; they pulled together a group of individuals from each setting—in effect, they created a new microsystem—it was called the Vault, and it was very powerful. This microsystem was made up of the top three leaders of the School Committee, the top business leaders in the city, the mayor himself, along with his director of administration and members of the Boston Municipal Research Bureau. This move added another powerful player to the table, the mayor. Finally, the City Council got involved. By drawing on their networks in ways that maximized their power and influence, the business community was eventually able to accomplish its goal for school governance.

These moves teach us a few things. One, the business community drew upon ever increasing positions of power within their own network in order to accomplish their goals. The African American community, not being part of this powerful network, tried to oppose the business community, and they almost succeeded once, when they allied themselves with the Senate Republicans. Unfortunately for the African American leaders, the Senate Republicans were also part of the business community's network. When forced to make a choice between members, they chose to go with the more powerful business lobby. The media, another member of the influence network, also played a role by publishing key stories at crucial moments in the debate.

Before this round of events, the business community especially had always operated as part of the schools' exosystem. Decisions made by those in a school's exosystem impact school leaders, teachers, and students. Businesses hired graduates and attempted to influence school policy, but they rarely, if ever, interacted directly with principles, teachers, or students. Business organizations also have a very strong and tightly connected network made up of the most powerful members of state and local government. The influence of these organizations is both deep and wide. The relationships within the business community's network rely mostly on contractual trust, which helps explain the original Boston Compact between the business community and the BPS, and the offense taken at the initial failure of BPS to hold up its end of the contract. This is in contrast to the relational trust needed to help schools thrive. By placing representatives from various business organizations within the public high schools, the business community made the high school part of its network. Likewise, the business representative also became part of the school's network. In these schools, including DHS, business was no longer operating as a complete school outsider. This relationship allowed for the building of relational trust between the business partner and those in the school, in this case the teachers and students, which in turn led to a deepening of the commitment of the business community to the schools, evidenced in the hard work of the 1990s. The PIC representative also gave those in the school access to the wider influence of power available to the business community.

The higher education community did the same thing. They began by working together within their own microsystem both through the Higher Education Partnership and the College President's Steering Committee. This allowed the members of the college microsystem to have sustained conversations among themselves about issues facing the schools; these conversations were an important first step. Next, each college began meeting with teachers and administrators from the high schools they were paired with, becoming part of each other's network. This was the beginning of relationship formation between university personnel and high school personnel.

EFFORTS IN THE EXOSYSTEM LEAD TO IMPROVED STUDENT OUTCOMES

By 1984, almost ten years later, which demonstrates how long it can take to bear fruit, these relationships finally paid off for students at DHS through the creation of Compact Ventures. Compact Ventures was the successful program created for ninth graders at DHS. The reader may remember that DHS had a very active business partner in New England Telephone and a Private Industry Council representative who worked at the high school. They also had a very active university partner in UMB. These were all people and organizations working with schools from the outside. On the inside, DHS had a group of teachers who had formed a community and wanted to work together with the ninth grade students. It was through these connections, relationships, and resources from the outside coupled with a committed community of teachers on the inside, that Compact Ventures was initiated. Once off the ground, another partner, the local media, got involved by profiling the students. This served not only to highlight the program, but also to validate the school and the students. The articles offered some much needed positive publicity about the school at a time when most news was negative.

By all accounts, Compact Ventures was a successful program in terms of raising student achievement. When we look at Compact Ventures according to the ecological systems model laid out here, we see the spotlight on the student. Compact Ventures created a tight web of support around the student through an interconnected network made up of members from the school, the business and higher education community, and the home. The students moved in cohorts with the same teachers, youth workers, classroom assistants, counselors, and tutors. In turn, all of these adults met weekly to discuss student issues. Parents were also included in the network through the youth worker who contacted student homes and spent time in the neighborhood. Unlike programs in operation today, Compact Ventures also made sure to build in activities that built student character. They went on trips and attended plays and performances as a group. These activities helped create a sense of community for the students and teachers in the program and provided students with a differentiated high school experience. Key to Compact Ventures success was that the program was able to create a common culture around it, one in which students were getting the same message in all their microsystems. The support did not stop with the student however. Compact Ventures, as a program, also had a strong web around it. The members of DHS's exosystem had become members of Compact Ventures' relational network. For Compact Ventures, they were no longer outside forces impacting the school from afar. Compact Ventures had strong support from the business community who had two staff in the building, from UMB, and from the legislature.

This progression of events provides us with one example about how activity that began within the school's exosystem ultimately impacted students both academically and socially. In the case of Compact Ventures three things came together, and they came together through a network of support. One, the state, a member of the school's exosystem, was looking for a way to support at-risk students in urban schools. Two, members of the business community, now part of both the state's and the school's network, brought the two together, and, three, there was a viable and willing small community of teachers in the school who shared a set of values and beliefs about students. On their own, these teachers most likely would not have heard about or been able to muster the resources to apply for the state funding. The business community, through the Private Industry Council, helped them write the proposal and no doubt advocated for them in the state capital. Compact Ventures is one example of how an ecological systems model works for effective urban high school reform. Sadly, the story of Compact Ventures also demonstrates what happens when the exosystem pulls out. Once the economy failed and the business community had other issues to contend with, the program fell apart. This happened even though the in-school community was still strong. The teachers remained, but without the web of support, they could not sustain the work alone. Even though it was a successful program that was recognized and replicated system-wide, Compact Ventures only lasted five years. This tells us something about the concept of capacity building.

Lesson Learned for troubled urban schools:

Real change in schools cannot originate within the school alone especially when that school does not have a strong internal school culture. The most successful programs in terms of student achievement get off the ground when the exosystem and the school's microsystem merge to become part of each other's network of support. Change is enhanced when members of the exosystem can find a community within the school with which to work, and, vice versa, school communities work when they are supported by the exosystem.

THE PROBLEMATIC CONCEPT OF CAPACITY BUILDING

The demise of Compact Ventures tells us something about the complicated notion of capacity building. Capacity building usually refers to learning, by individual constituents or by the organization as a whole, which leads to sustained change. Increased capacity makes possible individual and institutional development. Capacity building has been the stated goal of many reform efforts at DHS over the years. Often funders lend their resources, time, and effort in support of schools in the hopes that over time, the organization will "build capacity" within, by learning how to implement a particular reform, and keep it running on their own without the need for outside support. But what if this notion of capacity building is all wrong? The few successes at DHS over 60 years clearly demonstrate the impossibility of building internal capacity without a strong network of support. When members of a school's relational network pull out, those members and whatever sector of society they represent leave a huge hole in the network of support. This ends up severing one of the connections that held the network of support together. An ecological systems model tells us that success is in the connections; success is in the relationships. When just one connection is broken, one relationship severed, it hurts the whole system. This becomes a loss for the school, for the teachers, and for the students. In order for the members of a school's exosystem (business, higher education, and community organizations) to become members of that school's network of support, they need to work at building relationships and trust over time. This takes personal effort and commitment on both sides. It is not realistic for the outside partner to build these relationships with the idea that they will stay just long enough to help the school build capacity in the area of reform and then pull out.

Schools that do not have internal, cohesive cultures need these strong networks with the more powerful sectors of society. They need these connections and relationships, for it is the connections and the relationships that lead to the success. When educational reformers come in to work with a troubled school, they ought to focus on two things. The role they themselves play in *connecting* the school with other microsystems, and the role they play in helping the school form networks across those systems. Once school partners figure out their roles in making these connections, than it is the *connection* that must continue, rather than the transfer of some undefined capacity to members of the school community so they can now go it alone. The newly developed capacity for sustained change is really larger than the institution; rather than simply being a new intelligence or skill or motivation in just one party, the capacity grows in both partners, in terms of new relationships, collaboration, and possibilities for inspiration, creativity, and adaptability (and notice that sustained connections do not always imply endless financial support). Instead of targeting (and by implication, blaming) one group who are "incapacitated" and who need to build capacity, this definition of capacity expands the circle of responsibility and focuses on relationships. We maintain that going it alone most likely caused the problems in the first place.

One example, which we have seen happen at various instances throughout the history of DHS, demonstrates why capacity building is so difficult to achieve. DHS has had millions of dollars in grant money and partnership donations over the years. Unfortunately, and it is difficult to admit this, a great deal of the grant money that finds its way to schools like DHS is ultimately wasted, especially when measured against gains in student achievement. In most cases this is not the fault of the school. Most grant money comes to schools sporadically, unexpectedly and from school partners who have their own agendas about how to use the money. These agendas may or may not mesh with the school's own goals for moving forward. There are often a number of restrictions on how grant money can be used and most of it cannot be rolled over from year to year. This leaves school leaders scrambling to spend the money within the confines of the grant and the partners' own goals, without adequate planning or alignment with other school goals. In order to build capacity, extra school funds need to be utilized according to an overall plan where capacity building is an explicitly stated goal. When funds are allocated in the manner described above, the money often merely sustains previous efforts or introduces completely new ones, rather than contributing to incremental change within the confines of the school's own goals.

Last, capacity building requires new learning, and new learning takes time. Unfortunately, partnership efforts often end up creating more work for school leaders and teachers robbing them of the time needed to reflect upon the new approach. For example, schools leaders are often approached by outside partners who want to work with the school. Those who lead troubled urban schools know how crucial partnership resources are, so these advances are seldom turned down. What ends up happening is that the partner often funds a position on their end to handle the new relationship, while the school (which lacks the resources) simply adds the relationship to the list of many other daily responsibilities. So, for example, the Trefler-funded partnership between DHS and UMB created new management jobs at UMB, which allowed professors to come to the school to investigate, mediate, lead meetings, and push the agenda toward restructuring. However, no new management positions were created at DHS, although administrators and, in some cases, teachers were expected to attend the meetings and handle the new responsibilities. Each elaboration of the relationship—adding and monitoring interns in the Teach Next Year program, recruiting additional students into Upward Bound or Urban Scholars, tracking students in the dual enrollment program—required more work by school personnel which was simply added on top of their other responsibilities. Similarly, the LAB introduced the *Breaking Ranks* project and promptly hired a liaison from Salem State College to move the agenda forward. The school received no money and no position, but assumed more responsibility to achieve the goals of *Breaking Ranks.* When responsibilities are added to any group, without corresponding resources, authorities, and privileges, then one might assume that the target group is considered previously irresponsible or derelict in their duties. This ultimately hurts the ability of school personnel to build capacity and it definitely undermines the goal of building sustained, supportive, and responsible relationships.

Lesson Learned for troubled urban schools:

Capacity building is a real need, especially in our most troubled urban high schools, but it will not happen automatically. Those partners who want to work toward building the capacity of the high school to sustain reform efforts must do three things: put the goal of capacity building at the forefront of their agenda, build in explicit communication about how school personnel and partners will work together to build capacity in the school and the partnering institution, and be open to sharing authority and resources with the school toward the goal of capacity building.

THE EXOSYSTEM AND THE TRANSFER OF POWER

The Academy of Public Service (APS) offers us another, slightly different example of the crucial role the exosystem plays in school reform. APS was founded in the same way that Compact Ventures was. A group of committed and like-minded teachers built a small learning community within the school. This community was able to connect with school partners in order to make a real difference for children. In the case of APS, the business and university community representatives were already part of the school's network and had been for a long time. Once it was clear that the teachers were serious about creating something special within Dorchester High School, these partners stepped up to the plate with financial resources and support (see Figure 11.1).

Like Compact Ventures, APS placed the spotlight on students by creating strong interconnections between the student's face-to-face settings. In the early days, the APS students had direct face-to-face relationships with their teachers, parents, and family members, the Private Industry Council career specialist, the employer (for those who had jobs), and their peers. Some had a direct relationship with the funder, Pam Trefler herself. This was one difference between APS and Compact Ventures. APS's network contained a funder. In the beginning Pam Trefler became part of the student's support network. Her early work was entirely local, hands-on, and student-centered. She worked in an English classroom, funded a literacy lab, and mentored girls in the Academy of Public Service. APS provides a useful example of a program that was very successful because they put the student in the center of the spotlight. The APS teachers met together every day and discussed the kids and the plan. They called the parents and kept them in the circle of communication. The career specialist talked to the employers and then he talked to the teachers. Pam talked to all of them and enjoyed many face-to-face relationships with both teachers and students. At the same time, the peer group was supportive because of the powerful APS mystique.

Furthermore, APS as a program was also part of a network that contained business and university partners that gave the program access to the wider communities of influence. We know that when the network is

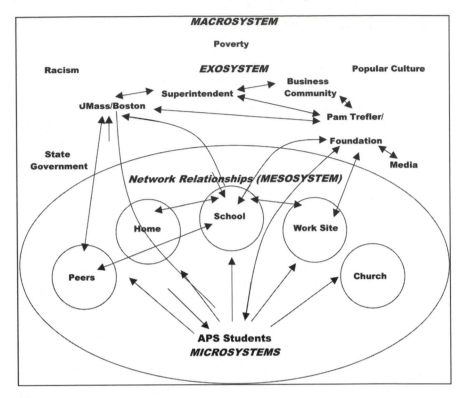

Figure 11.1   APS at the center of the ecological system.

strong and each individual setting shares the same message, the subject of the spotlight (in this case, the students and the program) will prosper. This was exactly what happened in APS.

APS supports the notion that a strong network improves student achievement, while also teaching us something about the transfer of power and the issue of scaling up successful reforms. Trefler was unique as a funder in that she wanted to be personally involved in the work with students. Once the success of APS was firmly demonstrated, Trefler's focus shifted to the entire high school. She funded the UMB/Dorchester High School partnership, and helped restructure the entire high school in the APS model. Soon after, in an effort to scale up this successful re-form, she reached out to the district to fund similar partnerships with high schools across the city. Eventually, she was working at the level of the superintendent and putting pressure on his office to support high school reform. Inevitably, APS saw less and less of her presence and her personalized, face-to-face work with students and teachers ceased.

What happened here was that when Trefler shifted the focus of her work through the foundation, she shifted the spotlight of development in other directions. We can say that in the early days, she was focused on the student. With greater resources, she focused on APS and contributed mightily to the development of this small learning community. Later, with the one million dollar gift, the focus of her spotlight was the entire high school and, still later, on the district high schools. With each shift of the spotlight, we must ask, "How do the face-to-face settings of the developing person shift? What happens to the interconnections within the network? This is not easy to answer. We cannot correctly say that "Pam Trefler developed APS" for the institution does not initiate and maintain relationships. Development must always focus on the individual and on human relationships. Perhaps it is correct to say that her focus shifted to the core teachers of APS. If so, then what were their face-to-face relationships? They met with each other and they met with students and parents. They met, reluctantly, with school administrators and, in this case, they did not share the same message. When Trefler removed herself from the teacher's network to work at the level of the exosystem (with the superintendent and district leaders) her influence was diminished because she no longer had face-to-face relationships with school administrators. Like most funders, she was now a part of the exosystem, communicating with some APS teachers but only indirectly with students.

Lesson Learned for troubled urban schools:

Sometimes members of the exosystem reach out to higher and higher levels of the educational hierarchy in an effort to scale up a specific educational reform or to gain some control over the outcomes at the local level. This is a noble goal, but runs the risk of undermining the original local school partnership. Partners can end up removing themselves from the students' and sometimes the teachers' networks of support, transferring the power of their resources away form the school rather than to the school. This reduces the capacity of the targeted individuals (in this case the teachers and students) and this, in turn, reduces the developmental potential of the reform effort.

PARTNERS CANNOT WORK WITH ONLY ONE SCHOOL CONSTITUENT: SCHOOL LEADERS ARE PART OF A WHOLE SCHOOL COMMUNITY

The work that the Northeast Region and Islands Educational Laboratory (LAB) at Brown University did with DHS in the late 1990s seemed promising. Born out of national education policy and funded by Carnegie, The LAB, as a representative of *Breaking Ranks,* was part of the school's exosystem. The LAB project at DHS was well funded and the idea of aligning the school with the 82 recommendations of *Breaking Ranks* seemed like a great idea. On the surface, this was the most comprehensive and research-based plan for whole school change ever seen at

DHS. The goals of the LAB were to improve student learning and achievement by working with teachers to examine student achievement data and then use those data to align their curriculum and teaching with the accreditation standards of the New England Association of Schools and Colleges. The LAB believed that when teachers work with student data they can raise student achievement significantly. Despite these beliefs, the bulk of attention from LAB staff was devoted to the head-master and the assistant headmaster. Contact with teachers was so infrequent that they often forgot what the *Breaking Ranks* project was. There was no contact with students.

Do the best investments in education always have to be student centered? We believe the answer is no. However, in keeping with the ecological systems model, when a member of the exosystem shines the spotlight on a set of individuals within a school, such as teachers, their efforts will be enhanced if they also become a member of those individuals' other networks of support. For example, if the LAB consciously chose to work with the headmaster and the assistant headmaster as the developing persons, their efforts would have the most benefit if they also worked with those who have direct, face-to-face contact with these individuals, such as teachers, counselors, the district, and the union. For instance, the assistant headmaster met daily with the headmaster and other school administrators, teachers, and students, whereas the LAB interacted only with the headmaster. We now know that development is maximized when messages across the network are complementary. Unfortunately, after an investment of three years, no one was developed at all, and the LAB failed in their efforts to effect real change at the school.

Lesson Learned for troubled urban schools:

Two things prevent an educational reform from taking hold within a troubled school: One, the partner also needs to maintain contact with the other individuals with whom the developing person has face-to-face relations. Two, in order to impact teachers, students, or school leaders, school partners must work directly not only with them, but also with all members of the teacher and student microsystems. Putting teachers or school leaders in the spotlight is an acceptable goal for a partner; however, working with these individuals in isolation, outside of their whole network, prevents the spread of a consistent cultural message across the network thus diminishing the work overall.

STUDENT SUCCESS DEPENDS UPON COMMUNICATION ACROSS THE SCHOOL COMMUNITY

Another example that will help us see this more clearly, and provide a useful contrast to the work of the Northeast Regional LAB and the

Academy of Public Service, is the work of the Institute for Student Achievement (ISA) in the late 1990s. ISA came to DHS through the mediation of Charlie Desmond at UMB, as did the LAB. Both were multi-year investments. However, ISA took a different approach. This program was based on campus and met with students daily. In this way, ISA was similar to the Academy of Public Service. We can ask the two critical questions. Who was the focus of the spotlight? In this case, the sixty students were clearly the focus of the program (although the actual sixty fluctuated somewhat over four years because of the high student mobility rate at DHS). So, unlike the LAB, the Institute for Student Achievement was on target, given the terms of its core mission to raise student achievement and get students into college.

However, in terms of its work with the student's network of support, ISA failed to take an ecological approach to student improvement, missing an opportunity to have a real impact. In contrast with the students in APS who spent at least half the day with their teachers, the students in ISA saw their core teachers after school or for brief periods of time during the day, such as lunch. ISA students still had relationships with six other Dorchester High School teachers, who often had different expectations and who communicated a different message. The ecological model stipulates that communication between the ISA teachers and the student's other teachers is necessary for optimal growth and development. The same thing happened with the student's peer relations. The APS students spent much of the day with a cohort of proud peers; the ISA students had far more opportunities to mingle and relate with non-ISA students throughout the day. ISA would have had a stronger program if they could have found a way to either create a peer network among their students or if they could have included the rest of the school in their program.

Furthermore, the networks of the APS and ISA students were quite different. APS teachers met with each other daily and managed to interact with the rest of the DHS teachers who had the same students when necessary. They were diligent to meet with DHS administrators whenever the core goals of the APS program were challenged. In contrast, the DHS staff often commented that they didn't know what ISA was doing. Many DHS teachers who had the same students were uninformed and the DHS administrative team went for weeks without contact with ISA. ISA functioned independently out in the satellites, further preventing communication, which is vital to the developmental success of the student. Thus, the ISA students ultimately did not prosper.

Lesson Learned for troubled urban schools:

The partner may have the student firmly in the spotlight, but if they work only with students, and not across the student's other microsystems, success will be minimal.

THE EXOSYSTEM IS POWERFUL PART ONE: IT CAN TRANSFORM SCHOOLS WITHOUT KNOWING IT

The above examples demonstrate the potential of the exosystem when its members are focused on working for school change. It is very important to note, however, that the exosystem also impacts schools when its members are not focused on school change. Sometimes the exosystem acts in opposition to the local school system, and sometimes it acts without an awareness of the local school system. In either case, these actions can cause great damage to local schools. Operation Exodus from the late 1960s provides us with an example of the exosystem acting in opposition to the schools. As we have seen throughout this history, one reason the exosystem is so powerful is because it has the ability, and the resources, to pull itself together and act as one when necessary. The exosystem does this by creating networks among various constituencies, who then act with one voice. When the middle class black parents of Boston got frustrated with the fight over desegregation going on above them at the legislative and court levels, they first began to organize within their own microsystem, or community of other concerned middle-class black parents, and transported their children to better schools within Boston. This got the attention of the media, who began publishing which schools had open seats. Through the media, the black parents got the attention of the surrounding suburban communities, who opened their doors to black children from the city. They also, finally, got the attention of the state legislature, this time for their own cause, which appropriated state dollars to pay for the newly formed METCO program.

These disparate microsystems—black middle class parents, the media, suburban middle-class communities, and the state legislature—in essence formed a new network of connected communities that then worked together to effect change for black children. Why were they able to do this fairly quickly and easily? One answer has to do with their shared culture. All the members of this newly formed network shared middle-class cultural values. Along with shared cultural values come shared knowledge and ideals, and a similar use of language. This is not to say that the motivations of all constituents were noble. Some members were acting out of fear that the state would sanction two-way city-suburban busing. Others were acting out of a sense of "liberal" white guilt. Despite their different agendas, their shared middle-class culture afforded them an underlying familiarity through which they could negotiate and combine their various agendas. This collaboration ended up having a profound impact, not only upon Dorchester High School but also on all of the schools in Boston. In effect, it removed middle-class and active and involved black parents from the Boston Public school system. Sadly, this was the last time that black parents in Boston were able to organize across constituents for positive change for their children.

The ecological systems model offers us one explanation for why black parents today have difficulty organizing in similar ways. The majority of children who attend the most entrenched urban high schools are from working-class or poor families. These families are not as well versed in the middle-class ways of doing things. They do not share the same kinds of knowledge, ideals, and uses of language as the middle-class constituents who run the major organizations that make up the exosystem. This prevents them from communicating in effective ways, not only with their children's teachers, guidance counselors, and tutors, but also with the business, higher education, and government organizations that may be working in their children's schools. Unfortunately, members of the exosystem seldom seek out the families and parents of urban adolescents as part of their work with urban high schools. Also unfortunate is the loss of middle-class, black parents, who are better able to advocate effectively for their children, from many of these schools. The parents of students at the Dorchester High School of today would have a much more difficult time repeating what it took to get Operation Exodus off the ground. The parents of today's urban high school students cannot advocate for their children in isolation. Just as they did in the late 1960s, they need the exosystem to partner with them for the optimal growth and optimal development of their children.

Ironically, the same business community that helped Boston's schools get back on track in the late 1980s really derailed progress at Dorchester High School in the late 1960s. The Boston Banks Urban Renewal Group (BBURG) created by leaders from the banking industry completely and rapidly disrupted the community surrounding DHS. The BBURG housing experiment demonstrates what can happen when other, more powerful segments of a city act without regard for local communities and local school systems. When business leaders take ownership of what happens within the local school district, as they did in Boston in the late 1980s, they will, it is hoped, become more aware of how their actions impact local schools. An ecological systems model does more than simply encourage members of the exosystem to take ownership of schools and communities. Rather, it urges them to become active, interacting participants with schools and communities. Once the business community becomes a member of a school's and a community's network of support, it is hoped that they would more carefully weigh the impact of their actions on schools and other community members.

What the history of Dorchester High School teaches us is that no school stands alone. It might look like some schools are able to fix themselves when problems arise or to easily adjust to the challenges of every national mandate that comes along, but what we are really seeing in these cases is the work of a underlying, unified, and cohesive culture, invisibly holding the community together. Schools in these communities are one link in a solid chain. When the internal culture of a high school mirrors the culture of a majority of the students' homes, the culture of the neighborhood in which the school is located, and the culture of the wider community, then what looks like a stand alone institution is really only one member of a strong network of support.

When the internal culture of a high school is dysfunctional or broken, or when the culture of a school differs markedly from the culture of the children's' homes and the surrounding neighborhood, the school simply will not function for the optimal growth and development of students, teachers, or school leaders. In this case, strong networks of support have to be consciously built around each individual and around the school as an institution. The exosystem plays a crucial role by providing a safe network of support, juxtaposing alternative healthy cultural values, and allowing teachers to tentatively let go of toxic cultural beliefs and to consider change in the direction of the new practices. Members of the exosystem accomplish this by maintaining connections and relationships with teachers, students, school leaders, and families. It is these connections and relationships, along with a cohesive and shared culture, that hold the school community together and that ensure optimal growth and development for students and other school constituents.

THE EXOSYSTEM IS POWERFUL PART TWO: IT CAN BE A STRONG FORCE FOR CHANGE WHEN ALL THE POWERS ALIGN

One of the most important lessons this history offers for other troubled school systems is that alignment among major decisions makers is crucial for educational reform to take hold. Looking at one school over time reveals who the major decision makers were, what drove their decisions and how those decisions ultimately impacted individual schools. Between 1953 and 1967 the major decision makers in terms of what happened in the schools were the Boston School Committee, the Federal courts, the State Legislature, the National Association for the Advancement of Colored People (NAACP), and local black and white parents. The School Committee made six major decisions during this time; of those, four focused on school facilities, one was a management-based decision, i.e., to add an assistant headmaster position to DHS in 1966, and one was a standards-based decision, to require the Metropolitan Achievement Tests in all Boston high schools. The School Committee was acting alone in making these decisions. The NAACP, the Federal Courts, the State Legislature and the local black community were also major decisions makers during this period. These four decision makers were aligned by their goal of achieving equity in the public schools. The decisions around equity began in 1954 when the NAACP sued in federal court. That same year, the Supreme Court decided in their favor in *Brown v. Board of Education*. In 1963, the NAACP supported the decision of

Boston's black parents to file a *de facto* segregation complaint with the Boston School Committee. Two years later, in 1965, the Massachusetts State Legislature passed the Racial Imbalance Act, which gave the State Board of Education the authority to withhold funding from schools that were racially imbalanced. Finally, in 1966, Boston's black parents, working with their white suburban counterparts, decided to form the METCO program that bused black students from Boston to schools in the surrounding suburbs. METCO had a tremendous impact on the schools by removing black middle-class families from the Boston Public School system. Note that the alignment of forces from local families up through the federal courts eventually overcame the racist tactics of the Boston School Committee.

The goal of achieving equity dominated school-based decision making until about 1974. Between 1968 and 1974, the School Committee made three decisions that impacted DHS directly. In the fight against desegregation, they voted to add the ninth grade to DHS, almost doubling the student population. In 1969, they added the satellite buildings to DHS to accommodate the new students. Finally, in 1974, they voted to hire special education and bilingual teachers at DHS. These decisions were all made in reaction to the push for equity. These decisions demonstrate how DHS became the focal point of the system's attempt to keep black students out of the other high schools. The NAACP, federal courts, and state legislature were still cooperating to push the Boston Public Schools toward a more equitable system. The NAACP filed Boston's famous desegregation suit in 1972 and the federal courts ruled two years later to force desegregation through busing. The state legislature amended the Racial Imbalance Act in 1974 to provide funding as an incentive for schools to reduce racial segregation.

It was also during this period that the business community and school partners became active. In 1972, the business community worked with the School Committee in an attempt to change the management structure of the BPS by transferring more power to the superintendent. At the local level, New English Telephone (NET) was forming the first business-school partnership in the country with DHS. Between 1969 and 1974, NET provided leadership training to DHS teachers and funded internships for students at company headquarters. At this point, the business community had yet to align their efforts for school change. They were still working individually with either the School Committee or local schools.

Up to this point the groups cited above were the only major players making school-based decisions. Except for their decision to form a union, the teachers were mostly silent. City government, higher education, and the BPS superintendent were conspicuously silent when it came to making decisions that would impact the schools. An interesting thing happened between 1975 and 1983. The federal courts and the business community were still the major players, but their focus shifted from

Table 11.1   The alignment of major decision makers.

Decision Years	1953–62	1963	1964–73	1974	1975–82	1983–92	1992–97	1998–2005
Decision Makers								
School Committee	Facilities '53, '59, '62	Standards (first city-wide test)	Facilities '68, '69	Equity (hires bilingual/SPED teachers)	Management '81	Management '89	Standards '94, '97	
NAACP	Equity '54							
Federal Courts	Equity '54	Equity		Equity	Management '74, '75, '82			
Black Parent Groups		Equity	Equity '66, '72					
Federal Government					Standards '82 (*Nation at Risk*)		Equity '97 (IDEA)	Financial awards '99, '00
State Legislature			Equity '65, '71	Equity (Racial Imbalance Act)	Equity '79	Management '82, '86, '87, '91	Standards '93 (MERA), '94, '97	Standards '01

Business Community	Management '72	Management '78, '79 and Standards '82	Management '84–87	Professional Development '94–96	Financial Awards '98 and Professional Development '00–05
NEASC	Facilities '72	Facilities '82	Standards '92–93, '96–97		Standards '01
School Partners		Standards '80			Financial Awards '98–'05
City and State Government			Management '88–91 (abolish elected SC)		
Superintendent		Standards '81, '82	Standards '85	Standards '93, '95, '96 and Professional Development '93	Management, Standards, and Professional Development '00–05

making equity-based decisions to making management-based decisions. The court created a management structure where businesses and universities would partner with individual high schools that resulted in the Boston Compact. This brought the business and university community together in their work with individual schools. During this time, the state legislature was still making equity-based decisions; they passed laws in 1974 and 1979 increasing school access to special education and bilingual students, so they had not yet joined the business community in their focus on school management.

The state legislature and the business community began to come together around the question of changing the management structure of the Boston Public Schools in 1981 with passage of the Tregor bill, which gave the superintendent the power to hire and fire school leaders. After this, the superintendent finally began making decisions that impacted the local schools. His first decision focused on standards. In 1981, the superintendent instituted a district-wide summative assessment system. The Boston Compact, signed in 1982 between the superintendent and the business community, also focused on raising educational standards. This was a key moment in terms of enacting authentic educational reform in Boston. The state legislature, the courts, the business community, higher education, and the superintendent, if not the School Committee, were finally aligned in their efforts to reform the Boston Public Schools.

This alignment was strengthened over the next ten years. The business community began funding education reform projects almost immediately. Between 1983 and 1987 they gave millions of dollars to the BPS. The State Legislature remained a major player, passing legislation that strengthened the superintendent's role in 1986 and 1987. Even the teachers union came on board by joining the Boston Compact and opening the door for more reform in the BPS. School partnerships with businesses and universities exploded during this time. By 1993, DHS had over thirty partnering relationships with organizations throughout the city. Even the city and state government got involved by pushing for an appointed School Committee in 1988. By 1991, the elected School Committee was thrown out by a citywide election, giving the mayor control of the schools through an appointed School Committee. All the major decisions made during this period were management-based. Once again, it was the alignment of powerful forces that finally changed the management of the Boston Public School system. Boston now had an appointed School Committee, which set the stage for the focus on educational standards that began to take hold in 1993 (see Table 11.1 on p. 178).

At this point, the stars were truly aligned. All the decisions made by key players between 1993 and 2003 were standards-based. In 1993 the state legislature passed the Massachusetts Education Reform Act (MERA) that called for a high-stakes graduation exam. The superintendent and the union reached a new collective bargaining agreement that called for more frequent teacher evaluations and the creation of pilot schools that could operate under relaxed union rules. The superintendent introduced citywide learning standards and a five-year education reform plan. The business community continued to give money, but they also began developing and supporting professional development programs for BPS teachers. Without the elected School Committee, which was more beholden to Boston's parents and families, the business community, the superintendent, and the School Committee could now work, basically unchallenged, for educational reform in the city's schools. This was a necessary step that we are convinced would not have happened without the alignment of the members of the exosystem. The Massachusetts Education Reform Act (MERA) toughened educational standards, raised teacher quality, and tied improvement to the examination of school data. All are vital components of a comprehensive educational reform plan. However, thirteen years into MERA it seems that the business approach to educational reform has become all-consuming. The voices calling for more of a balance between standards and social and life skills have not just been drowned out; they have been lost. We will discuss the impact of this in the final chapter.

Lesson Learned for troubled urban schools:

Examining the decisions made by powerful players at the state and local level in Boston demonstrates the incredible power of the exosystem to effect change. We have seen how schools are impacted for good or ill when the exosystem aligns. The progression of the motivators for change is also telling. The key decision makers moved from being motivated by equity concerns, to management concerns, and finally to concerns about educational standards. Other communities who are struggling to enact lasting educational reform should take note of the process that finally brought about real change in Boston. Our hope is that the next motivator will be relationship building and connections between schools, students' homes, and the power brokers of society. The exosystem is powerful; it can bring these settings together.

CHAPTER 12

Consider the Challenges of Urban Adolescents

We have seen that, all too often, those young people who attend our most troubled urban high schools live in settings that are disconnected from each other. Their community is fragmented. They may have supportive parents, yet be neglected and bullied at school because they are quiet and not disruptive and because their parents don't know how to navigate the system on their children's behalf. They may have strong relationships at school, but be isolated in their neighborhoods and neglected at home. Their homes may be supportive, but burdened by poverty and single parenthood, making it difficult for their parents to maintain strong connections with the school. All too often it seems that urban students trapped in failing high schools have been abandoned to sink or swim on their own. We have seen that in 60 years, despite many reform efforts and millions of dollars in investments, student academic outcomes never really improved at Dorchester High School. When student outcomes did improve they did so only in small, teacher created and teacher run learning communities: that is, in "units" within the school that had "a separate status and some independent powers although still constituting part of the parent"[1] school. The history of DHS affords us some insight into the experiences of students who attend failing urban high schools. This chapter outlines some of the major problems a subset of our urban students face at urban high schools. We then offer some recommendations for rebuilding the community around young people.

THE GOOD NEWS

The good news is that as a nation we have really matured in our efforts to address the many problems that plague urban high schools. We now have a tremendous amount of research on what promotes effective instruction and student engagement. We know more about the impact of teaching and teacher knowledge on student learning. We have several models of what successful urban high schools look like, allowing us to escape the one size fits all paradigm.[2] We finally understand the power of data, which has allowed both Republicans and Democrats to agree on the need for standards and accountability, even if we do not yet agree on how to implement those standards or how to hold schools accountable. Finally, real money has been put on the table to restructure high schools into caring and attentive communities that truly engage students while raising expectations that all students can successfully complete a more challenging and rigorous curriculum with the right student and teacher supports.[3]

Although many of these initiatives are fairly new, the data on their success to date have been promising. We define success as measurable improvements in academic achievement, in student engagement with school, in dropout rates, and in graduation and college attendance rates. So far we have seen the most improvement in terms of academic achievement. Data from the 2005 state assessments mandated by the No Child Left Behind Act and the federal National Assessment of Educational Progress exams show marked improvement in the reading and math scores of urban fourth and eighth graders. Unfortunately, the scores of urban high school students do not show similar gains and urban schools still lag behind their suburban counterparts. Despite the slower progress at the high school level, the Council of Great City Schools reported in 2006 that the achievement gaps between racial and ethnic groups "appear to be narrowing."[4] These data leave us hopeful that the academic trends evident in fourth and eighth grade can and will persist into high school. We still do not have reliable measures to determine true dropout, graduation, and college attendance rates.

THE BAD NEWS: A CONCENTRATION OF INDICATORS OF FAILURE IN URBAN HIGH SCHOOLS

Despite these improvements in our efforts to reform urban high schools, there remains a class of inner-city high schools that has proven impervious to reform. These schools have the lowest attendance rates; the lowest test scores, the lowest graduation rates, and the highest mobility and dropout rates. Many of the students who attend these high schools are not reading on grade level; their math scores on state assessments are extremely low; many of the students are court involved or from homes plagued by drug abuse, poverty, and violence. The majorities of students who attend these schools are African American and Latino, are immigrants, and are poor. Robert Balfanz and Nettie Legters have created a measure to identify some of these schools. They call it "promoting power, which compares the number of freshmen at a high school to the number of seniors four years later."[5] Using this measure to identify those high schools that had "sixty percent or fewer seniors then freshman" they found 2000 failing high schools in this country. These persistently failing high schools make up 18 percent of all high schools in this country and educate over 2.5 million students. Where are these schools located?

> What is significant about promoting power in many of the nation's largest cities, however, is not the number of high schools with weak promoting power but their concentration. In half of the nation's largest 100 cities, fifty percent or more of high school students...attend high schools with weak promoting power. In twenty-one cities, this climbs to seventy-five percent of high school students and... [in] 2000 it reached an incredible 100 percent in [two cities].[6]

As to who these students are, Balfanz and Legters point out, "the nation's dropout factories are overwhelmingly the province of minority students."[7]

In 2001, Dorchester High School had the highest dropout rate in the city and the state, at 26 percent. This should not have been a surprise to anyone, and in fact was quite predictable. We know that students who have a history of academic failure are more likely to drop out of high school.[8] At DHS, 60 percent of the students entering the school as freshman had failed two or more core classes in the eighth grade. This includes English, math, social studies, and science. In short, they were unprepared for high school. Students with weak academic skills often get retained in one or more grades before entering high school. Often, these students find themselves in ninth grade at the age of seventeen. The older a student is when he enters high school, the more likely he will be to drop out.[9] Nationwide, we know that the poorer a school district, the higher the dropout rate.

Before Dorchester High School was broken down into small schools, 76 percent of the students were low-income and on the federally funded free or reduced lunch program. The two new small schools that replaced DHS have 66 percent and 53 percent of low-income children. Schools that have high percentages of minority students have higher dropout rates.[10] In 2001, 3 percent of the students at DHS were white. We know that the higher the percentage of special education programs in a school the higher that school's dropout rate.[11] Near the end, the special education population at DHS was about 32 percent. That was when the school had over 950 students enrolled. Three years into the small school structure, the Noonan Business Academy still has a 32 percent special education population out of about 270 students. The special education population at APS is a bit higher, at 33 percent out of 310 students. We also know that students who transfer to a new high school are more likely to drop out of school.[12] In the last year, Dorchester high school had a 43 percent mobility rate. Last, students who have poor attendance rates also tend to have higher dropout rates.[13] The attendance rate at DHS in 2002, and at the new small schools now, is about 80 percent.

Students who display these kind of academic indicators often suffer from other social, emotional, and behavioral difficulties. As one teacher from DHS explained,

> We have fifty to sixty kids in the [Learning and Adaptive Behavior] cluster [designed for kids with emotional/behavioral problems]. We have The Accelerated Academy program [for older age students] that is probably the most challenging program in the school. The kids run amuck. They are all over the building. They answer to no one. Now that's 240 kids in the building who are discipline problems and who have social problems. That's 240 problems right there. We have 300 special education kids in the building total. So we have almost 600 students in the school who have special needs out of a population of about 986 kids. That leaves about 386 students who can be considered to be your average high school adolescent.

The level of failure evident on all of these indicators screams out to us, not only because so many kids are suffering, but, more importantly, because a very large percentage of these students are concentrated in one school. As the promoting power data indicate, there are schools like this in major cities all over the country. Like DHS, these schools become the dumping ground schools in their respective cities. We focus on the dropout data because high schools with large numbers of dropouts are high schools where students are suffering. How can we sit back and let over 2.5 million children suffer silently in this nation's urban high schools? Why are we allowing these children to languish in failing schools?

ACADEMIC ACHIEVEMENT IS POSSIBLE

It does not have to be this way. We know what works in terms of educating students who attend high-minority and high-poverty inner-city schools. Research on these "high impact" schools is consistent and encouraging,[14] even when high impact schools are not successful across the board.

> They are not yet among the highest-performing schools in their respective states or even where their staffs hope they will be soon in terms of student proficiency. In fact, most still have a long way to go. But they have been able to make greater than expected gains with previously underperforming students.[15]

Nevertheless, these schools have several characteristics in common. They have a strong internal culture that is shared by all the staff in the building. These adults convey a consistent message to the students throughout the school day. The instructional focus is paramount.

Academics, rather than school rules, are emphasized. The outside organizations that partner with these schools focus on college and career preparation by providing internships and other authentic experiences for growing adolescents.[16] By contrast, the partnerships of average schools tended to focus exclusively on the social and emotional needs of students. Teacher collaboration focused on student work is the norm. Data drive most decision-making. For these schools,

> data are not mere numbers collected for accountability purposes but human stories. Data help them identify the child whose reading score shows that without careful help and instruction he will lead a life of dependency and insecurity. Data reveal to them the teacher who is expert in teaching statistics and probability but hasn't figured out how to teach measurement. Data tell them when a program they have instituted is having the effect they intended or whether it wasn't worth the time put into it. Data, in other words, is information about people that is used with meticulous care.[17]

We believe an ecological approach to current reform efforts could push these schools into the high achieving realm. For example, school partners need not have a single focus when working with needy high schools. They can work with schools to tackle both academics and the social and emotional needs of students. We will recommend ways that schools can begin to take a more ecological approach at the end of this chapter. First, there are two more aspects of the experience of attending troubled urban high schools for us to consider.

THE PROBLEMS ASSOCIATED WITH ATTENDING A TROUBLED URBAN HIGH SCHOOL

Difficult Transitions from Middle to High School

Dorchester High School was one of the least chosen schools in the city for about the last twenty years of its existence. Unfortunately, the two new small schools that took its place are now suffering the same fate. The whole high school community is diminished when first-year students do not enter the building with excitement and enthusiasm for attending their new school. The students' initial lack of enthusiasm for DHS appears to stem from the reputation of the surrounding neighborhood and the overall community of Dorchester as it is portrayed in the media. Unfortunately, the area surrounding the school is one of the most violent areas in the city. The school's location within the Dorchester neighborhood, and the fact that it shares the neighborhood's namesake, ends up infecting the reputation of the school itself. Unfortunately, most of the students know that their fellow classmates did not choose the school, causing further damage to their own sense of self-worth. As one student explained, "I didn't want to come here. They said it was like a fight school. All these bad stuff happen there."

What we need to understand is that the transition from middle to high school is very difficult. Young adolescents entering high school look forward to having more choices and making new and more friends; however, they also are concerned about being picked on and teased by older students, having harder work, making lower grades, and getting lost in a larger, unfamiliar school.[18] These fears are exacerbated for young adolescents at DHS for two reasons. One, their preconceptions of the school have been tainted by the larger reputation of the neighborhood, and two, because of the choice system, many students enter high school without their established friendship groups. When students experience a difficult or fearful transition to high school it impacts their academic achievement. They often experience a decline in grades and attendance;[19] they tend to view themselves more negatively and experience an increased need for friendships.

Difficulty Making Real and Lasting Friendships in High School

Sadly, the need for friendship is especially difficult to fulfill at DHS. The quality of the friendships described by DHS students is very troubling. Much research has been done on the impact of adolescent friendships. For example, having close friends contributes to the social adjustment of students. Students who report having close and supportive friends have higher self-esteem, and a healthy sense of self-worth is dependent on having friends.[20] Friendship and peer acceptance has been linked to children's level of success when making transitions into a new school environment.[21] Also "disturbances in self-concept and social adjustment are reduced when school changes occur in the company of one's good friends."[22] Because of Boston's choice assignment system, DHS freshmen are separated from their established middle school friendship groups when they enter high school; they then enter an environment where the students are suspicious and fearful of their own peers, thus making it very difficult to establish new friendships. This type of fear also leads to social isolation. Research shows us that by the end of 10th grade, as many as 6 percent of isolated students drop out of school.[23] Experiencing a difficult transition from middle school to high school surely impacts the high dropout rates that plague many troubled urban high schools.

Another important dimension of adolescent friendships is that similarities among adolescent friends have been found to increase over time thus having a direct impact on social adjustment.[24] A host of research has demonstrated that the "company one keeps" influences behavior and social adjustment.[25] "Friends contribute either positively or negatively to adolescent socialization. Because friendships derive only partly from choice: whether two individuals become friends depends on their opportunity to meet, and which individuals meet depends on the organization of their social world."[26] Unfortunately, the student social world at DHS is not one that is conducive to high levels of student achievement; thus it has the potential to reinforce negative socialization toward high achievement. The reader may recall Steinberg et al., quoted in Chapter 10, who concluded that the peer group undermines the efforts of black parents in terms of school achievement.

Just before DHS was converted to three small high schools, we saw that the students' perceptions of their peers were negative, judgmental, and intolerant. They were also afraid of their peers. As one student said, "you can't put black people in the same place for more than an hour. We just can't get along. We should not be in the same place." Holding these kinds of attitudes about one's peers, about the people who look like oneself, is internalized racism. Internalized racism impacts an individuals' own level of self-esteem. The beliefs and attitudes exhibited by the students at DHS are examples of internalized racism at work. Internalized racism has been given as one explanation for the achievement gap between African American and Latino students and white students.[27]

People who grew up, or who now live, in the suburbs would simply be aghast at this situation. Many suburban children go to school with the same set of peers for their entire twelve years. In many cases, the friendships that suburban children formed in high school remain for a lifetime. In contrast, the children who live in the city get separated from their peers at two points, between fifth and sixth grade when they have to choose a middle school, and then again between eighth and ninth grade when they have to choose a high school. These difficult transitions are eased for those children who have parents at home who are helping them make the choice, and guiding them to a school that fits their child's needs.

Unfortunately, this is a problem whose solution is not as easy as it seems. There is no one person or institution to blame, or who could easily fix this situation. There are three facts that lead to this problem. One, the kids who end up at DHS do not have anybody at home to help them choose a school or to inquire about what choice the child was making. At best this is due to a lack of knowledge about the school system, or to an inability to speak English. At worst, it is due to inattention, neglect, or indifference. Two, because DHS is located in a poor, violent, and crime ridden neighborhood, a fact that is known across the city, those kids who do have parents who are paying attention would never send their kids to DHS. We have already reported that those families who live near DHS send their children to West Roxbury, South Boston, and East Boston, quite a distance from home, rather than send them the few blocks to DHS. Three, when all the other schools get filled by the children whose parents are overseeing their educational choices, Dorchester High School is left with empty seats. This is where the late choosers or the no choosers end up. This is why DHS is filled with court appointed children, children who didn't get their forms in, and children who enter the system late. Many of these struggles are the result of poverty and its consequences.

The Many Impacts of Poverty

The impact of poverty on academic achievement and school behavior has become clearer and clearer over the last decade. Unfortunately, many middle-class whites, including teachers, still struggle with understanding two aspects of poverty. First, those who live in poverty over long periods of time begin to develop norms and beliefs that shape their approach to life. These cultural norms and beliefs make it more difficult for the poor to function in mainstream society.[28] Second, race and poverty are not the same thing, but this fact gets confused in the minds of many middle-class people.[29] In other words, there is a culture of poverty that shapes behavior, and this culture is often confused as being a "black" or race-based culture when it really is a culture of the poor.

The interrelationships between class and race are important to understand because both race and class work to shape the various cultural backgrounds of blacks and whites in this country. The classroom is one place where the cultural differences between blacks and whites gets highlighted, especially the urban classroom. In discussions of class and race there is often the urge to privilege one over the other. However, the privileging of either race or class as the major force behind black oppression is misleading. As shapers of culture, the two are intimately related and perhaps equally influential. Raymond Franklin illustrates the interrelationship of race and class in black oppression:

> The present state of the race-class debate remains confused or misinterpreted because it fails to embrace the interplay between black overcrowding in the lower class where race and class are sometimes fused and "pure" racial discrimination in the middle and upper ranges of the economic hierarchy where class differences defined in terms of income, occupation, and education may be absent. This, of course, does not imply the absence of racial criteria in the determination of the status of the black poor...poor blacks suffer from the burdens of race and class simultaneously, while poor whites suffer from that of class....The overrepresentation of blacks in the lower class casts shadows that stigmatize working- and middle-class blacks for reasons of race alone.[30]

One reason for the salience of race and class is that they manifest themselves as visible markers of cultural difference. For example, Lisa Delpit uses the term "culture of power" to indicate the ideas and norms of middle-class America.[31] She says, "children from middle-class homes tend to do better in school than those from non-middle-class homes because the culture of the school is based on the culture of the upper and middle classes—of those in power."[32] She defines the culture of power as "codes or rules...that relate to linguistic forms, communicative strategies, and presentation of self; that is, ways of talking, ways of writing, ways of dressing, and ways of interacting."[33] Thus the culture of power, as with other cultures, is detected by the visible and audible manifestations of language (linguistic forms and communicative strategies) and class which are represented in presentations of self. Therefore, when urban teachers explain the "behavioral problems" of black boys in the classroom as a manifestation of their cultural background, they are seeing race and class. As Delpit says, a white student "who exhibits problems is an individual with a problem." A student of color "who exhibits problems immediately becomes a representative of his cultural group."[34]

Poverty and Academic Achievement

Delpit, Shirley Brice Heath, and others demonstrated long ago how cultural differences between teacher and student, based upon the class structure, hurt children academically. The next thing we really have to understand is how poverty is at the root of many of the difficulties students in our most challenging urban schools face. Poverty impacts how students approach writing and story telling;[35] how they speak to their teachers and other adults, and how they handle conflict.[36] Last, as Elijah Anderson, James Garbarino, and others have shown, the use of violence and physical assault to solve interpersonal conflict is more common among poor families. This results in a higher incidence of child abuse and neglect within poor families.[37] This is not because poor parents do not love their children. It happens because the stresses on the life of a poor, most likely single mother, are enormous.[38] "One result of the chronic stress of living in poverty-stricken and violence-ridden communities is that parents cannot meet the needs of their children. Depressed, overwhelmed, and their own needs unmet, such parents are not able to care for or nurture their children adequately."[39]

Teachers and other school personnel must pay attention to these consequences of poverty, for we now know how damaging violence and neglect are to the academic ability and cognitive functioning of children.

> For some children, a safe community and school may help buffer the impact of violence in the home. The highest-risk children, however, are safe no where; their home is chaotic and episodically abusive, their community is fragmented and plagued by gang violence and the schools are barely capable of providing structure and safety from intimidation and threat. These children must adapt to this atmosphere of fear. Persisting fear and the neurophysiological adaptations to this fear can alter the development of the child's brain, resulting in changes in physiological, emotional, behavioral, cognitive, and social functioning.[40]

Our most challenging urban high schools, like Dorchester High School, are filled with children who live under these stressful conditions, and the developing brain especially is extremely sensitive to stress. Abuse and neglect alter the brain in very specific ways by damaging those brain structures most crucial for learning. For example, abuse and neglect damage the cortex, which controls rational thinking and the hippocampus, which regulates emotions and memories. Both are smaller and underdeveloped in abused and neglected children.[41] The corpus callosum, a bundle of fibers that allows the left side of the brain to communicate with the right side, is also smaller in abused and neglected children. "The result of a smaller corpus callosum can be that children can 'reside' in one hemisphere of the brain, rather than shifting seamlessly between the two.... A lot of individuals who have survived childhood trauma reside in their left hemisphere when they function well. But when traumatic thoughts arise, they retreat into their right.... They can get very emotional, without any of the logic of the left side there to guide them."[42]

Verbal abuse is equally as damaging.[43] Much of the damage results from changes in the chemistry of the brain. It turns out that our experiences release a host of chemicals that wash over the brain. Positive experiences release chemicals that keep the brain healthy, while too many negative experiences release chemicals that inhibit brain growth. "Positive experiences that contradict a traumatized child's negative expectations are critical to helping the brain to readjust itself. For example, just saying to a child that you are sorry the event happened changes brain chemistry."[44] That quote is worth repeating. Simply "telling a child that you are sorry" that a traumatic event happened to him or her "changes brain chemistry." Teachers should know that a kind word and some emotional support to children who are suffering in silence can actually have a physical impact on their brain development. Bruce Perry provides us with a good example of how this damage manifests itself in the classroom:

> When a child is in a...state of low-level fear that results from exposure to violence, the primary areas of the brain that are processing information are different from those in a child from a safe environment. The calm child may sit in the same classroom next to the child in an alarm state, both hearing the same lecture by the teacher. Even if they have identical IQ's, the child that is calm can focus on the words of the teacher and, using the neocortex, engage in abstract cognition. The child in an alarm state will be less efficient at processing and storing the verbal information the teacher is providing. This child's cognition will be dominated by [the emotional areas of the brain] focusing on non-verbal information—the teacher's facial expressions, hand gestures, when she seems distracted.... This child will have more selective development of non-verbal cognitive capacities. The children raised in the vortex of violence have learned that non-verbal information is more important than verbal.[45]

Ruby Payne defines poverty as "the extent to which an individual does without resources."[46] She then identifies eight resources that help all people get through life. Those resources are financial, emotional, mental, spiritual, physical, support systems, relationships/role models, and knowledge of hidden roles. Poor families often do not have access to many of these resources. Schooling intersects with at least three of these resources, emotional, mental, and relationship/role models. Students who can read, write, and compute well are better able to think themselves out of difficult situations and to use their cognitive abilities to solve problems and make better and more informed choices about life. Students who can regulate their emotions are better able to navigate daily frustrations without resorting to violence or "self-destructive" behavior.[47] Last, students who develop a strong and healthy relationship with just one adult role model do better in school. "All individuals have role models. The question is the extent to which the role model is nurturing or appropriate....It is largely from role models that the person learns how to live life emotionally."[48] Schooling can play a crucial role in giving poor children access to these vitally important mental, emotional, and relationship resources. One of the major purposes of schooling is to teach children how to acquire mental resources. An ecological systems approach to educational reform makes the provision of emotional and relationship resources central to the goal of educating children.

MAKING SCHOOL CULTURE THE FOCUS OF EDUCATIONAL REFORM

A first step toward doing this is to acknowledge the importance of culture in shaping both individuals and schools. The children who attend our most troubled urban high schools need culturally based and community-based reforms that involve health care and mental health services, violence prevention, mediation, and family intervention services. We already know how to provide these services, mostly outside of the high school context. When educational reform movements began to focus on improving academics in the 1980s, urban high schools, which were very far behind their suburban counterparts in terms of offering students a rigorous curriculum, began doubling up on the core academic courses such as English and math. Before we knew it, out of six or seven periods a day, urban students were required to take two periods of English and two periods of math, leaving the other periods for science, history and if they were lucky, an elective. There is no longer any room for art, music, and other activities to be built into the school day. Students who want to participate in these activities have to stay after school. A very challenging task when the school is located in a violent and unsafe neighborhood, and further complicated by students' other family and work responsibilities.

Led by the business community, we came to believe that after school programs, community organizations, and health care institutions could focus exclusively on the social and emotional needs of urban high school students and that schools should only have to focus on academics. We cannot, we must not, continue this separation. Anyone who works in troubled urban high schools knows that the vast majority of students, no matter how distressed, go to school every day—willingly! They go to school for safety, for friendship, for food, and for adult attention and often for learning. Yes, the schools these children attend need to be reformed. We can reform them with a mix of cultural, curricular, and structural reforms. We can keep academics at the forefront without taking away those life enhancing aspects of schooling that make school relevant and engaging for students.

As we have seen from the success of the three small learning communities that grew up at Dorchester High School, there are many organizations and institutions working to improve troubled urban high schools. They provide countless hours of service, many needed materials and sometimes vast resources to improve schools for all stakeholders, especially students. Oftentimes, after years of effort, many of these reforms fail to achieve authentic academic improvement for students. We argue that it is time for the imaginations, materials, and resources of outside partners to be redirected toward the student's face-to-face settings (the home and the workplace) toward what is needed to ensure optimal growth and development for the student (activities, trips, and opportunities to take on various roles) and toward repairing school cultures and building relational trust. The following six cultural reforms, enacted in genuine and authentic ways, can help us get there.

THE IMPACT OF KNOWLEDGE, BELIEFS AND ATTITUDES

In most cases, failing inner-city schools in impoverished neighborhoods did not lose so much ground over night. As the history of DHS demonstrates, there is a long, slow decline, with a few bright spots. As part of any school history, everyone usually remembers when "things were good" and when the school worked for teachers and students. The history of failing schools often becomes idolized, but not utilized to reflect on and improve the present. The knowledge, beliefs, and attitudes that school personnel have about parents, families, and neighborhoods are often forged through a school's historical experiences. The beginnings of cultural change are also rooted in a school's history. This is why cultural reform is so crucial to the task of explicitly helping school personnel mine their past and uncover the meaning behind the beliefs and attitudes they hold about parents and families. The negative beliefs and attitudes that some urban teachers have, particularly of African American parents, has been well documented in the literature.[49] It has been demonstrated that racial and ethnic differences, especially between African American students and families and white school personnel make it even more difficult to build trust in schools.[50] The tensions that spring up around racial and ethnic misunderstandings make it more difficult to implement certain educational reforms.[51]

Cultivating relationships and building trust across these types of interpersonal divides is extremely complex but necessary work. Resources are needed to help schools uncover, discuss, and reflect upon the attitudes and beliefs they harbor toward their students' families and neighborhoods, as well as the level of knowledge they have about the neighborhood, and how these both help and hurt the job of creating an educational environment that provides students with optimal opportunities for growth and development. This problem goes both ways. Given their often conflictual history with schooling, poor parents and families also harbor negative beliefs and attitudes about teachers and their children's schools. Their knowledge of school processes and operations is also most likely weak. Improving parent and family involvement is a necessary piece of cultural reform in urban schools. Schools simply cannot do this kind of relationship building within and across their students' face-to-face settings alone. They need the same kind of supports they get to improve school curriculum and structures.

DISTRIBUTING ACCURATE AND UP-TO-DATE INFORMATION AND FOSTERING COMMUNICATION

Transitions are key points in a child's life. The manner in which children experience key transitions can aid or hinder their overall development. For example, when making the transition between middle and high school, students' roles and expectations for themselves shift. This same shift happens among the adults in the student's life. As Bronfenbrenner points out, the possession of accurate and up-to-date information about the new setting facilitates these types of role shifting transitions for both the student and the family. The transition to high school is also easier when made in the company of a supportive adult or friend. It is improbable for inner-city parents to accompany their teenagers to school on the first day, but if the student also comes without friends, this hinders his or her entry into the new system. Given the convoluted assignment policies of many urban districts, a majority of urban high school students begin high school without the benefit of a strong friendship group. This situation differs drastically from schools in suburban communities where students enter high school with peers they have known since elementary school.

Communication between the school and the home before a key transition is made facilitates the student's entry into the new setting. If communication is not possible before a transition is made, having a process in place to facilitate communication once entry is made goes a long way toward easing the transition for both parent and student. This becomes even more crucial when families have misconceptions about the school, especially if the school has a history of failure and/or is located in an undesirable neighborhood. Often, urban schools have partnerships with community organizations or with businesses and universities located in proximity to the school. Connections between the school and the home are enhanced if the school's partners also become part of the communication circle and help to distribute information about the school in the community. Schools that have weak communication with families, or that are filled with students whose families have little to no information, or inaccurate information, about the school, have weaker links with the student's home and therefore will have a more difficult time creating an environment of optimal growth and development for students.

Unfortunately, high schools often unwittingly make it more difficult for parents to communicate with teachers. Parent-teacher conferences are often scheduled during times when working parents cannot attend. Many schools lack translation services for parents who do not speak English. Calling schools is often very difficult for parents seeking to talk with someone about their child's progress. These difficulties in connecting with teachers are common in all high schools, but the lack of contact leads to more negative feelings when the school serves poor parents who often don't have the resources or the means to assert themselves on behalf of their children.

Viewing school reform through an ecological systems model also encourages schools to broaden the roles parents can play at the school site. Laura Abrams and Jewelle Gibbs identified four roles parents play in schools: helper, monitor, decision-maker, and advocate.[52] Parent helpers tend to volunteer in classrooms, go on field trips, and help raise funds for a school. Parents who play the role of monitor work to ensure that their own and other children are succeeding and being treated fairly. The decision-making role is often fulfilled by those parents who serve on school site counsels or other school boards. Last, parents who play the role of advocate tend to rally around an issue such as inclusion, bilingual, or special education and work to make sure the school is in compliance with district and state law.

Parents who want to be involved in their children's school naturally gravitate to one of these four roles. Schools have the power to include or exclude parents from exercising these roles. They can create structures that highlight these and other roles for parents to play, or they can make it difficult for parents to have access to all but the helper role. However, as stated above, "home-work" is very difficult, and ineffective, for parents of high school students. Rather than cut parents off from other avenues of involvement, an ecological systems model of reform encourages schools to consider and actively promote a wide range of roles that parents can play in relation to their children's education.

We already know that parent involvement leads to higher levels of student achievement. Supporting and promoting a variety of in-school roles for parents also strengthens the home-school connection and enhances the student's opportunity for optimal growth and development by providing the parent with more information, more knowledge about school processes, and responsibility, choice, and control over their child's education. As Bronfenbrenner states, "it is by introducing changes in the traditional role expectations...that new activities involving new patterns of social interaction are set in motion. The creation and allocation of roles is an especially powerful strategy for influencing the course of human development."[53] We argue that expanding role opportunities makes this true not only for students but for inner-city parents as well.

THE TRANSFER OF POWER TO THE DEVELOPING PERSON AND HIS OR HER PARENTS

We return now to the importance of transfer of power. We see this notion operating on two levels, between the school and the student and between school partners and school personnel. Adolescents are in high school during a key developmental span in their lives. Students' evolving conceptions, of themselves and the world, change dramatically between the ages of thirteen and nineteen. They mature cognitively, emotionally, and socially, becoming less and less egocentric and more able to accommodate their growing knowledge about the world. The grade structure of schools, grouping students by age and experience, can actually facilitate the transfer of power to students. Gradually gaining more power over their lives, through increasing opportunities to take responsibility and make decisions for themselves, enhances student growth and development.

The above recommendations go a long way toward improving communication and knowledge between the school and the home. This is not enough to provide for all the needs that troubled urban adolescents face, but creating relationships with parents is an important first step toward being able to provide more comprehensive services for students. The structural and curricular reforms now in place in many urban districts, including Boston, provide the absolutely necessary academic foundation upon which all school services can be built. We must now provide the social and emotional structures that will allow students to take full advantage of the academic offerings.

Similarly, the high standards that have emerged for high schools sometimes translate into reduced power for school personnel. Teachers struggle with strict pacing guides and miss the joy of designing new curriculum. Administrators resent the reduction of creative leadership opportunities. Effective school partnerships are built around two worthy objectives: one is the need to simply accomplish certain tasks and the other is the desire to further develop the individuals who are doing the task in terms of initiative, creativity, and motivation. The gradual transfer of power to those doing the work is the only way both objectives will be met.

CHAPTER 13

The Ecological Systems Model and the Development of the School Leader

The story of Dorchester High School illustrates how dramatically the role of the urban high school leader has changed over the last 60 years. Unfortunately, professional development for school leaders has not caught up with these changes. This is true especially in terms of the relational skills an urban high school principal needs in order to successfully manage a troubled urban high school. Just as our efforts to reform urban high schools have focused on curricular and structural changes to the exclusion of cultural reform, so too has our work with school leaders focused on the mechanical, technical, and instructional aspects of leading urban high schools to the exclusion of the relational qualities necessary to successfully transform the culture of failing urban high schools. Once again, this is where we turn to an ecological systems model for help in charting a new course for developing urban school leaders.

THE CHANGING ROLE OF THE SCHOOL LEADER

Over the last 60 years, there have been ten major shifts in the work responsibilities of an urban high school principal. In the beginning of this history, in 1945, the demands on the school leader allowed him to spend much of the day in his office where he could handle the minor incidents of student misbehavior. The work year of the principal was only two days longer than that of the teachers. The students never saw him, except for when he addressed them at graduation. The civil rights movement in the 1960s precipitated the first major shift in the urban principal's job, bringing new faces and new alliances into the high school. Now the school leader had to negotiate with the Boston Teachers Union and, later, with the Boston Association of School Administrators and Supervisors. He also had to contend with student and parent advocacy groups. The second major shift came in the 1970s when the courts and State Legislature succeeded in increasing access in urban schools for bilingual and special education students. This influx brought new legal responsibilities for access, as well as individual education plans, and mandated reporting requirements. Each program became an entire department in its own right increasing the staff and the reporting requirements for school leaders.

The third shift required the school leader to pay more attention to student and school safety as the increasingly diverse student body moved from occasional ethnic fistfights to the armed racial conflicts of the 1970s. The principal and school staff needed additional skills and training in "cooperative discipline" and, in today's atmosphere of school shootings and terrorist threats, in "crisis prevention and intervention." These first three shifts in the school leader's responsibilities were still focused inward, on what happened inside the school building. They involved managing the staff and students and creating a school atmosphere that was inclusive and safe.

The fourth shift, which came about with the school choice movement in the 1980s, required the school leader to project outward. Now she had to think more carefully about her public reputation, as well as recruiting and advertising for the school. The introduction of the Annual School Report card in 1984 allowed the public to compare school results and the media was quick to jump on comparative figures in student attendance, dropout rates, disciplinary incidents, and standardized test scores. The fifth shift came in the 1990s with the standards-based reform movement that presented new challenges to align curriculum, test students, and analyze and respond to test data. School leaders found themselves buried in weeks of test administration, test results analysis, and test preparation and remediation that just did not exist previously. They were responsible for leading their staff in using these data to inform instruction, but they lacked the experience to accomplish this task. Sixth, this new attention to academic results was accompanied by a greater emphasis on supervision and evaluation of teaching, as well as professional development to remedy the deficiencies in instruction. The school leader spent a lot more time in the classroom and was expected to intelligently lead discussions of curriculum and pedagogy. The performance evaluation document swelled to twelve pages and required many hours to complete.

The standards-based reform movement brought with it the institution of site-based management and shared decision-making. This seventh shift in principal responsibilities required new meetings with parents and teachers and called upon new leadership skills. At a time when the school leader needed, more than ever, to streamline his own work and make tough decisions, he faced the requirement to train a board of empowered but not necessarily knowledgeable parents, teachers, and community members and run the big decisions by them. This also required a different kind of leadership style for which school leaders had not yet been adequately prepared. The growth in school site councils brought even more partners into the building. This added challenge of working with community partners has grown incrementally since Judge Garrity required the creation of partnerships of all schools in the 1970s. With each decade, the partnerships increased in number and complexity to include health, business, university, philanthropic, and judicial partners as well as various advocacy groups. The eighth shift in principal responsibilities has been the new and increasingly complex need to raise funds, reach out and cultivate new partners, stroke and assuage the current partners, and organize the often disparate resources into a seamless network of support for teachers and students.

Ninth, the pressure to succeed in the face of limited resources has meant that many school leaders now make grant-writing and fundraising part of their schedule. Finally, the school leader himself has been the recipient of much more professional development, requiring more time out of the building and more attention to district standards and expectations. This includes the addition of having a principal coach who can act as a needed soundboard when issues crop up, but who also demands a portion of the school leader's increasingly limited time.

The increasing complexity of the job of school leadership was accompanied by a steady increase in the size of the administrative team. The headmaster, seen alone in yearbooks through 1964, was after accompanied by assistant headmasters and program directors for special and bilingual education, until the team swelled to ten full-time administrators during the tenure of Bobby Belle in the late 1990s. This was in addition to the five teacher-leaders of the small learning communities. The responsibility for developing the leadership team also fell to the headmaster. When Dorchester High School was converted to three small schools in 2003, the administrative team in each school was reduced to the headmaster and one assistant. Unfortunately, the new headmasters faced all the responsibilities outlined above with far fewer people to help, requiring the school leader of the new small high school to become, in effect, a "jack-of-all-trades."

THE PERSONALITY REQUIREMENTS OF THE URBAN SCHOOL LEADER

The changing nature of the headmaster's position has been accompanied by a change in the personality requirements for the job. The headmaster of the 1950s had the appearance of a "gentleman-scholar" who could quote Latin, the Bible, and the classics. He (or she, in deference to the one female headmistress in this history) wrote elegantly and had time to compose speeches in advance for the assembled students. In reality, this leader oversaw a humdrum academic program for boys and girls where many failed to complete high school and only a handful went to college.

A new leadership style appeared in the 1960s and 1970s: the "coach-leader." This leader was far more visible in the hallways of the school, a hands-on practical leader who had to address the many critical issues that arose in that era in the school. Many of these leaders first developed their dynamic leadership style as high school sports coaches; others were athletes in their own right. Almost all of the headmasters from 1965 to 2003 had previously been coaches or star athletes. These headmasters were not known for their knowledge of curriculum and teaching. Instead, they were valued for their ability to handle crises and unite the staff in devising solutions. As time went on, the need for creativity in crisis management was subverted by the need for compliance. The intense micromanagement of the Boston schools, stemming from the oversight of federal judge Arthur Garrity from 1974 to the mid-1980s, necessitated a school leader who could follow orders, make do with limited resources, maintain the peace, and provide ample reports.

The shifting requirements of the headmaster's job—the increasing focus on standards and curriculum, on assessments and the use of data, and on the supervision and evaluation of teachers—called for a new leadership style in the 1990s, i.e., the "instructional leader." In theory, this leader would spend far more time in the classroom, observing instruction, and then meeting collaboratively with teachers in common planning time. Payzant, in particular, expected this kind of leadership. Instructional school leaders were also being asked to look more carefully at the results of standardized assessments. Standardized tests had been around since the 1950s, but for twenty years they were used as placement exams. Beginning in the 1970s, students were targeted for remedial services based upon the results of standardized tests and finally, in the 1980s, there was a push to hold students back from graduation if they failed to succeed on certain tests. The MCAS, however, was the ultimate, no-way-around-it gateway test for graduation. During this era, professional development for school leaders became a serious topic and reflected the new standards-based reform efforts. These leaders were expected to know the latest curricular innovations, including literacy across the curriculum, math pedagogy, accommodations for students with disabilities, and how to assist English language learners in the classroom. They were introduced to each new curriculum package that was adopted by the district to address the shifting state standards.

However, at Dorchester it was difficult for the administrative team and the school leadership to shift to this new instructional approach to leadership. This is one of the ways that the most challenging urban high schools get left behind in terms of educational reform. At DHS, the lingering problems with unruly students, the attending fights, and false fire alarms still called for a dynamic "coach" leader who could marshal his forces to keep out intruders, guard the fire alarm pulls, clear the hallways, and prevent students from skipping classes and leaving early. For this reason, instructional leadership was late in coming to DHS. For example, Dorchester's last headmaster, Bobby Belle, had no teaching background and limited experience in curriculum, pedagogy, and assessment and was unable to fulfill the expectations of the superintendent for instructional leadership.

He was, however, able to get discipline and student behavior under control so that learning could take place in the classrooms. The district did not appreciate the scope of these challenges, however, and as a result, the position of Chief Academic Officer was created in 2000 to fill the instructional leadership role, causing dissention on the leadership team. When the school was reconstituted in 2003, instructional leaders were called upon to run the three new schools, but this was done without regard for the real social and behavioral challenges with which the leaders of two of the three small schools still had to contend. Now that we know how things turned out for those new small schools, perhaps it was a mistake to ignore the need for both an instructional leader and a "coach" leader, for both skills were clearly needed at the school. The history of Dorchester High School indicates that the notion of a "lead-the-charge" instructional leader who spends most of his time in the classroom is unrealistic and counterproductive. This model ignores the many competing demands upon the headmaster's time, from central administration, the administrative team, parents, and students, as well as from community partners.

Last, while the expectations and responsibilities of the headmaster have increased exponentially in recent decades, the authority and security of the position have decreased. The school leader is now accountable to the superintendent and the School Committee, as well as the School Site Council and, in some cases, a board of advisors. The proliferation of data on student achievement has resulted in specific standards of school improvement to which the headmaster is compared. At the same time, some contractual rights of the position have been reduced since the 1980s, making it easier for the superintendent to remove ineffective school leaders.

THE NEW RESPONSIBILITIES OF URBAN HIGH SCHOOL LEADERSHIP

When we examine the changing role of the headmaster through the lens of the ecological systems model, we see very clearly how managing relationships, maintaining connections, and building networks of support is both central to the school leader's job and the very thing that threatens his or her effectiveness. The ecological systems model necessitates direct, face-to-face relationships between the school leader, the teachers, the staff, and the students who make up the school's microsystem. These parties, in turn, can do their job more effectively if they are also part of a strong network of support that extends beyond the schoolhouse walls both to the families and communities of the students and to the business, higher education, and community members who make up the exosystem. The exosystem also supports or confounds these networks of support.

However, the evolving responsibilities of the headmaster's position require more and more direct, face-to-face relationships in the microsystem and across the network of support. He or she must be in the classroom and cultivate relationships of trust with teachers so they can grow professionally; the perfunctory annual evaluation of the 1950s is no longer adequate. There are other school personnel—guidance counselors, secretary, other administrators, school police—who look to this leader for guidance. The headmaster must be accountable to the superintendent, the central administration team, and the members of the School Site Council. Parents cannot be ignored. Then there are partnerships to be cultivated; most business and university leaders do not want to meet with a lesser authority in the school. In the end, the headmaster is overloaded with personal relationships, which hinders his ability to develop many of them effectively. Delegation of responsibilities seems like the obvious answer, but most of the responsibilities just listed cannot be acceptably passed off. One can easily see that these necessary relationships in the microsystem and across the exosystem will inevitably be shallow relationships, leaving the headmaster, and those with whom he or she is trying to relate, unsatisfied and their working relationship unfruitful. This prevents the effective optimal growth and development of the headmaster, who is left with little time for reflection, long-range strategic planning, leadership development, or team building (see Figure 13.1).

The challenge of too many relationships is further complicated when the networks of support are weak, when there is poor communication between the members of the microsystem and the members of the exosystem, and when the school culture is such that different messages are being conveyed to the school leader from the various constituencies with which he or she has to deal. An urban high school with as many problems as Dorchester High invites many relationships with outside partners who come offering answers to the schools many ills, and often, the answers conflict. For example, the *Breaking Ranks* solution for school improvement did not match the district's Six Essentials of Whole School Change. We have seen that the district administrators did not always see eye-to-eye with the Boston Plan for Excellence, a member of the Boston Compact.

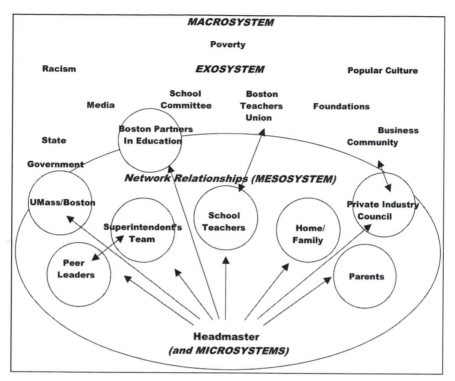

Figure 13.1   The school leader (headmaster) at the center of the ecological system.

As a result of these mismatching solutions, teachers and school leaders hear different messages, depending on who has visited and observed their classroom. When the members of the network of support are not communicating the same message, then optimal growth and development (be it of the headmaster or an administrator or a teacher or a student) is delayed.

We must understand that the responsibilities of the headmaster have increased without an equivalent increase in help. This history demonstrates that various members of the exosystem create new projects for which the school leader is, at least in part, responsible. Each school partnership puts new demands on the school leader. For example, the Flexible Campus program of the 1970s and Compact Ventures of the 1980s required numerous meetings for planning, coordination, implementation, and evaluation. When state legislators passed the Massachusetts Education Reform Act in 1993, school leaders discovered that they lost an entire week of their annual schedule to the administration of the new state assessments. In subsequent years, this only increased as the state experimented with fall and summer retests and new springtime test dates. Weeks disappeared without any resources to aid in this new testing regimen. More recently, the five-year partnership with the Trefler Foundation required many planning meetings as well as a monthly steering committee meeting and the annual day devoted to selecting the next crop of Teach Next Year interns, as well as countless informal meetings that took place from week to week. Meanwhile, the stream of work required for the district, NEASC accreditation, School Site Council meetings, and other partnerships and grants went undiminished. The new central model for leadership—the instructional leader—was offered in addition to these other responsibilities. No wonder many school leaders lament the lack of time to be in the classroom.

The alternative to this complexity of relationships is to simply turn some down. But this is unrealistic. Urban school leaders know that partnerships with the exosystem especially are crucial for the survival of struggling urban high schools. No headmaster will turn down these partnerships, for the schools are resource-starved and leaders are constantly looking for opportunities for their students, but with each new relationship, some other relationship—with another partner, or with students, or parents, or teachers—inevitably suffers. We have seen that urban school leaders have hundreds of relationships to maintain, but the relationships that are truly supportive and that lead to optimal growth and development in the school leader must be few in number and deeply cultivated. These kinds of relationships, unfortunately, are easily compromised.

THE DEVELOPMENT OF THE SCHOOL LEADER

Finally, until recently, the urban school leader has not had access to a comprehensive program of leadership development. In Boston, coaching for school leaders was not instituted until 2001. Superintendent Payzant's Focus on Children II explicitly stated that developing leadership at the school level was one of six major goals. Unfortunately, this released a cascade of programs for school leaders. For example, Bobby Belle, the last headmaster to lead Dorchester High School, was receiving special attention from many sources during the final years of his tenure.

He had many consultations with UMB professors; he had an Annenberg coach, and he was working with representatives from the LAB at Brown University. There are many reasons why one would expect to see real leadership development with this kind of focused attention. First, Belle was involved in the kind of face-to-face relationships with multiple partners for which we have been advocating. He was relating directly with the superintendent's team, with leaders from the New England Association of Schools and Colleges (NEASC), as well as with other headmasters also going through professional development. Also following our ideal, many of these same individuals were in conversation with each other through the network of support built up at DHS. For example, the

LAB and NEASC worked closely together toward accreditation; UMB was cognizant of the superintendent's goals, and the headmasters shared common goals.

However, we have seen that there were many inconsistencies. For example, the superintendent's In Depth Review team was panning Dorchester High School at the same time that NEASC was praising the school and restoring accreditation. Clearly there was little discussion between these two members of the headmaster's network of support. Likewise, in 2001, some central BPS administrators were instructing the headmaster to use program directors to oversee and evaluate the small learning communities, while other central administrators insisted that math teachers be evaluated by math program directors and English teachers by English program directors, and so on. Finally, none of the coaches or school partners seemed to be aware of what was happening day to day in the classroom. Had these partners also been talking with teachers, they would have learned about the high level of teacher frustration during this time. The teachers felt that there were too many disruptive students in the school and that instruction was being compromised. The teachers held Belle accountable for this, and became critical of his leadership while others, such as NEASC and the LAB at Brown, were praising his accomplishments and touring him all over the country. The conflict between these internal criticisms and the outside advisors was stressful; this kind of conflict of goals leads to compromises, superficial compliance, and a failure to really develop and practice new leadership skills. It was clear that this set of partners had Belle, as the school leader, in their spotlight. However, in the end the network of support was ineffective because although they were talking to each other, they were not talking to the other members of Belle's in-school microsystem, namely the teachers and students.

The ecological systems model of educational reform returns us to the network of support. Too often, and for good reason, the spotlight of educational reform shines on the students in urban high schools. We cannot forget, however, that in our most challenging schools, school leaders and teachers all *need* to be the focus of the spotlight, especially if they are to fulfill their responsibilities for raising student achievement. When districts and school partners elect to focus on developing the school leader, they must not lose sight of the demands outlined above. Urban schools need strong partners, and urban school leaders need the web of support that a strong exosystem provides. The problem is that new responsibilities often sneak up on school leaders and school systems. By the time an issue is recognized as a problem, that issue has already become entrenched in the "system." Any solution at this point is often just another "add-on" which demands additional attention and is difficult to dismantle. There are many examples in this history: the needs of bilingual students, special needs students, alternative students, and, most recently, students who fail the MCAS, have all led to the creation of "add-on" programs which have complicated the work of school leadership. Years later, after much anguish and effort, these programs are gradually phased out in exchange for programs that are more integral to the school and inclusive of all students.

Looking across time has revealed the complexity of leading urban high schools. We have also learned that the best times at the school were times of collaboration between outside partners and small teams in the school. We have maintained throughout that it is impossible for the average urban high school to fix itself. We have also learned that it is also impossible for the headmaster—no matter how dynamic, charismatic, and connected—to single-handedly save the school. The history demonstrates that salvation comes through teamwork and partnerships. The next step is for school partners to consciously work within the context of the school leader's many microsystems. Rather than always introducing new programs and new initiatives, some school partners must take it upon themselves to simply work with, and for, the school leader as a true network of support for his or her optimal growth and development as a leader.

CHAPTER 14

School Values and Moral Authority

Our use of the word "moral" here is deliberate. We have often felt that those on the religious and political right have hijacked the term. This is unfortunate, not just for those of other religious and political persuasions, but for the public in general, for those who don't have strong political or religious leanings, but who want, for themselves and their children, to live a moral life. Moral is defined first as "relating to the principles or considerations of right or wrong" and secondly as, "expressing or teaching a conception of right behavior."[1] "Right behavior" is not religious behavior. If we think of morality as focusing on "right behavior," then we can see that there are so many ways that the term applies in our civic and educational lives. We should not be afraid to talk about our morals for "right behavior" or to design systems that teach these morals and hold others to them—not through force or punishment, but through persuasion and the strength of human relationships. We ask that you keep this definition in mind as you read this chapter on school values and moral authority.

A large portion of this book is devoted to the role that school culture plays in overall student success. This history has shown us that student outcomes improved when a small community of like-minded teachers who shared cultural norms formed a strong network of support around students with the help of a strong school leader and outside school partners, usually from the business, higher education, and philanthropic communities. Unfortunately, these small in-school communities never really impacted the school as a whole. They remained small and isolated enclaves separate from the wider school community. We have tried to understand these success stories in terms of ecological systems. In this chapter, we explore the outermost layer of Bronfenbrenner's "Russian doll" model of environmental influences. The macrosystem represents the "ideological, cultural and value laden belief systems"[2] in which we all live. In our study of the "trees" of school influences, the macrosystem is the "forest" that is easily overlooked.

When we think about the macrosystem, we think about the underlying values that shape the work of schools. Like the air we breathe, shifts in our prevailing cultural values are difficult to detect while we are living through them. This is why, when we consider the macrosystem we really need to take a historical approach, for only then can we see how school-based values have changed over the years. The main limitation of many school studies is that they miss the impact of overarching cultural values because they are so focused on the immediate picture. We cannot forget, however, that it is the prevailing values of the day that really drive educational policy. Examining the history of Dorchester High School helps us see this process at work.

We find that, in each decade, students who attended Dorchester High School grew up within a macrosystem which was largely undefined and often unrecognized; nevertheless the macrosystem defined their curriculum and school experiences. The macrosystem shaped the convictions of the members of the microsystem (and the exosystem) and helped determine the stability and strength of the networks of support. These, in turn, influenced student development. When we examine the vocabulary of the time, we can spot the prevailing values and fairly accurately describe the macrosystem, recognizing that in certain decades there was greater unanimity and, in others, greater divisiveness and debate. We should ask, however, what are the prevailing values of today as they relate to the education of our most needy urban students? And just as important, who should be determining and promoting and upholding those values? We start by identifying the shifting values over time.

The 1950s at Dorchester High School exemplified some of the social purposes of education, when learning to get along with others was just as important as mastering a foreign language or exploring Physics or Chemistry. The goals of the school included helping students become responsible adults and good parents. It was important that students have workforce, but not necessarily academic, skills; thus we see the focus on industry and business tracks that were so popular with the working class students who attended DHS. Academics were much less rigorous in the 1950s. Home economics was an acceptable part of the high school transcript, as well as a Household Science sequence that included classes in Clothing, Cooking, and Millinery.

If one had any doubt about the prevailing values of schooling during this decade, one need only examine the yearbooks, report cards, and other publications at DHS. In the 1950s, the report cards convince us that social skills were as important as academic achievement, for right alongside the test scores and grades in math and English and science we find marks in "Reliability, Manners (sometimes penciled over as 'Courtesy'), Cooperation, Faithfulness, and Appearance." Parents everywhere remind their children to cooperate, be respectful, avoid trouble, and get along with others. In the 1950s, then, we see that students were being lectured and trained on the same character traits in school as they were at home. In other words, they were facing the same expectations for socially acceptable behavior across two of their microsystems, home and school. Of course, the school community was predominantly white. They were not yet challenged with the diverse social standards and expectations of different racial and ethnic groups nor were they troubled by the need to accommodate those students with special or bilingual educational needs.

In the 1960s, the political purposes of education began to appear and supplant the social goals of the 1950s. The headmaster's message in the 1966 yearbook was filled with lofty calls to duty. "High on the agenda of the unfinished business of this generation is the achievement of the rightful place of your Negro brother in the social, political, and economic spheres of American society. Part of this same problem, although not exclusively a Negro problem, is the question of poverty. Should malnutrition and slum housing exist in a nation of abundance?"[3] Now the curriculum included courses ranging across the social spectrum such as "Seminars in United States History to African Studies, History of China and the Far East, Black Studies, Urban Problems, and Urban Civilization."[4] In this era, students organized into the Black Student Union and walked out of classes while teachers organized into teachers' unions and walked out of school. Protest, confrontation, conflict, and court battles were not shunned, but encouraged. Notions of civic responsibility replaced the relational values of the 1950s. The desirable characteristics noted on report cards also shifted in the 1960s to Initiative, Seriousness of Purpose, Industry, Influence, Concern for Others, Responsibility, Emotional Stability, and Social Adjustment, reflecting the civil rights era and national concern for the welfare of others.

By the 1970s, character marks had disappeared from the report cards altogether. Why? Perhaps the deliberate inclusion of bilingual students and diverse cultures challenged the simplistic belief systems of earlier years. Maybe the same court decisions that resulted in the removal of prayer from the public schools made the public uneasy with any value-based codes for behavior. No longer was the school, in any systematic or public way, holding forth the same values as the parents when it came to student behavior. We know this, in part, because the parents in cities all over the country were themselves so violently divided as a result of battles over school desegregation. Some parents modeled racism for their children, while others lamented the divisiveness and violence. At the same time, the teachers were exercising their new union muscles and demonstrating how to challenge authority. In many of our cities, the guiding authorities of the 1970s—teachers, parents, public officials—were

not speaking with the same voice. Given this, the mayhem in student relationships is easier to understand. No longer were students hearing the
same value laden message from each of their microsystems.

In the 1980s, the values of the business community began to prevail as
they organized and stepped in to address the woefully unprepared workers graduating from urban high schools like Dorchester. In time, the values of civic responsibility and individual rights expressed within school
contexts were replaced by values of achievement reflected in the new
focus on standards, data, accountability, and benchmarks. This is the language of the competitive business world, and it came to predominate in
the schools. For many reasons, we believe these values have prevailed
in public schools for the last 25 years, leading to certain overall changes
in educational philosophy.

The first of these changes was the shift in emphasis from access to
achievement. In the 1970s, the emphasis was on serving all the students
(African American, special education, and bilingual) in public schools.
Teachers from this era recall that "self-esteem" was a prevailing value;
it was most important to help students feel good about their abilities
and the things they could do. In the 1980s, the emphasis shifted to encouraging high academic achievement for all students. Educational excellence
was defined in terms of uniform standards. Educators spoke of benchmarks and alignment. During this time, the curriculum shifted from a
wide array of history courses to an increasing emphasis on literacy and
math. This was also the beginning of the loss of nonacademic activities
that were once offered in urban high schools. Unfortunately, the self-
esteem movement never really took advantage of how the standards-
based reform movement made it possible to tie self-esteem to real accomplishments. Equally unfortunate is the fact that the main measure of academic accomplishment is achievement tests, which are inevitably
competitive, leaving some students scoring near the bottom. This serves
to exacerbate the glaring gaps in achievement between minority and
white students adding one more symptom to the long list of why under-
funded urban high schools were failing.

In the 1950s and 1960s, the few standardized assessments that were
given to students were given at the beginning of the year to help school
leaders decide how best to place students in various career tracks and lev-
eled courses. Although more student centered, because the "placements"
took student strengths and weaknesses into account and tried to match
those with a similar academic and career path, this approach was problematic because students ended up getting stuck in those "tracks" for
their entire school career and beyond. By the 1980s, the assessments
shifted to the spring to measure advancement and, in time, all students
were held to the same standards, especially in math and English language
arts, a more fair and desirable outcome, but one that slowly squeezed out
other dimensions of adolescent growth and development.

We see by looking at the educational offerings at DHS over time that the curriculum became increasingly narrow and the attention to student interests, both in and outside of the classroom, waned. In our 25 year effort to help our students master math and reading, we have slowly eliminated elective courses, student activities, free periods, and many out of school experiences such as field trips. For example, 50 years ago, Dorchester High School offered multiple world languages, including French, Spanish, Italian, and Latin. In the 1960s, the school offered an arts program that drew students from all over the city. In addition to the wide variety of courses, students could choose from 33 after school clubs and activities in which to engage. In the 1970s there were courses in history, civics and politics, and students were believed responsible enough to leave the building during their free periods or study halls. By the 1990s, the art requirement was reduced to one year of study. Eventually, the arts options at DHS disappeared altogether. Today, DHS students have two clubs to choose from, a debate club and a business club. There are no free periods or study halls. The headmaster has to scramble every year for funds to provide other activities such as dance or art. If he can't find the money, the students go without. For the past five years, for example, there has been no music program at the school. What can we say of a curriculum that invests so little in stimulating and developing creativity? Why are we surprised that urban high school students are not engaged in school?

Even more troubling, this single focus on academics accompanied by the dearth in activities and the lack of opportunity to take on new roles and responsibilities severely limits our ability to cultivate the optimal growth and development of urban students. We have argued that an ecological systems approach to educational reform keeps the focus of our reform efforts on relationships and human development. The relational focus points toward the importance of a supportive school culture and the developmental focus reminds us of the teenage need for options, choices, and the exploration of alternative roles. We seem to have forgotten one of the historical missions of the high school: to give students the opportunity to try on new adult roles. Suburban schools still uphold this mission. Students in suburban schools are more likely to be able to exercise choice, greater responsibility and decision-making in their high school careers. Opportunities for choice, greater responsibility and decision-making are sorely lacking in many inner-city high schools. For example, many urban students are prevented from experiencing an open campus, not only because their schools are located in impoverished neighborhoods that lack choices for lunch or because those same neighborhoods are violent and we are concerned for student safety. There is merit to these reasons, but there is also something else at play here, something that conveys a lack of trust in our urban students. Teachers and school leaders do not believe they will return to school or act responsibly

while away from campus; therefore, we have simply removed the option
for them to exercise responsibility and face the consequences when they
are unable to do so. This lack of trust ultimately hurts urban children.

Many inner-city schools have also taken choice and decision-making
completely out of the course selection process. In service to standards
and accountability we have taken the life—literally—out of urban high
schools. No longer do some of the most impoverished urban high schools
offer electives in language, art, or music, or any variety in the standard
history or science courses. In the effort to enhance the "basics" we have
taken away other aspects of the curriculum that might engage students.
Clearly, these decisions have not been made with the optimal development of the student in mind. Student growth and development is
enhanced when students have the opportunity to participate and perform
successfully in an ever-broadening series of related roles. Development is
enhanced even further when students play similar roles across their other
face-to-face settings. Now more than ever, the roles available to urban
students should be expanded not diminished. The cultural/developmen-
tal reform model posited here, because of its priority on building relations
and enhancing student development, serves to remind schools of the
need to provide more role opportunities for students.

Roles are partly defined by the activities in which one engages. For
example, part of being a high school student involves completing assignments in class and at home, studying for exams, and engaging in class
discussions. Clubs and after school activities also become more differentiated and specialized for high school students, opening the door for them
to be more independent and to play more adults roles. Activities are
driven by intentions, and have some meaning to the participants in a particular setting. According to Bronfenbrenner, the activities engaged in by
the student "constitute both the internal mechanisms and the external
manifestations of psychological growth."[5] The activities available to adolescents at the high school level should reflect the growing developmental
complexity of this particular stage of life. Urban high schools can play a
crucial role in providing opportunities for teenagers to engage in a variety
of activities that contribute to their development as young adults.

Sadly, many urban high schools lack real variety in the activities available to students. This has happened for the same reasons cited above—
the push for standards and accountability has forced schools to focus on
the basics, thus removing all "extras" from the curriculum. In terms of
after school activities available to urban students, a comparison between
DHS and Newton, a neighboring suburb, says it all. Today, in 2006, the
students at the Dorchester Education Complex have the typical sports
teams and then just two clubs from which to choose. Outside partners
offer a few additional options in academics (Upward Bound, for example,
at UMB) or leadership development (Teen Empowerment). Some students have independently hooked up with community agencies, such as

the YMCA or the Dorchester Youth Collaborative, while others cobble together small after-school activities that lack faculty supervision. Sometimes, the headmasters of the small schools try to bring in a dance or music program when they can find the funds for it.

The students in Newton have 68 clubs and after school activities. For the artistically inclined they have dance, art, film, anime, improv, theater, and music clubs. For those focused on academics they have astronomy, philosophy, math, and science clubs. For the politically minded they have Amnesty International, animal rights, N.O.W., violence prevention, human rights, and community action clubs. For diverse students they have the Asian, Irish, Israeli, Italian, Jewish, Latino, and Russian culture clubs, as well as the Black Leadership Advisory Council. They also have book, Bible, chess, board games, and recycling clubs. Aside from providing activities for students to engage in, these clubs also provide students with various identities. The clubs broaden the roles students can envision themselves playing in life. For some reason, it appears that many urban schools are operating under the belief that prohibiting or cutting back on activities is beneficial for students with poor academic records. This could not be further from the truth. Extracurricular activities have been shown to increase student engagement in school, especially for underachieving students. Students who participate in after school activities actually perform better in the classroom.[6] These activities also aid parent involvement because they provide another, non-punitive reason for parents to spend time at the school. Most importantly, participation in extracurricular activities enhances the optimal growth and development of students.

Having a wide range of available activities to engage in is so important for young adults. Having a variety of activities to choose from enhances human development because the choice allows the young person to initiate and maintain new interests beyond the scope their parents' influence. As young people get older, the roles they envision for their adult selves and the activities they engage in tend to become one and the same. Activities propel students forward into their future and help them make decisions about who they want to "be" and what they want to do with their lives.

Last, student growth and development is enhanced when students are exposed to a variety of settings and when they take on different roles and engage in increasingly complex activities in those settings. This is supported by the fact that students who have lived away from home or who have held apprenticeship type jobs or internships adjust more quickly and perform better in college.[7] These students have benefited from experiencing contexts where they can take on a variety of roles and engage in different activities. Development is enhanced even further for those individuals who have experiences with people who are different from them either culturally, racially, ethnically, or economically, or when young people get to spend time with individuals who are older. For example, we know that African American students who live in the inner city but who attend predominantly white high schools tend to do better in college.[8] The reason is not necessarily because those high schools are superior; rather, these students benefit from crossing cultures. They have more experience relating across very different settings, are exposed to varying role expectations and engage in different sets of activities. Those students who spend all or most of their time in one setting will have more difficulty adjusting when they attempt to leave that setting. Urban high schools can help expose inner-city students to settings that are culturally, racially, ethnically, and economically different from their neighborhoods. They can do this by working with their business and university partners to increase opportunities for students to get out of the neighborhood and have different sets of experiences.

It appears that in our efforts to bring every student to the table of academic achievement—a table at which they definitely need to be—we have neglected to pay attention to the meal we were serving. Our measurements reveal our values and most of our measurements lack the spice of life. There is little in the educational servings of our most troubled urban high schools to meet the needs of young people to dream, to hope, and to create and to craft their ideals. We are asking more and more in the way of academic achievement of our students, as we should, but we are doing it with less and less to really inspire them. Once again, an ecological systems approach to school reform remains mindful of all aspects of human development—not just academics. This mindfulness suggests that educators put as much effort into structuring the roles and activities available to urban students as they do in structuring the academic program. All are needed for optimal growth and development.

Our last and most important point about the macrosystem is that our sole focus on academic standards, often narrowly defined around math and literacy, appears to have replaced traditional values. This history reveals that there was a violent clash of values throughout the 1970s, the most turbulent period in history for many urban schools. We needed the business community to step in at the turn of the decade to remind the School Department of one of the most fundamental reasons for going to school: to get an education that will prepare a student for a job. It is important to acknowledge that the business community did not reject the social and civic values that drove our earlier educational agenda; rather, they offered a simpler idea, which was to identify rock-bottom standards on which everyone could agree. Data would measure progress against these new standards. The emphasis on data, which began in the 1980s, offered a tempting way out of the turbulent debates of the 1970s which pitted the rights of one group against another as constituents were divided by age, race, gender, language, ethnicity, occupation, or political persuasion. Data were perceived as being scientific, and thus neutral and unbiased. Data avoided the squishy subjectivism of the 1970s self-esteem evaluations. In addition, the use of data avoided the messy clash of values in schools that had been cut loose from the Biblical value systems of the 1950s. Data-driven decision-making promised a fair and equitable pathway to the future.

The fact that we have now created an elaborate system that is driven by the values reflected in standards, data, and academic measurements obscures the fact that we now have urban schools that operate without the balance of more humanistic, developmentally focused values. This has created a moral vacuum. There are numerous problems with this "scientific" system of standards and data-collection methods.

First, we have only to think about where we have well-defined standards and where we don't and we spot a serious problem. Currently, many urban school systems have written, grade-level standards in math, English, history, science, health, and the arts, while we have no comparable, written, grade-level standards for behavior. Social skills such as punctuality, preparedness, responsibility for materials, teamwork, cooperation, respect, dress, and socially acceptable vocabulary are also necessary for school success. Yet these are unaddressed and undefined. In our most troubled urban high schools, we wrestle with sexual abuse, physical violence, drug abuse, and vandalism because, in part, we have not said, "This is what we expect in grade 9, grade 10, grade 11..." and "This is what you will need to demonstrate in order to graduate." This short list only includes some of the most obvious social skills. We have likewise ignored the political skills, once heralded in the 1960s, of advocacy, public service, debate, and civic duty.

We have seen over and over again in the history of DHS that when the microsystem was weak, the exosystem stepped in, creating a strong network of support that often carried students toward academic and social success. Currently, the school's microsystem is weak when it comes to moral guidance. The Boston Public Schools only developed a code of discipline in the 1980s and we continue to rely upon iterations of this document to define the most egregious behaviors. There are no well-defined and published standards for moral improvement. There are no "high-stakes tests" in "right behavior" that guard the way to graduation. Thieves and drug users and weapons carriers and sexual predators can still graduate from many urban high schools without any real interventions on their behalf. The school system does not send a powerful message. Too often, the message from home is faint, for single parent homes and poverty leave families strained, stressed, and broken. The values of the business community led them to team up and bring us academic standards in the 1980s and an appointed School Committee in the 1990s; surely now the community partners of the Boston Public Schools can address school safety issues and "right behavior" with the same effectiveness.

Students cannot effectively engage in schools where they do not feel safe. We have known for years that school safety is tops on the list of concerns among young people. We know that it takes more than metal detectors and security cameras to make a safe school. These instruments are no defense against verbal abuse, intolerance, racism, sexual advances, gang recruitment pressures, or the more subtle pressures that students face every day. The school says, in general, that these behaviors are unacceptable, but the system has no plan to define them or to teach alternative behaviors.

The experiences of students in their final years at DHS reminds us that students do not even feel safe with their closest friends in school. This year, a science teacher conducted a simple experiment in his freshmen class. During a unit on evolution, he asked the students, "If you could have one of the following adaptations, which one would you pick: wings, claws, or eyes on the back of your head?" Over 90 percent of the students chose the eyes, because then "we could see who was sneaking up behind us." This does not indicate a safe learning environment.

We have learned from Bryk and Schneider that trust is a "core resource" for school improvement.[9] Yet in our most troubled urban high schools students do not trust their closest friends. Teachers do not trust administrators. School leaders are too harried to cultivate trusting relationships among their staffs. But how can trust be established in an amoral environment? Bryk and Schneider have demonstrated that trust can be measured in a school. They have focused on characteristics of respect, competence, compassion, and integrity.[10] Hugh Sockett, on the other hand, predicates trust on "five interlocking conditions: predictability of behavior, agreement on ends, dialogue, a belief in the good will and rationality of others, and reflection and self-critique."[11] These words carry moral meaning. Currently, they do not appear on the average teacher performance evaluation document. We do not evaluate students on these dimensions. We have not yet found the moral leadership needed to help students and faculty define the parameters of trust, learn its essential value, understand how to cultivate it, and work to create a truly safe school environment.

We are looking for more than just the elimination of abusive behaviors, however. Students are spiritual, idealistic beings. We long to see the energy and idealism of our young people encouraged and directed into great endeavors. We cannot and would not return to the quasi-religious atmosphere of the public high school of the 1950s, but it is a shame we have nothing to put in place of the "character marks" of that era. In our determination to get on top of math and literacy achievement, we have completely eliminated character education. We no longer know how to talk to the students about values, morals, self-control, service, duty, and sacrifice. In fact, we are more likely to run into these concepts outside the classroom and on the athletic fields, where there are no standardized assessments but great challenges and authentic contests which inspire students to do their best.

Not only do we lack moral standards for our schools, but our moral language has atrophied, so we lack the vocabulary needed to define or recognize certain school problems. Schooling is a moral enterprise, which requires moral leadership.

> We have to see our professionalism as primarily moral in conception....Education does not have a sophisticated moral language, and the specific tasks of teaching and of understanding education are made extraordinarily difficult by this vacuum. I am using "moral" here as descriptive of a discourse in which words like good, care, love, virtue, compassion, ought, right, person, loyalty and so on are found. It is a language which may, or may not, be framed within a religious belief. It is practical, not theoretical.[12]

The lack of what Sockett calls a "thick" moral vocabulary leaves educators and school partners without the concepts or convictions to guide students in what is clearly a moral exercise. One thing we have noticed in writing this book is how often the problems in Dorchester High School were right out in the open, but they were not named or addressed. Somehow they were overlooked in all the other conversations. The segregation of the 1950s, the overcrowded conditions of the early 1970s, the high teacher turnover, the over-assignment of special needs and bilingual education students to this one high school, the prevalence of students from the Department of Youth Services, the racial disparities, the dangers of sending students on foot through the "hot zones" identified by the Boston Police Department—there are so many examples over the years—all these should have been obvious and easily corrected, but they lingered and were debated and were forgotten as other problems pressed to the surface. We lacked the language to recognize these moral abuses and call them what they were; in hindsight we are shocked that we allowed these things to happen. There is not a national moral consensus that focuses on the worth of every child and places the child at the center of every educational decision.

PARENTS, THE MISSING CONSTITUENCY

One microsystem that has been difficult to capture throughout this history is the student's home. We know the families of Dorchester High School are poor and, from that, we can make some safe guesses about their lives, priorities, and decisions. For the most part, we argue from absence, for parents have not played a significant role in school decision-making, ever. In recent years, they have attended the School Site Council in tiny numbers. Nevertheless, parents are involved with the school every day. They attend the daily Individual Education Plan meetings with the special education staff. They call in the morning to let us know their child will be absent or late to school—and would we keep the front door open? They sign the permission forms for field trips and after-school activities. We talk to them on the phone, usually around student behavior, and the less fortunate come in for suspension hearings. But unlike suburban parents, these parents do not organize, advocate, or wield power in any significant way.

There are many reasons for the piecemeal parent engagement of the urban high school, but certainly one is that we—the school staff and the parents—speak different languages. When we listen to parents, they do not talk to us about achievement gaps, MCAS scores, inclusion strategies, assignment patterns, and similar educational technical jargon; they talk about their children and their desire to see good behavior, hard work, and progress toward graduation. These are moral concerns. The fact that our language "has been corrupted by the technical"[13] and we have lost our moral vocabulary and convictions means that we have excluded parents from the conversation.

In our conceptual framework, we discussed a home-based versus a school-based model of parental engagement. The technical jargon of high school education indicates how far we have drifted from the home. While generalizations are almost always wrong, we find that many of our parents are conservative and religious. Many of the home-based standards we hear from the mouths of parents fly in the face of current educational policy. We promote access, tolerance, and inclusion, while parents will not uncommonly say, "I don't want my daughter hanging out with those kids." We hold convoluted suspension hearings, endeavoring to protect the legal rights of students, with multiple forms, signatures, and timelines to be followed, while the parents are outraged at bad behavior and just want swift consequences. They do not understand why any institution for children should need metal detectors at the front door; they certainly don't have one at home, but they will vociferously advocate for them once they understand that weapons are a distinct possibility in our school. The school is so unlike their home that they hardly know where to connect. Our neglect of the moral in education has denied parents the one language they speak articulately and passionately.

We have discussed the long-standing tension between access and achievement in public education; it is difficult to include everyone in public education and also have every student succeed at high standards. This tension makes little sense to a parent, however, where the focus is always on the individual child. No reasonable parent would stand for an either-or situation. Imagine a home without sufficient food and a parent thinking, "Which is better—having all my children sit at the table to eat a little food or having the brightest children eat a full meal?" Another parent might ask, "Do I want all my children to have access to medical care, even if it's inadequate, or do I want to use the resources to make sure the strongest are healthy and let the others get sick?" No parent would stand for these choices and neither should we!

In all of our inner cities, there is one institution which represents the moral interests of parents, and that is the church or "faith-based organization." We acknowledge this while still maintaining our conviction that to speak in moral terms is not to focus solely on religion, but on "right behavior" in a just society. Far more inner-city parents claim affiliation with a church than any other institution. Many urban areas, similar to Boston, have enjoyed a documented revival of religion over the past fifteen years, thanks in part to the steady stream of immigrants who have brought their faith with them and planted hundreds of small churches throughout the inner city.[14] Oddly enough, the church has also been the one institution in many areas—in contrast to the business and finance community, the universities, the foundations and philanthropies, and the health system—which has had little engagement with the public school system. Why is this so?

In the 1960s, the church was foundational to the civil rights movement and the integration of schools. Martin Luther King Jr. and others forged their message in the church and returned to the church again and again to address willing audiences. Since that decade, the voice of the church has been absent when it comes to public education. As a result, parents are left on their own to voice their concerns. While the courts have erected strict guidelines against proselytization in public schools, they have also carefully defended the place of the church in the public square. The national conviction regarding separation of church and state should not silence the voice of parents and their churches when it comes to moral concerns regarding their children. In Boston, where the need for moral leadership is so acute, the church could play a useful role. The church is an important member of the microsystem for parents and children and a disconnected member of the exosystem in public education.

In conclusion, we find that the local school has no defense against the macrosystem. This history demonstrates that the school is often sabotaged and beat up by major, national forces. The economy sags, neighborhood demographics change, racism and poverty undermine progress, and popular culture undermines student achievement. In the face of ever increasing and large-scale threats to the urban high school, we now must turn to the larger community of the exosystem to provide moral leadership.

Notes

PREFACE

1. Angus and Mirel, The Failed Promise, 1999
2. Ibid.
3. Ibid.
4. Payne and Kaba, "So Much Reform, so Little Change" ; Steinberg et al., *Beyond the Classroom* 1996; Tyack and Cuban, *Tinkering Toward Utopia*.

CHAPTER 1

1. In Boston, high school leaders are called headmasters and elementary and middle school leaders are called principals.
2. Balfanz and Legters, "Locating the Dropout Crisis."
3. Anderson, *Code of the Street*.
4. Deal and Peterson, *Shaping School Culture*, 48.
5. Deal and Peterson, *Shaping School Culture*, p. 2.

CHAPTER 2

1. From the class history of the 1964 yearbook.
2. The graduation rate for these early years was calculated by dividing hte number of transcripts marked "graduation" by the total number of transcripts for all enrolled students no matter how long they were enrolled, but who never graduated.
3. Interview with the first African-American staff member hired at DHS.
4. King, *Chain of Change*, 32.
5. Allen, "Segregation and Desegregation in Boston's Schools, 1961–1974," 114; King, *Chain of Change*, 38.

6. Formisano, *Boston Against Busing*, 45.

7. Committee Chairwoman Ellen Jackson as quoted in The *Boston Globe*, December, 1965.

8. Levine and Harmon , *The Death of an American Jewish Community*, 171.

9. Ibid., 176.

CHAPTER 3

1. Louis and Miles, *Improving the Urban High School*, 60.

2. From the 1972 DHS yearbook.

3. Formisano, *Boston Against Busing*, 166.

4. From the 1971 DHS Yearbook.

5. Letter from DHS faculty to Judge Garrity in 1976.

6. Formisano, *Boston Against Busing*, 216–17.

7. Louis and Miles, *Improving the Urban High School*, 62.

8. From the headmaster's letter to the New England Association of Schools and Colleges in 1974.

9. From the headmaster's letter to the New England Association of Schools and Colleges in 1979.

10. Taylor, *Desegregation in Boston and Buffalo*, 53.

11. From the New England Association of Schools and Colleges Evaluation Report, 1972.

12. Dentler, *Moving Forward*.

CHAPTER 4

1. Norma Love, "Girl Shot at Dorchester High," *Boston Globe,* February 9, 1982; James McBride, "Victim Called Scared, Uncertain," *Boston Globe*, February 10, 1982.

2. Interview with teacher, quoted in Louis and Miles, *Improving the Urban High School,* 63

3. Former Boston Public School's superintendent, April 18, 2001. Interview by John Leonard.

4. City Wide Education Commission, "A brief history of student assignment," *Focus on the Boston Public Schools,* March 1997.

5. Interview with DHS's Verizon business partner liaison (formerly New England Telephone). Interviewed by John Leonard, March 16, 2001.

6. Business evaluation of Partnerships, 1976, Boston Public School Archives.

7. Ibid.

8. Neil Sullivan (executive director, Private Industry Council), interviewed by Lisa Gonsalves, May 22, 2006.

9. The next chapter explores the School Committee's problems in more detail.

10. Dooley, *The Culture of Possibililty*, 16.

11. Interview with teacher, quoted in Louis and Miles, *Improving the Urban High School,* 64.

12. Ibid., 65.

13. Ibid.

14. From the New England Association of Schools and Colleges Report, 1982.

15. Interview with teacher, quoted in Louis and Miles, *Improving the Urban High School*, 66.

16. Louis and Miles, *Improving the Urban High School*, 66.

17. From the DHS 1985 Yearbook.

18. Charlie Desmond (UMB liaison to DHS), interviewed by John Leonard, April 2001.

19. Louis and Miles, *Improving the Urban High School*, 68.

20. Ibid.

21. Paul Casilli (former DHS teacher), interviewed by Lisa Gonsalves, June 5, 2006.

22. Irene Sege, "Dorchester High School: Tilting with math at Midyear," *Boston Globe*, January 17, 1985.

23. Ibid.

24. Written by Diane Simmons, from the 1985 DSH Yearbook.

25. Louis and Miles, *Improving the Urban High School*, 71.

26. Ibid., 73.

CHAPTER 5

1. Samuel Tyler is the director of the Boston Municipal Research Bureau, the fiscal watchdog agency for the city of Boston. Interviewed by Lisa Gonsalves, May 23, 2006.

2. Quote from Dorchester High School's business partner liaison Verizon, formally New England Telephone.

3. From interview with Samuel Tyler, Boston Municipal Research Bureau.

4. The parties in this case were the white school committee leadership, the mayor, and the business community.

5. Steven Marantz, "City Council Proposes Panel to Study Schools, Some See it as Threat to Elected Committee," *Boston Globe*, February 2, 1989.

6. Michael Rezendes, "Senate Boosts Effort to Eliminate City's Elected School Board." *Boston Globe*, May 29, 1991.

7. Ibid.

8. Tracy Jan and Maria Sacchette, "An Uphill Battle for Better Schools," *Boston Globe*, May 22, 2005.

CHAPTER 6

1. A number of factors made a difference for Cohen's leadership at DHS. First, he was a leader in a time of system-wide innovation when diligent cooperation with Court Street was probably more important than independent genius. In addition, he was surrounded by a solid core of talent from the late 1960s including the members from the "class of '69" mentioned earlier. Last, he benefited from the many partners who stepped up to work with the school. The Boston Compact was one such partner, along with the staff from New England Telephone and UMB. Cohen was fortunate to have these resources, among others, for they allowed him to nurture the pockets of success maintained by the faculty.

2. Patricia Wen, "Boston Gangs: A Hard World Officials Fear For Schools," *Boston Globe*, May 10, 1988.

3. Doris Sue Wong, "Teenage Thief Gets School, Not Jail Term," *Boston Globe*, September 8, 1989.

4. Ellen O'Brien, "Student, 17, Fatally Stabbed in Roxbury," *Boston Globe*, January 29, 1990.

5. Ibid.

6. From the New England Association of Schools and Colleges Report, 1993, 41.

7. Albert Holland, *High School Accreditation Problems* (Boston: Boston Public Schools, 1995).

8. Report by the Boston City Council's Finance Commission 1995, pp. 2, 9, and 14.

9. From "Transforming Boston's Schools: A Decade of Focus on Children and the Challenges of the Future" (Boston: Boston Public Schools, 2005).

10. Ibid., 3.

11. Ibid., 2.

CHAPTER 8

1. New England Association of Schools and Colleges letter.

2. Beth Daley and Francie Latour, "Dorchester High Student Stabbed After Argument," *Boston Globe*, October 22, 1999.

3. Beth Daley and Judy Rakowsky, "Teen's Brutal Slaying an end to Difficult Life," *Boston Globe*, November, 6 1999.

4. From the New England Association of Schools and Colleges Report, December 16, 1999.

5. Anand Vaishnav, "Payzant Names Three to Lead Overhauled High Schools," *Boston Globe*, December 16, 2002.

6. From a Special Progress Report and Curriculum Audit conducted at DHS in the fall of 2000.

7. Edward Hayward, "Reform Ax May Cut Hub School Managers," *Boston Herald*, October 22, 2000.

8. From the Curriculum Audit conducted fall 2000.

9. From the 2001–2 UMB and Dorchester High School Evaluation Report researched and written by Lisa Gonsalves.

10. "Transforming Boston's Schools," p. 4.

11. Neil Sullivan, interviewed by Lisa Gonsalves, May 8, 2006.

CHAPTER 9

1. When teachers are excessed, it means that they have been given a pink slip, and that their job is no longer available. Many excessed teachers do return to the system, but they often do not hear about whether or not they are being invited back until very late in the summer.

2. Notes from Design Team meeting, 2003.

3. Email correspondence sent from Pam Trefler to school partners, April 2003.

4. Education Matters is the outside evaluator for high school restructuring in Boston. They have written a report on the progress of restructuring for the last three years. These reports can be found at http://www.edmatters.org/reports.html.

5. From the September 2004 Education Matters Evaluation, 7.

6. APS teacher, interviewed by John Leonard, 2006.

7. Teacher quoted in the Education Matters Evaluation, September 2004, 22.

8. Union rules stipulate that teachers have to vote on any schedule changes.

9. Education Matters, September 2004, 42.

10. Collaborative Coaching and Learning is a Professional Develoment model developed by the Boston Public Schools in which teachers work together in inquiry groups to discuss content and student work.

11. Education Matters, September 2004, 18.

12. Ibid., 42.

13. Ibid., 22.

14. Ibid., 26.

15. Ibid., 46.

16. Ibid., 42.

17. Vaishnav, "Payzant Names Three."

18. Quote from Boston's School Truancy Project.

LESSONS LEARNED FOR URBAN EDUCATION: INTRODUCTION

1. Balfanz and Legters, "Locating the Dropout Crisis," 61.

CHAPTER 10

1. Armstrong and Savage, *Secondary Education*, 25.

2. Bronfenbrenner, *The Ecology of Human Development*, 22.

3. Ibid., 59.

4. Bronfenbrenner calls this level of the environment the macrosystem.

5. Deal and Peterson, *Shaping School Culture*, 3.

6. Bronfenbrenner, *Ecology of Human Development*, 226.

7. The Federal No Child Left Behind legislation is one example of this.

8. Bryk and Schneider, *Trust in Schools*; Sergiovanni, "Moral Authority, Community and Diversity"; Payne and Kaba, "So Much Reform."

9. Steinberg, *Beyond the Classroom*.

10. Comer, *Waiting for a Miracle*.

11. Louis and Miles, *Improving the Urban High School*.

12. Fullan, *Leading in a Culture of Change*.

13. Newman, *Student Engagement and Achievement in American Secondary Schools*; Ames, "Classrooms"; McCombs and Pope, *Motivating Hard to Reach Students*; Steinberg, *Beyond the Classroom*.

14. From the Boston Public Schools Carnegie Proposal, 10.

15. Steinberg, *Beyond the Classroom*, 67.

16. Ibid., 22.

17. Steinberg, *Beyond the Classroom*; Dornbusch et al., "The Relation of Parenting Style to Adolescent School Performance"; Stevenson and Baker, "The Family-School Relation" ; Grolnick and Slowiaczek, "Parents Involvment in Children's School."

18. Bryk and Schneider, *Trust in Schools*, 20.

19. Louis and Miles, *Improving the Urban High School*; Fullan, *Leading in a Culture of Change*.

20. Sarason, *The Culture of the School and the Problem of Change.*
21. Bryk and Schneider, *Trust in Schools,* 20.
22. Bronfenbrenner, *Ecology of Human Development.*
23. Ibid., 86.
24. Payne and Kaba, "So Much Reform, so Little Change."
25. Epstein, "Parents' Reactions to Teacher Practices of Parent Involvement"; Anguiano, "Families and Schools.".
26. Lawson, "School-Family Relations in Context."
27. Ibid., 80.
28. Lawson, "School-Family Relations in Context"; Epstein, "Parents' Reactions to Teacher Practices"; Anguiano, "Families and Schools"; Abrams and Gibbs, "Disrupting the Logic of Home-School Relations"; Harry, Klingner and Hart, "African-American Families under Fire."
29. Lawson, "School-Family Relations in Context," 94.
30. Ibid., 95.
31. Dornbusch and Glasgow, "The Structural Context of Family-School Relations."
32. Dunst, "Family-Centered Practices."
33. Ibid.
34. Steinberg, *Beyond the Classroom,* 125.
35. Ibid.
36. Ibid., 134.
37. Hartup, "Adolescents and Their Friends."
38. Anderson, *Code of the Street,* 76.
39. Ibid., 77.

CHAPTER 11

1. Shear et al., *Creating Cultures for Learning.*
2. Fullan, "Leadership for the 21st Century"; Johnson, *Teachers at Work*; Newman, *Authentic Instruction*; Deal and Peterson, *Shaping School Culture.*
3. Deal and Peterson, *Shaping School Culture,* 29–30.
4. Hampel, in *The Last Little Citadel,* recounts the history of the growth of teachers unions and the tensions this created between teachers.
5. Balfanz and Legters, "Locating the Dropout Crisis."

CHAPTER 12

1. This definition is from *Webster's Third New International Dictionary—Unabridged,* 2002.
2. U.S. Department of Education, *Turning Around Low-Performing High Schools,* Issue paper prepared by the Leadership Summit (December 2005).
3. Much of this money has come from the Gates Foundation and the Carnegie Corporation of New York.
4. Casserly, "Beating the Odds."
5. Balfanz and Legters, "Locating the Dropout Crisis," 58.
6. Ibid., 66.
7. Ibid., 62.

8. *Too Big to be Seen: The Invisible Dropout Crisis in Boston and America*, a report from the Boston Youth Transitions Task Force (May 2006). The report was sponsored by The Private Industry Council and The Boston Compact.

9. Ibid.

10. Balfanz and Legters, "Locating the Dropout Crisis."

11. Ibid., 8.

12. Ibid., 9.

13. Losen, "Graduation Rate Accountability under the No Child Left Behind Act and the Disparate Impact on Students of Color."

14. The Education Trust, "Gaining Traction, Gaining Ground"; The Education Trust, "The Power to Change".

15. The Education Trust, "Gaining Traction," 3.

16. Ibid.

17. The Education Trust, "The Power to Change," 24.

18. Phelan, Yu, and Davidson, "Navigating the Psychosocial Pressures of Adolescence."

19. Barone, Aguirre-Deandreis, and Trickett, "Means-Ends Problem-Solving Skills."

20. Bukowski and Hoza, "Popularity and Friendship."

21. Keefe and Berndt, "Relations of Friendship Quality to Self-Esteem in Early Adolescence,"; Berndt and Keefe, "Friends' Influence on Adolescents' Adjustment to School,"; Gary W. Ladd, "Having Friends, Keeping Friends, Making Friends, and Being Liked by Peers in the Classroom"; Ladd, Kochenderfer, and Coleman, " Friendship Quality as a Predictor of Young Children's Early School Adjustment,"; Erdley, Nangle,Newman, and Carpenter, "Children's Friendship Experiences and Psychological Adjustment."

22. Seidman,Aber, Allen, and French, "The Impact of the Transition to High School on the Self-System and Perceived Social Context of Poor Urban Youth."

23. Peng and Lee, "Educational Experiences and Needs of Middle School Students in Poverty."

24. Hartup, "Adolescents and their Friends."

25. Ball, *Beachside Comprehensive: A Case Study of Secondary Schooling*; Cairns and Others, "Social Networks and Aggressive Behavior: Peer Support or Peer Rejection?" ; Kandel and Andrews, "Processes of Adolescent Socialization by Parents and Peers."

26. Hartup, "Adolescents and their Friends."

27. Weissglass, "Infusing Equity into Reform."

28. Mayer, *What Money Can't Buy*; Harrington, *The Other America*.

29. Franklin, *Shadows of Race and Class*.

30. Franklin, *Shadows of Race and Class*, 117–18.

31. Delpit, "The Silenced Dialogue"

32. Ibid., 283.

33. Ibid.

34. Ibid., 291–92.

35. Heath, *Ways with Words*; Delpit, *The Silenced Dialogue*; Balester, *Cultural Divide*.

36. Mayer, *What Money Can't Buy*; Anderson, *Code of the Street*; Payne, *A Framework for Understanding Poverty*.

37. Gelles, *Intimate Violence*.

38. Halpern, "Poverty and Early Childhood Parenting."

39. Garbarino, Dubrow, Kostelny, and Pardo, *Children in Danger*.

40. Perry, "The Neurodevelopmental Impact of Violence in Childhood," 230.

41. Teicher and others, "Early Childhood Abuse and Limbic System Ratings in Adult Psychiatric Outpatients."

42. Raja Mishra, "Gauging Toll of Abuse on a Child's Brain," *Boston Globe*, December 15, 2000.

43. Teicher, "Wounds that Time Won't Heal."

44. Jose Kendall, "How Abuse and Neglect Damage the Brain," *Boston Globe*, September 24, 2002.

45. Perry, "The Neurodevelopmental Impact of Violence," 230.

46. Payne, *A Framework for Understanding*, 12.

47. Ibid.

48. Ibid., 9.

49. Harry, Klinger, and Hart, "African-American Families"; Lawson, "School-Family Relations."

50. Bryk and Schneider, *Trust in Schools*.

51. Payne, *A Framework for Understanding*.

52. Abrams and Gibbs, "Disrupting the Logic."

53. Bronfenbrenner, *Ecology of Human Development*, 54.

CHAPTER 14

1. *Webster's Third New International Dictionary—Unabridged*, 2002.

2. Bronfenbrenner, *Ecology of Human Development*, 26.

3. From the DHS 1966 Yearbook.

4. From the Evaluation of Dorchester High School by the New England Association of Schools and Colleges, 1972.

5. Bronfenbrenner, *Ecology of Human Development*, 240.

6. Reis, Colbert, and Hebert, "Understanding Resilience in Diverse, Talented Students in an Urban High School"; Clark, "Building Student Achievement," in *NCREL Policy Issue* eds. Ferguson, Clark, and Stewart; Brown and Evans, "Extracuriculuar Activity and Ethnicity"; Hebert, "Defining Belief in Self "; Heath, "Making Learning Work,"; Posner and Vandell, "After-School Activities and the Development of Low-Income Urban Children."

7. Knouse, Tanner, and Harris, "The Relation of College Internships, College Performance, and Subsequent Job Opportunity," ; McCormick, "Critical Thinking, Experimental Learning, and Internships,"; Taylor, "Effects of College Internships on Individual Participants."

8. Valentine, "Deficit, Difference and Bicultural Models of Afro-American Behavior"; Clark, "Social Identity, Peer Relations and Academic Competence of Black Adolescents," ; Gardner, "Postsecondary Education Opportunities as Perceived by Black High School Seniors," eds. M. Lang and C.A. Ford.

9. Bryk and Schneider, *Trust in schools*.

10. Ibid.

11. Sockett, "Caveat Emptor."

12. Ibid., 37.

13. Ibid., 43.

14. EGC Inside: A Monthly Report from the Emmanuel Gospel Center, 10:1, 2002.

Bibliography

Abrams, Laura S. and Jewelle T. Gibbs. "Disrupting the Logic of Home-School Relations: Parent Involvement Strategies and Practices of Inclusion and Exclusion." *Urban Education* 37, no. 3 (2002): 384–407.

Allen, Henry L. "Segregation and Desegregation in Boston's Schools, 1961–1974." In *From Common School to Magnet School: Selected Essays in the History of Boston's Schools,* edited by J. Fraser, H.L. Allen, and N. Barnes. Boston: Trustees of the Public Library of the City of Boston, 1979, 109–118.

Ames, Carole. "Classrooms: Goals, structures, and Student Motivation." *Journal of Educational Psychology* 84, no. 3 (1992): 261–71.

Anderson, Elijah. *Code of the Street: Decency, Violence, and the Moral Life of the Inner City.* New York: W.W. Norton & Company, 2000.

Anguiano, Ruben P. V. "Families and Schools: The Effects of Parental Involvement on High School Completion." *Journal of Family Issues* 25 no. 1 (2004): 61–85.

Angus, David L., and Jeffrey E. Mirel. *The Failed Promise of the American High School, 1890 to 1995.* New York: Teachers College Press, 1999.

Armstrong, David G. and Tom V. Savage. *Secondary Education: An Introduction.* 3rd ed. New York: Macmillan College Publishing Company, 1994.

Balester, Valerie, M. *Cultural Divide: A Study of African-American College Level Writers.* Portsmouth, NH: Boynton/Cook Publishers, 1993.

Balfanz, Robert, and Nettie E. Legters. "Locating the Dropout Crisis: Which High Schools Produce the Nation's Dropouts." In *Dropouts in America: Confronting the Graduation Rate Crisis.* Edited by G. Orfield. Cambridge, MA: Harvard Education Press, 2004, 57–84.

Ball, Stephen J. *Beachside Comprehensive: A Case Study of Secondary Schooling.* Cambridge: Cambridge University Press. 1981.

Barone, Charles, Ana I. Aguirre-Deandreis, and Edison J. Trickett. "Means-Ends Problem-Solving Skills, Life Stress, and Social Support as Mediators of

Adjustment in the Normative Transition to High School." *American Journal of Community Psychology* 19, no. 2 (1991): 207–19.

Berndt, Thomas J., and Keunho Keefe. "Friends' Influence on Adolescents' Adjustment to School." *Child Development* 66, no. 5 (1995):1312–29.

Booth, Alan and Judith F. Dunn, eds. *Family-School Links: How Do They Affect Educational Outcomes?* New Jersey: Lawrence Erlbaum, 1996.

Bronfenbrenner, Urie. *The Ecology of Human Development: Experiments by Nature and Design.* Cambridge, MA: Harvard University Press, 1979.

Brown, Randall and William P. Evans. "Extracurricular Activity and Ethnicity: Creating Greater School Connection among Diverse Student Populations." *Urban Education* 37, no. (2002): 41–58.

Bryan, Julia. "Fostering Educational Resilience and Achievement in Urban Schools Through School-Family-Community Partnerships." *Professional School Counseling* 8, no. 3 (2005): 219–28.

Bryk, Anthony S., and Barbara Schneider. *Trust in Schools: A Core Resource for Improvement.* New York: Russell Sage Foundation. 2002.

Bukowski, William. M., and B. Hoza. "Popularity and Friendships: Issues and Theory, Measurement, and Outcome." In *Peer Relationships and Child Development.* Edited by T.J. Berndt & G.W. Ladd. New York: Wiley, 1989.

Cairns, Robert B. and Others. "Social Networks and Aggressive Behavior: Peer Support or Peer Rejection?" *Developmental Psychology* 24, no. 6 (1988): 815–23

Casserly, Michael. "Beating the Odds, A City-by-City Analysis of Student Performance and Achievement Gaps on State Assessments: Results from the 2003–2004 School Year." Council of Great City Schools, March 2005.

Clark, Maxine L. "Social identity, peer relations and academic competence of Black adolescents." *Education and Urban Society* 24, no. 1 (1991): 41–52.

Clark, Reginald. "Building Student Achievement: In-School and Out-of-School Factors" In "Closing the Achievement Gap in Suburban and Urban School Communities," Edited by R. Ferguson, R. Clark, and J. Stewart. Special issue, *NCREL Policy Issue*, no. 13 (December 2002).

Comer, James. *Waiting for a Miracle: Why Schools Can't Solve our Problems and How we Can.* New York: Plume Books, 1998.

Deal, Terrence E., and Kent D. Peterson. *Shaping School Culture: The Heart of Leadership.* San Francisco: Jossey-Bass, 2003.

Delpit, Lisa. "The Silenced Dialogue: Power and Pedagogy in Educating Other People's Children." *Harvard Educational Review* 58, no. 3 (1988): 280–98.

Dentler, Robert A. *Moving Forward.* Boston: Boston Commission on Secondary Education, 1973.

Dooley, Edward. *The Culture of Possibility: The Story of the Boston Plan for Excellence in the Public Schools.* Boston: The Boston Plan for Excellence, 1994.

Dornbusch, Sanford M., and Kristan Glasgow. "The Structural Context of Family-School Relations." In *Family-School Links: How do They Affect Educational Outcomes?* Edited by A. Booth and J. Dunn New Jersey: Lawrence Erlbaum, 1996, 35–44.

Dornbusch, Sanford M., Philip L. Ritter, Herbert P. Leiderman, Donald F. Roberts, and Michael J. Fraleigh. "The Relation of Parenting Style to Adolescent School Performance." *Child Development* 58, no. 5 (1987): 1244–57.

Dunst, Carl J. "Family-Centered Practices: Birth through High School." *Journal of Special Education* 36, no. 3 (2002): 139–47.

The Education Trust. "Gaining Traction, Gaining Ground: How Some High
    Schools Accelerate Learning for Struggling Students." Washington, DC: The
    Education Trust, 2005.
———. "The Power to Change: High Schools that Help All Students Achieve."
    Washington, DC: The Education Trust, 2005.
Epstein, Joyce. "Parents' Reactions to Teacher Practices of Parent Involvement."
    Elementary School Journal 86, no. 3 (1986): 277–94.
Erdley, Cynthia A., Douglas W. Nangle, Julie E. Newman, and Erika M.
    Carpenter. "Children's Friendship Experiences and Psychological Adjustment:
    Theory and Research." *New Direction for Child and Adolescent Development*, no.
    91 (2001): 5–24.
Ferguson, Ronald F., Reginald Clark, and Judy Stewart, eds. "Closing the
    Achievement Gap in Suburban and Urban School Communities." Special issue,
    NCREL Policy Issue, no. 13 (December 2002).
Formisano, Ronald P. *Boston Against Busing: Race, Class, and Ethnicity in the 1960s
    and 1970s.* Chapel Hill, NC: University of North Carolina Press, 1991.
Franklin, Raymond S. *Shadows of Race and Class.* Minneapolis: University of Min-
    nesota Press. 1991.
Fraser, James W., Henry L. Allen, and Nancy Barnes. *From Common School to Mag-
    net School: Selected Essays in the History of Boston's Schools.* Boston: Trustees of the
    Public Library of the City of Boston, 1979.
Fullan, Michael. "Leadership for the 21st Century: Breaking the Bonds of Depend-
    ency." *Educational Leadership* 55, no. 7 (1998): 6–10.
———. *Leading in a Culture of Change.* San Francisco. Jossey-Bass, 2001.
———. "Moral Purpose Writ Large." *The School Administrator* (September
    2002). Available from the American Associations of School Administrators,
    http: // www . aasa . org / publications / saarticledetail . cfm ? ItemNumber =
    1916&snItemNumber=950&tnItemNumber=951 (accessed January 15, 2003).
Garbarino, James, Nancy Dubrow, Kathleen Kostelny, and Carole Pardo. *Children
    in Danger: Coping with the Consequences of Community Violence.* San Francisco:
    Jossey-Bass Publishers, 1992.
Gardner, Oscar S. "Postsecondary Education Opportunities as Perceived by Black
    High School Seniors." In *Strategies for Retaining Minority Students in Higher Edu-
    cation.*Edited by M. Lang and C.A. Ford. Illinois: Thomas Books, 1992.
Gelles, Richard J. *Intimate Violence.* New York: Simon and Schuster, 1988.
Giles, Hollyce C. "Three Narratives of Parent-Educator Relationships: Toward
    Counselor Repertoires for Bridging the Urban Parent-School Divide." *Profes-
    sional School Counseling* 8, no. 3 (2005): 228–36.
Grolnick, Wendy S., and Maria L. Slowiaczek. "Parents Involvement in Children's
    School: A Multidimensional Conceptualization and Motivational Model." *Child
    Development* 64, no. 1 (1994) 237–52.
Halpern, Robert. "Poverty and Early Childhood Parenting: Toward a Framework
    for Intervention." *American Journal of Orthopsychiatry* 60, no.1 (1990): 6–18.
Hampel, Robert L. *The Last Little Citadel: American High Schools Since 1940.* Boston:
    Houghton Mifflin Company, 1986.
Harrington, Michael. *The Other America.* New York: Simon and Schuster, 1962.
Harry, Beth, Janette K. Klingner, and Juliet Hart. "African-American Families
    under Fire: Ethnographic Views of Family Strengths." *Remedial and Special Edu-
    cation* 26, no. 2 (2005): 101–112.

Hartup, William W. "Adolescents and Their Friends." *New Directions for Child Development*, no. 60 (1993): 3–22.

Heath, Shirley Brice. "Making Learning Work." *Afterschool Matters* 1, no. 1 (2000): 33–45.

———. *Ways with Words: Langauge, Life and Work in Communities and Classrooms.* Cambridge: Cambridge University Press, 1983.

Hebert, Thomas P. "Defining Belief in Self: Intelligent Young Men in an Urban High School." *Gifted Child Quarterly* 44, no. 2 (2002): 91–114.

Johnson, Susan. M. *Teachers at Work: Achieving Success in Our Schools.* New York: Basic Books, 1990.

Kandel David B., and Kevin Andrews. "Processes of Adolescent Socialization by Parents and Peers." *International Journal of the Addictions* 22 (1987): 319–42.

Keefe, Keunho and Thomas J. Berndt. "Relations of Friendship Quality to Self-Esteem in Early Adolescence." *Journal of Early Adolescence* 16, no. 1 (1996): 110–29.

King, Mel. *Chain of Change: Struggle for Black Community Development.* Boston: South End Press, 1981.

Knouse, Stephen B., John R. Tanner, and Elizabeth W. Harris, "The Relation of College Internships, College Performance, and Subsequent Job Opportunity." *Journal of Employment Counseling* 36, no. 1 (1999): 35–43.

Ladd, Gary W. "Having Friends, Keeping Friends, Making Friends, and Being Liked by Peers in the Classroom: Predictors of Children's Early School Adjustment?" *Child Development* 61, no. 1(1990): 1081–1100.

Ladd, Gary W., Becky J. Kochenderfer, and Cynthia C. Coleman. "Friendship Quality as a Predictor of Young Children's Early School Adjustment." *Child Development* 67, no. 3 (1996): 161–78

Lawson, Michael. "School-Family Relations in Context: Parent and Teacher Perceptions of Parent Involvement." *Urban Education* 38, no. 1 (2003): 77–133.

Leonard, John. "History of a High School Community: 1950–2000." PhD Diss., Boston University, 2002.

Levine, Hillel, and Lawrence Harmond. *Death of an American Jewish Community: A Tragedy of Good Intentions.* New York: The Free Press, 1992.

Losen, Daniel J. "Graduation Rate Accountability under the No Child Left Behind Act and the Disparate Impact on Students of Color." In *Dropouts in America: Confronting the Graduation Rate Crisis*, edited by G. Orfield. Cambridge, MA: Harvard Education Press, 2004, 57–84.

Louis, Karen S., and Matthew B. Miles. *Improving the Urban High School: What Works and Why.* New York: Teachers College Press, 1990.

Mayer, Susan E. *What Money Can't Buy.* Cambridge, MA: Harvard University Press, 1997.

McCombs, Barbara L., and James E. Pope. *Motivating Hard to Reach Students.* Washington, DC: American Psychological Association. 1994.

McCormick, Donald W. "Critical Thinking, Experimental Learning, and Internships." *Journal of Management Education*, no. 17 (1993): 260–262.

Nelson, Adam R. *The Elusive Ideal: Educational Opportunity and the Federal Role in Boston's Public Schools, 1960–1985.* Chicago: University of Chicago Press, 2005.

Newman, Fred N., ed. *Student Engagement and Achievement in American Secondary Schools.* New York: Teachers College Press, 1992.

Newmann, Fred M. and Associates. *Authentic Instruction: Restructuring Schools for Intellectual Quality.* San Francisco: Jossey Bass, 1996.

Orfield, Gary, ed. *Dropouts in America: Confronting the Graduation Rate Crisis.* Cambridge, MA: Harvard University Press, 2004.

Payne, Charles M., and M. Kaba. "So Much Reform, so Little Change: Building-Level Obstacles to Urban School Reform." Lecture, Harvard University, Cambridge, MA, June 13–14, 2002.

Payne, Ruby K. *A Framework for Understanding Poverty.* Highlands, TX: aha! Process Inc., 1996.

Peng, Samuel S. and Ralph M. Lee. "Educational Experiences and Needs of Middle School Students in Poverty." Washington DC. National Center for Education Statistics, 1993.

Perry, Bruce D. "The Neurodevelopmental Impact of Violence in Childhood." In *Textbook of Child and Adolescent Forensic Psychiatry.* Edited by D. Schetky and E.P. Denedek. Washington, DC: American Psychiatric Press, Inc., 2001.

Phelan, Patricia, Hanh C. Yu, and Ann L. Davidson. "Navigating the Psychosocial Pressures of Adolescence: The Voices and Experiences of High School Youth." *American Educational Research Journal* 31, no. 2 (1994): 415–47.

Posner, Jill K., and Deborah Lowe Vandell. "After-School Activities and the Development of Low-Income Urban Children: A Longitudinal Study." *Developmental Psychology* 35, no. 3 (1999): 868–79.

Reis, Sally M., Robert D. Colbert, and, Thomas P. Hebert. "Understanding Resilience in Diverse, Talented Students in an Urban High School." *Roeper Review* 27, no. 2 (2005): 110.

Sarason, Seymour B. *The Culture of the School and the Problem of Change.* Boston: Allyn and Bacon, 1971.

Seidman, Edward, Lawrence J. Aber, LaRue Allen, and Sabine E. French. "The Impact of the Transition to High School on the Self-System and Perceived Social Context of Poor Urban Youth." *American Journal of Community Psychology* 24, no. 4 (1996): 489–527.

Sergiovanni, Thomas J. *Moral Leadership: Getting to the Heart of School Improvement.* San Francisco: Jossey-Bass, 1996.

———. *Building Community in Schools.* San Francisco: Jossey-Bass, 1999.

———. "Moral Authority, Community and Diversity: Leadership Challenges for the Twenty-first Century." In *Leadership for Quality Schooling: International Perspectives.* Edited by Kam-Cheung Wong and Colin W. Evers, London: Routledge, 2003, 1–11.

Shear, Linda, Mengli Song, Ann House, Ben Martinez, Barbara Means, and Becky Smerdon. *Creating Cultures for Learning: Supportive Relationships in New and Redesigned High Schools.* The National Evaluation of High School Transformation. American Institutes for Research. April 2005.

Sockett, Hugh. "Caveat Emptor: Children and Parents as Customers." Paper presented at the meeting of the Curriculum and Pedagogy Institute of the University of Alberta, Alberta, Canada, 1997.

Steinberg, Laurence. *Beyond the Classroom: Why School Reform Has Failed and What Parents Need To Do.* New York: Simon & Schuster, 1996.

Stevenson, David L., and David P. Baker "The Family School Relation and the Child's School Performance." *Child Development* 58, no. 5 (1987): 1348–57.

Taylor, Steven J.L. *Desegregation in Boston and Buffalo: The Influence of Local Leaders.* Albany: State University of New York Press, 1998.

Taylor, Susan M. "Effects of College Internships on Individual Participants." *Journal of Applied Psychology* 73, no. 3 (1988): 393–401.

Teicher, Martin H. "Wounds that Time Won't Heal: The Neurobiology of Child Abuse." *Cerebrum* 2, no. 4 (2000): 50–65.

Teicher, Martin H., and Others. "Early Childhood Abuse and Limbic System Ratings in Adult Psychiatric Outpatients." *Journal of Neuropsychiatry and Clinical Neurosciences* No 5 (1993): 301–306.

Tyack, David B. and Larry Cuban. *Tinkering Toward Utopia: A Century of Public School Reform.* Cambridge, MA: Harvard University Press, 1995.

Valentine, Charles A. "Deficit, Difference and Bicultural Models of Afro-American Behavior." *Harvard Educational Review,* 41, no. 2 (1971): 137–57.

Vera, Elizabeth M., and Richard Q. Shin. "Promoting Strengths in a Socially Toxic World: Supporting Resiliency with Systemic Interventions." *The Counseling Psychologist* 34, no. 1 (2006): 80–89.

Weissglass, Julian. "Infusing Equity into Reform." *Leadership* 30, no. 4 (2001): 34–37.

Williams, Trina R., Larry E. Davis, Julie M. Cribbs, Jeanne Saunders, and James H. Williams. "Friends, Family and Neighborhood: Understanding Academic Outcomes of African-American Youth." *Urban Education* 37, no. 3 (2002): 408–431.

Wong, Kam-Cheung, and Colin W. Evers, eds. *Leadership for Quality Schooling: International Perspectives.* London: Routledge, 2003.

Index

About the Authors

Both authors have an inside view of Dorchester High School. Dr. Leonard has been at DHS since 1996, as a teacher, assistant headmaster, Chief Academic Officer, and now the headmaster of one of the new small schools created out of DHS. Dr. Gonsalves has worked closely with the Boston Public High Schools since 1996 and with Dorchester High School since 2000 in her role as university partner. She wears many hats in this role: providing professional development for teachers in English language arts, analyzing the school's standardized assessment scores, overseeing student teachers working with the DHS/UMB professional development school partnership, researching the school's climate and culture, and evaluating the school's implementation of the Reader's Workshop curriculum model. Dr. Gonsalves also teaches her university courses at the high school.